Ethnicity
Racism, Class and Culture

Steve Fenton

MACMILLAN

First published 1999 by
MACMILLAN PRESS LTD
Houndmills, Basingstoke, Hampshire RG21 6XS
and London
Companies and representatives
throughout the world

ISBN 0–333–66224–5 hardcover
ISBN 0–333–66225–3 paperback

A catalogue record for this book is available
from the British Library.

This book is printed on paper suitable for recycling and
made from fully managed and sustained forest sources.

10 9   8   7   6   5   4   3   2   1
08 07 06 05 04 03 02 01 00 99

Editing and origination by
Aardvark Editorial, Suffolk

Printed in Hong Kong

Contents

Contents   vii

Acknowledgements

I wish to thank all my colleagues at the University of Bristol, Department of Sociology, including Rohit Barot my friend and colleague for so long. More than anyone else, Harriet Bradley has given me huge support, encouragement and invaluable advice; without her encouragement I am not sure I would have kept going through the worst spells. I am grateful to Ivan Huey for reading the first typescript and giving me canny advice and to Steve May for our lively discussion and every kind of assistance. Sole responsibility for the text is the author's.

I owe a special debt of gratitude to the University of Hawai'i and its distinguished Department of Sociology. They welcomed me as a Visiting Professor in 1978, 1981 and 1986 and as a visitor again in 1996. I am very grateful for the help and guidance I received from the late Andrew Lind, and from Kyoshi Ikeda, David Chandler, Gene Kassebaum and many others. I was greatly assisted by the University Library and its fine Hawai'i and Pacific collection and their patient and kind staff.

I would like to dedicate this book to Jenny, Alex and Lynda who have been wonderful throughout. They may not read it but I'll bet they're glad it's finished.

Preface

The demise of the sociological idea 'race relations' has been slow but certain. As a phrase in popular discourse it retains a meaning as signifying the better or worse state – the presence or absence of ill-feeling – of relations between peoples perceived as different. But it founders on the analytic ambiguity of the term 'race' implying as it does peoples who are inescapably different and between whom relations are essentially problematic. The term ethnic, and hence 'ethnic groups' and 'ethnic relations' escapes the invalidity of the term race. But the term ethnic relations is flawed by the implication that there is a special type of relationship in which ethnic sentiment preponderates. In all those social situations marked by some measure of 'ethnic relevance' we cannot presume how strong the ethnic dimension is.

Historically, the difficulty with the term ethnicity has been its largely anthropological provenance and its seemingly central focus on the concept of culture. For this reason a concern with ethnicity has appeared to sidestep the problem of racism and to neglect the hard-edged inequalities which are evident in racialised societies – societies which are marked by the belief in racial difference and the practice of social domination. In this book we have, by reuniting ethnicity with the economic and the political, sought to reap the benefits of the focus on culture without omitting economic inequalities or the subtle and not-so-subtle exercise of power. The fact that racist doctrines have encompassed ideas of racial divisions and cultural difference further ensures that a concern with ethnicity does not become a cue for a retreat from class and power.

To achieve this end we have insisted on contextualising ethnicity, on setting the study of ethnicity within the characteristic contexts of economy and polity whose historical and present forms constitute the stage on which ethnic dramas are played out.

We have set out to define the characteristic contexts of ethnicity. Three historical trajectories are specified: that of slavery and post-slavery in the modern world; that of the world as colonial and post-colonial; and the formation of nation-states in the capitalist West and beyond. That is to say that the enslavement of Africans in the 'New World', the domination of large tracts of our world by European states and the aftermath of post-colonialism in those states and the zones which they occupied, and the formation of nation-states – these three have provided the setting within which ethnicity has taken shape.

We have argued through this volume that there are real dangers in seeing ethnicity and ethnic groups as everywhere the same phenomenon. The different kinds of settings have given rise to some rather different types of ethnic groups – or, more precisely, to significantly different modalities of ethnicity. Only if we shade our eyes from these differences can we conclude that there is some kind of universal 'ethnic phenomenon' or indeed anything so dramatic as an 'ethnic revival'. To be sure, relatively enduring social classifications – predicated in ancestry, language and culture – are found virtually everywhere we look. But it takes closer inspection to see whether these are the same kind of phenomenon.

To give emphasis to the idea of characteristically different contexts of ethnicity, we have built the volume around five 'types' of ethnic groups, each with a discernible place in the historical trajectories we described. Slavery and post-slavery societies have given rise to one set of ethnicities, commonly marked by a discourse of racialised difference; the land dispossession societies are marked by historical marginalisation and the cultural devaluing of indigenous peoples; the plural societies of the colonial and post-colonial world are ones in which migrant worker populations have taken root, compete with each other for economic and political space, and compete with groups with a claim to being indigenous; the proto-nations are found in established nation-states within which cultures were imperfectly integrated, and peoples were marginalised but not to the point of disappearance; urban minorities are the product of global patterns of migration of both labouring and trading populations. This schema owes a great deal to the work of Thomas Hylland Eriksen; we took the further step of situating them within the historical settings they imply. This kind of typology is a guide to organising our thoughts, the historical settings a guide to organising our explanations.

The book has also tried to avoid a descent into two other familiar disputes: whether ethnicity is to be seen as primarily material or symbolic and whether ethnic is a 'real' or 'constructed' phenomenon. The convincing answer, easily said but less easily argued, is that ethnicity is both grounded and constructed, and both material and symbolic. It is possible to show that ethnicity is constructed by showing how ethnic categories shift their ground, import and content as circumstances change. But ethnicity also has a 'real' social basis in the enduring significance which people attach to ancestry, cultural difference and language. These ethnic differences are not 'merely cultural' but are organised and mobilised within contexts of political and economic structure. Ethnicity is manifested as a dimension of cultural meanings and as a dimension of social structure; ethnic formations are material, symbolic and social facts. The way in which this can be traced through a specific case is illustrated in the later chapters of this book.

In the Introduction we present the key themes which guide much of the remainder of the book. These are: the distinction between the terms 'race/racial' and ethnic, the discourse of race and the discourse of ethnicity; the idea of ethnicity as socially constructed and as socially grounded in culture, ancestry and language; ethnicity in its global and local and macro- and micro-social forms; treating ethnicity as simultaneously material and symbolic; followed by the outline of the argument that ethnic groups and ethnic identities should be seen within their political and economic contexts.

In Chapter 1 we argue that there are three key historical trajectories within which ethnic formations have emerged in the modern world: slavery and its aftermath, colonialism and post-colonial social orders; and the formation of modern nation-states. Within these we define, following Eriksen (1993b), five types of ethnicity, more concretely five types of ethnic groups: urban minorities, proto-nations, ethnic groups in plural societies, indigenous minorities, and post-slavery minorities. We discuss the economic and political contexts which ethnic groups have in common and the lines along which they differ. Urban minorities, ethnic groups in plural societies, and post-slavery minorities have all arisen from contexts of labour migration, varying from free movement, through degrees of compulsion, to unfree movement. Among proto-nations the central problematic is political and among indigenous peoples there are leading interests at stake which are both economic and political – economic marginalisation, land dispossession and political autonomy. Examples of proto-nations are given as illustrations throughout the book. The other four 'types' are illustrated by way of our four leading examples: Britain and urban minorities, Malaysia as a post-colonial 'plural' society; Hawai'i and Hawaiians as an instance of the dispossession of an indigenous people; and African Americans as a post-slavery minority. In the last part of this chapter we examine the intersection of cthnicity and gender.

In Chapter 2 we examine the concept of racism and the discourse of 'race', following important arguments about its modern character and its modern origins. We look at science and Christianity as the origin of ideas about universal humankind and about 'natural' difference; some of the earliest European adventurers provoked fierce debates about the kinds of peoples they encountered. The enslavement of Africans in America has founded a language of racial difference which has become an enduring component of American culture, although changing radically and always contested. We also look at a non-European instance of a discourse of race (in China) which raises questions about the European white pre-eminence in the generation of racist ideas.

In Chapter 3 we discuss two of the key points of dispute within the sociology of ethnicity – its characteristic as 'primordial' as against situational and instrumental; and its portrayal as 'calculating' as against passionate or 'irrational'. This debate is presented through a discussion of an early essay by Clifford Geertz (1973) and the support and criticism which his arguments have subsequently received. A central point to the debate is whether primordial identities undermine and overwhelm civic ties in the modern state, particularly in new states. We suggest that primordial ties may be strong where civic ties are weak – the unstable, even 'collapsing' state giving way to primordial identities.

Chapters 4, 5, 6 and 7 are all substantively based on the historical cases of the USA, Malaysia, Britain and Hawai'i; the USA as a case study of a post-slavery society, Malaysia as a plural post-colonial social order, Britain as a post-colonial coloniser society receiving in-migrants from its former colonies, and Hawai'i, now incorporated within the USA, as an instance of the dispossession of an indigenous people. Chapters 4 and 5 concentrate on the economic, class contexts of these examples, Chapters 6 and 7 concentrate on the political contexts, especially the politics of culture and ethnic identity.

Chapter 8 addresses a central question in the sociology of ethnicity – can we speak of a revival of ethnicity in the contemporary world? We phrase this as a facet of the argument that the 'liberal expectancy' foresaw a decline of ethnic ties in a context of modernity – an expectancy which many see as having been unfulfilled. By seeing this modern expectation in its economic, political, sociological and cultural 'versions', we suggest that the omnipresent power of ethnicity has been overstated.

Introduction

Conceptualising Ethnicity

In this chapter we introduce four principal themes of the book: the distinction between the terms 'race' and 'ethnic'; the concept of macro-, meso- and micro-social settings within which ethnicity is relevant; the distinctions between ethnicity as voluntary and imposed and as grounded and constructed; and the political and economic contexts of ethnicity.

Discourses of race and ethnicity

The terms 'race' and 'ethnic' have become not only terms of social science discourse, but familiar terms of everyday conversation and description. In the USA in 1996 the trial of a black American accused of killing his white wife is described routinely as being surrounded by 'racial tensions'. Events in the former Yugoslavia are described as 'ethnic conflict' and movements of people there are described in that ominous phrase 'ethnic cleansing'. Conflict in Northern Ireland is described as 'sectarian', rarely as 'ethnic', never as 'racial'; black–white conflict in South Africa is most commonly termed 'racial' but 'black–black' conflict is likely to be described as 'ethnic' or even 'tribal' (Horowitz 1985, Marks and Trapido 1987). In South East Asia, India and the Caribbean (Hirschmann 1987, Vertovec 1992, Yelvington, 1993), group identities, and especially political competition based on group identities, are commonly referred to as 'communal' and the political manipulation of these identities is described as 'communalism' (Ratnam 1965, Hua Wu Yin 1983, Khan and Loh Kok Wah 1992).

These ethnic or racial terms are used in casual conversation and in press reportage. In February 1998 the press reported that the Malaysian government expected a temporary relaxation of legal provisions favouring Malays, as against Chinese Indians and others,

1

in access to jobs and business opportunities. The sub-headline read 'Malaysia's racial laws' and the story related that the 'decision to ease *racial* laws favouring *ethnic* Malays was only temporary' (*Financial Times* 26 February 1998, my emphasis). The Malaysian constitution refers to Malays and defines a Malay as 'a person who professes the Muslim religion, habitually speaks the Malay language, conforms to Malay custom and was born in the Federation' or a person whose parents meet those criteria (section 160 Malaysia, The Federal Constitution).

Section 153 of the Malaysian constitution refers to 'the special position of the Malays and the legitimate interests of other *communities*' and section 161 refers to 'natives of the Borneo states' and lists the natives of Sarawak as including as many as twenty '*races*'. (my emphasis). In the same document the terms race (racial), ethnic and community are used with no evident distinction between them and at the same time Malays are defined by reference to religion, language, custom, ancestry and birthplace.

In the American census the word 'races' is commonly used and 'race, races and racial' remain central to American social and political discourse. But the same census also uses the word 'ethnic', and a table listing 'Hispanics' as an ethnic category contains the curious footnote 'Hispanics may be of any race' (Lee 1993). The British census nowhere uses the word race but British law has a Race Relations Act and the census offers respondents ethnic categories, one of which is 'black' and another 'Pakistani', the first a 'race'/colour term and the second a national origin/ethnic term (Fenton 1996). Ethnic differences within the 'white' population in Britain are virtually ignored in the census so that there is only indirect enumeration of the ethnic Irish, despite the fact that the Irish are shown to have a disproportionate share of social disadvantage, the measurement of which was stated as a primary reason for the measurement of ethnic groups (Fenton 1996). Indeed, one curiosity of the British census with respect to ethnic groups is that about 94 per cent of the enumerated population fall into a single category, 'white', itself not strictly an 'ethnic' term (Ballard 1996).

There is difficulty both with creating and using categories, that is, in deciding how many categories there should be and determining who fits where, and with being sure what it is that is being measured. In the Malaysian census the major divisions are now between 'Malay', 'Chinese' and 'Indian' which correspond, as Hirschmann (1987) describes, to the 'popular conception of "race", the everyday term'. But Hirschmann goes on to describe how:

The Indian population encompasses Hindus, Muslims, Sikhs, Buddhists, and Christians and is also differentiated by a variety of Indian Pakistani and Sri Lankan mother tongues. The Chinese population is similarly cross-cut by religion and language. A minority of Malaysian-Chinese, known as Perakan or Baba Chinese, have adopted much of Malay culture, including language, dress and cuisine. Conversion to Islam and the adoption of Malay language and custom typically allow a person of any ancestry to be considered a Malay. (see also Nagata 1974)

The precise list and definition of categories in most censuses changes from one census to the next (for the American case see Lee 1993). But just what is being measured is also both contentious and unclear. The Malaysian census in the 19th and early 20th centuries was very much informed by ideas of racial difference, reinforced by the hierarchies of a colonial social order, and this was the case in many similar colonial situations. By the 1970s and 80s there had been a shift to a phraseology which included 'community' and ethnic group, while the term 'race' has persisted in popular or public discourse. In the USA the terminology of 'race' persists both in popular *and* academic discourse despite the acknowledgement that it conveys a notion of discrete, inherently different and permanent divisions of humankind which are not matched in reality (Rodriguez and Cordero-Guzman 1992). In academic discourse the ideas of race and ethnicity have existed side by side (see Anthias 1992), intertwined and overlapping and we should not expect to make a final and decisive break. Nonetheless, as this book progresses, we shall begin to make important clarifications and make distinctions as to where the respective emphases lie.

Ethnic and racial – what's in a name?

The actual use of ethnic group and race in popular, political and administrative discourses gives no immediate guide to any analytic distinction since, as we have already seen, the terms are frequently used interchangeably, swapping places over a number of years or even in the same sentence. But historical usage, and the legacy of now discredited theories of the division of humankind into funda-mentally different 'types', link the term 'race' with *physical* or visible difference, and explicitly or implicitly convey the idea that populations marked by characteristic appearance are constitution-ally or biologically different. By contrast the term 'ethnic' or 'ethnic group' is used primarily in contexts of *cultural* difference, where cultural difference is associated above all with an actual or commonly perceived shared ancestry, with language markers, and with national or regional origin. This reference to the physical/ biological (race) and the cultural/ancestral (ethnic) provides the reader with a broad guide to the centre of gravity of the two terms with respect to their place in popular, political and academic discourses. But the observation regarding usages in Malaysia, the USA, and Britain shows that there is a high degree of inconsistency. Groups marked by ancestral and cultural difference in Malaysia are described as races, and 'black' is offered as an 'ethnic group' category in the British census.

The two key contentions of this book are:

1. The term 'ethnic' has a much greater claim to analytical usefulness in sociology because it is not hampered by a history of connotations with discredited science and malevolent practice in the way the term 'race' is.
2. A discourse in which the idea of 'race' is present remains a powerful feature of common-sense thinking and of the ordering of social relations.

It is this second fact that prevents us from simply abandoning a terminology which includes 'race', although we reject the notion of 'races' as an analytic term in sociological theory and conceptualisation. In the USA in particular we have to accept that we are dealing with a social order which has incorporated, in a pervasive and persistent way, the idea of 'racial difference', and that this in many ways matches real divisions and inequalities in the American social structure. This is precisely what is meant by 'racialisation' – that there is both a set of powerful ideas and beliefs about 'race' and also a matching of this set of ideas with the differential social incorporation of groups commonly perceived as 'racially different'.

Historical associations of the idea of race

Throughout much of the 19th century and more than half of the 20th the idea that humankind was divided into races which were inescapably different and unequal in their capacities held sway in a broad band of social, political and scientific thought, and particularly so in a white Western Euro-American discourse which almost invariably placed the 'whites', 'Europeans' or 'Caucasians' at the pinnacle of a hierarchy of humankind (Kiernan 1969, Miles 1989, Malik 1996). The divisions of the populations of the world into postulated 'races' were almost entirely defined by externally observable physical features of skin colour, hair type, stature and facial appearance and the science of races significantly pre-dated modern knowledge of genetics. The proponents of what was viewed as race science believed – in ways which will be explored in Chapter 2 – that in the concept 'race' they held the key to history, culture and civilisation; race was believed to determine culture, human capacities, temperament and dispositions of all kinds.

There are three main reasons why this science of races has come to be discredited. First, it proved impossible to sustain any single classificatory system because the degree of variation within postulated races came to be recognised as greater than the variation between them. Second, the postulate that racial difference could account for many other differences – presumed to be racially inherited – was replaced by the sociological and anthropological observation that historical circumstance and cultural difference accounted for these differences much more satisfactorily. And third, by the middle of the 20th century it was cruelly evident that the science of racial difference had been allied to the denial of dignity and the very right to life of 'races' perceived as lower and dispensable. It is for these reasons that we discard the concept of race as an analytical tool and it is in this sense – the discredited science of racial inheritance and the idea of discrete divisions as the bearers of a great inescapable compound of social cultural inequality and difference – that we cannot sustain the term as part of the language of sociological observation and explanation.

While being clear about what we discard, we must also be clear about what remains. There remain throughout the world broad population clusters where characteristic appearance types can be found. There are evidently more people of dark-skinned appearance in Lagos, Nigeria, than in Stockholm, Sweden. What the sociologist does is not to fail to observe this but to decline to accept that a whole edifice of a theory of civilisations can be built on such observations. What is sociologically significant are the social meanings attributed to such differences rather than the differences themselves. The second thing which remains is a cultural or ideological inheritance of ideas about race – of which the central one is the idea of inescapable difference and inequality – which is reproduced on the one hand as ideas and on the other hand is matched in the social orders we have described as 'racialised'. In the chapters discussing the USA, we explore the ways in which racialisation has developed historically, and in Chapter 2 we examine racism as the belief in inescapable difference and inequality.

Ethnic, ethnicity, social discourse, sociological discourse

We shall engage, throughout this book, with a discourse of race and a discourse of ethnicity, but not in an even-handed way. The reason for the different treatment of the term 'ethnic' is that it does not suffer from the historical association of error in the way that the concept of race does. If the centre of gravity of the concept 'ethnic' is ancestry, culture and language then it is unmistakable that ancestry and beliefs about ancestry have real sociological meaning, that cultural difference is a central facet of life-as-lived on both a global and a local scale and that we can observe both a factual distribution of language use and the social meanings which are attributed to language difference. To explain this last point by way of examples, there are Welsh speakers in Wales and French speakers in Quebec as 'simple' facts of language difference and these differences are construed into ethnic or national identities in which language survival is a core element of a wider social movement. Language is a fact of life but it is also a dimension of the politics of culture.

All commentators on the concept of ethnic group agree that it refers to the social elaboration of collective identities whereby individuals see themselves as one among others like themselves. Collectively, people – whose boundaries may be loosely or tightly defined – distinguish themselves from other people. Thus ethnicity is about social classifications emerging within *relationships*, as Eriksen (1993b) especially has emphasised. There are not simply groups – a static category – but social relationships in which people distinguish themselves from others. But how do people make these distinctions and cultivate these identities? The enduring dimensions of social life around which ethnic identities are built are the ones which just above we have called the 'centre of gravity' of the concept 'ethnic' – ancestry, culture and language. But the relational nature of ethnicity means that we cannot speak of ethnic groups as peoples who share ancestry, culture and language. This sharing may be more or less the case but for ethnicity to spring to life it is necessary that *real or perceived differences of ancestry, culture and language are mobilised in social transactions.* People know or say that 'we are different from them' because of the way we speak, the customs and ways of life we hold dear, and the continuity of our people through the generations.

Ancestry

The concept of ancestry illustrates perfectly the way in which ethnicity constitutes a socially grounded, a culturally elaborated and a socially constructed phenomenon. People commonly know of their fathers and mothers and their grandparents and of a wider network of kin – both dead and alive – to whom they are connected. The way in which these relationships are remembered, in societies with stronger or weaker kinship systems, is the social foundation of ancestry. But the way in which people connect themselves to their ancestors is also a function of how ancestry is socially constructed and culturally elaborated. People may choose to remember or forget aspects of their past and may choose to venerate some ancestors and discard others. Not only will people value some ancestors and not others, they will also play fast and loose about who their ancestors are. What is true of ancestry is true of ethnicity – both are simultaneously socially grounded and socially constructed.

People particularly remember their ancestors when they believe them to have died nobly defending their folk or at the hands of a terrible foe. In the accounts of the Yugoslav civil wars of the early 1990s (Glenny 1990, 1992, Bennett 1995) we find examples of both the most remote and the very immediate memory of ancestors. To stimulate Serbian loyalties, the ideologue of the Serbian cause Milosevic ordered the bones of Prince Lazar to be displayed in every town in the Serbian heartlands. The Prince had died over 600 years earlier defending 'his people' against the 'invading hordes' of infidels. Here ancestry is stretched as far as it can go in connecting a collective contemporary identity with a noble past. Much more immediate is Bennett's (1995) account of the Serbian ethnic warrior whose devotion to his cause draws upon his memory of watching his parents murdered by Croatian fascists. Here the glorious and slain ancestors are the immediately remembered father and mother; for others in violent struggles it will be brothers and sisters, parents, grandparents and beyond.

Ethnic communities which convey a historically enduring sense of peoplehood are defined by Anthony Smith (1981, 1986, 1991, 1995) as *ethnie* and his conceptualisation expresses the importance of ancestry as a dimension of ethnicity so well as to merit a longer quotation:

> Ethnie have vied or colluded with other forms of community – of city, class, religion, region – in providing a sense of identity among populations and in inspiring in them a nostalgia for their past and its traditions. In periods of grave crisis, it has even been able to arouse in them powerful sentiments of anger and revenge for what were seen as attacks on a traditional lifestyle and identity. For the most part, however, ethnie have provided foci of identification with ancestors and thereby a means of confronting death, especially violent death at the hands of enemies. By invoking a collective name, by the use of symbolic images of community, by the generation of stereotypes of the community and its foes, by the ritual performance and rehearsal of ceremonies and feasts and sacrifices, by the communal recitation of past deeds and ancient heroes' exploits, men and women have been enabled to bury their sense of loneliness and insecurity in the face of natural disasters and human violence by feeling themselves to partake of a collectivity and its historic fate which transcends their individual existences. (Smith 1986)

Culture and language

For both sociologist and anthropologist the concept of culture is simultaneously a central one and a tantalising diffuse one. For much of its history it has played the part of emphasising the importance of learning as against innate bio-psychological universals, and of therefore underscoring the seemingly endless variation in the construction of cultures. At its widest, the term has incorporated so-called material culture – the objects created, the material reproduction of human societies – but its principal reference is to the symbolic, to valued styles and ways of life, to manners and to ritual and custom with respect, for example, to birth, marriage and death, food and dress. The student of ethnicity is interested in those dimensions of culture which are connected to the construction of group boundaries. Culture should not be thought of as a fixed quality; cultures shift both in small incremental steps and in seemingly dramatic moments wherein we imagine we glimpse the end of a way of life or the beginning of a new one. Neither should it be thought of as 'attached' to a group, community, nation or people in such a way that we can, without qualification, define 'this people' as the people who share 'this culture'. Within an ethnic group we will typically find that cultural standards are contested and variable. Among Sikhs in Britain for example the importance attached to dress, the wearing of turbans by men, the non-cutting of hair, the ways in which marriages are negotiated, and relationships structured by gender, are all subject to dispute; they vary and they change. Among Welsh people in Britain – a nation rather than an ethnic group, but the principles are the same – the importance attached to Welsh speaking is not uniform, just as the ability to speak Welsh itself is very unevenly spread through Wales. In this sense Welshness in Britain or Sikhness in Britain cannot be described by reference to a unitary set of cultural traits. Devotion to specific cultural forms varies across a group and the forms are frequently contested and constantly being defined and redefined.

Similarly there is not a one-to-one relationship between ethnic groups and language. Languages 'stretch' across many groups who may think of themselves as ethnically distinct. Among English-speaking Americans there is a common tongue but within that population of English speakers, attachments to ancestral ethnic identities persist. At the same time language is undoubtedly a powerful group marker, especially since, if the language is unknown to outsiders, it is a means of social exclusion. But where language is part of an ethnic or ethnonational claim, it is frequently right at the heart of the boundary-making process as the examples of the Welsh, Catalans, Basques, Quebecois and many others illustrate (May 1999). The importance of language does not simply correspond with its widespread use. The value attached to a language is often coupled with a sense of loss as its speakers decline in number, or a sense of unwonted change when a language changes or, as its defenders would see, is corrupted and hopelessly misused. England has its defenders of good plain English (uncorrupted by American – at school I was reprimanded by a teacher for using that lazy Americanism 'OK'), France charges its Academie Française with the sacred task of preserving proper French, and German speakers worry about the encroachment on their language of American English. Language use is surrounded by ideas of what is proper and what is pure, and language domains are surrounded by a sense of sacredness and defence against violation or neglect.

These constructions of culture and language in relation to ethnic and national identities cannot be utterly divorced from the 'appearance type' and visible differences which have long been associated with the concept of race. There are two reasons for this. The first is that conceptions of colour difference and appearance type are themselves culturally constructed and inserted into popular views of us and them and into ideas of what constitutes beauty and worth. The second is that where ancestry and culture/language differences are construed into ethnic identities, they are frequently accompanied by visible differences whether permanent or transient. Where people share ethnic identity and common experience it is likely that out of this common experience come characteristic mannerisms of speech, dress and posture which make people instantly recognisable as X or Y to all the Xs and Ys who are initiated into the system of social recognition. It remains true that physical differences do not disappear over generations whereas people may learn and unlearn cultures, learn and forget languages, change their styles of dress or worship, change the way in which they select marriage partners, and do all this in a generation or two or less. But even if the physical differences do not disappear it is certainly true that the social significance attached to them can change radically, quickly and dramatically. South Africa moved, in the space of less than ten years from the late 1980s to 1994, from an apparently resolute racist state to a country which, with admitted difficulty, is transforming itself into a multi-ethnic democracy (Adam and Moodley 1993).

Ethnicity as relationships, as process

Ethnic identities are articulated around ancestry, culture and language which are subject to change, redefinition and contestation. Thus we cannot talk simply of 'ethnic groups'. It follows that if ethnic groups are not fixed and uncomplicated entities, then our subject is not 'intergroup relations' or 'ethnic relations' as it was once mistakenly conceived. Rather we should understand ethnicity as a *social process*, as the moving boundaries and identities which people, collectively and individually, draw around themselves in their social lives. Central to this process is the production and reproduction of culture, of acknowledged ancestry and ideologies of ancestry, and the use of language as a marker of social difference and the emblem of a people. The social relations which are only in part predicated on these systems of social classification are not a special and limited type, 'ethnic' or 'racial relations'. They are social, political and economic relations which have an ethnic dimension, and this dimension is activated – or suppressed – in a wide variety of contexts.

At the level of individual action ethnicity is a signal of identification. At the social system level ethnicity refers to the 'systematic and enduring social reproduction of basic classificatory differences between categories of people who see themselves as culturally discrete' (Eriksen, 1993). These categories are not stable or permanent orderings of people or symbols.

Once we begin to think of ethnicity as a dimension of social relationships, and not of 'ethnic relations' as a specific type of relationship, then it becomes possible to deconstruct some of the language used in talking about ethnicity. This may be best illustrated by an example. In the case of the former Yugoslavia we read of Serbian-Croatian conflict described as 'ethnic conflict'. This conveys at least two common-sense implications, that Serbian and Croatian are unambiguously different groups and that this profound historical and cultural difference is the cause of the conflict, as if the ethnic difference made the conflict almost inevitable. Both of these common-sense implications could be frankly wrong or at very best misleading. In the cities of old Yugoslavia, a considerable number of Serbians and Croatians intermarried so that many people described themselves as neither Serb nor Croat but as Yugoslavian, and the list of cultural attributes which they shared could be made at least as long as the ways in which they diverged (Glenny 1990, 1992, Bennett 1995). And we cannot be at all sure of what the principal 'causes' of the conflicts were: did they arise from skilful manipulation by a minority of ruthless Serbians (or Croats) or were the mutual animosities deeply felt and widely shared in the respective groups? Even if we allow that there were some long-standing animosities, we would still need to explain how these animosities were translated into murderous conflict. Our answer to these questions would affect our view of whether the conflict was adequately described as 'ethnic'. The same could be said of a multitude of conflicts worldwide which are routinely reported in the public discourse as 'ethnic'.

The construction of categories and identities

The conceptual language of *constructionism* (Nagel 1994) has become increasingly prominent in the last part of the 20th century. This does not represent a genuinely new departure but an elaboration of a much older theme in sociology, that is the importance of social definitions, the importance of labels, and the social power mobilised by those who are in a position to create and sustain both the labels and the meanings the labels confer. We have been thus far emphasising the way in which ethnic identities may be accentuated or suppressed and how they may change their conformation. But while Thomas' (1966) famous dictum that 'if men define situations as real they are real in their consequences' carries in it this important kernel of truth it has to be counterposed to an understanding that the 'material' situations or contexts of social life are capable of being very compelling.

Men and women are not simply 'free' to change the definition of the situations in which they live; whether conceived as material and economic circumstances, as political and legal power and control of the means of violence, or as social and moral cultures, the 'situations', are compelling and constraining in themselves. So a social constructionist approach to ethnicity is a guard against an assumption of the essential permanence of groups or cultures. This has to be balanced against a view that ethnic identities are not made and remade at will. We need to consider the *manner* in which ethnic identities and classificatory systems are constructed and the *contexts* within which ethnicity takes shape as a dimension of structure and action.

Ethnicity: global and local, the grand and minor scale, *de jure/de facto*

Three important modalities on which ethnicity varies are scope, scale and formality. The scope of ethnic identities may reach from the most local to the global, the scale may vary from the macro-social to the interpersonal exchanges of micro-social life, and ethnicity may be a matter of regular but informal practice or formalised into legal and constitutional principle.

Global and local

Some ethnic identities, and, in particular, religious identities, are played out on a global stage, the most evident contemporary example of which is Islamic identity. This is not to say that Islamic identity takes a single global form – far from it – but that it has a global presence in such a way that local forms are seen within an international framework. Language cultures too have a universal scope; consider the phrases the 'English-speaking world' and 'Francophonie'. These are not ethnic identities in precisely the way we have described them but they do constitute religious and linguistic cultures which are global in their impact and inform local expressions of cultural difference. Similarly the idea of 'race', as we discussed it earlier in this chapter, has locally situated forms as in, for example, the caste-like black/white racialised order of the old southern states of the USA. But it also became part of a global racialised ordering of peoples – a world of white ascendancy.

This global use of racial distinctions was the hallmark of a world dominated by (white) European colonialisms over the last four centuries and lasting into the present century until the collapse of the Portuguese empire in 1974. As Balibar and Wallerstein (1991) have argued, racialisation was worldwide. The white–black, European–native, advanced–primitive distinctions were applied across the globe in forms of thinking and practice which classed together huge numbers of people who had no social organic connection with each other. In the local system, black people in Indianola, Mississippi, knew each other or knew of each other, and so did white folk. But black–white and African–European became global categories participated in by French, British, Dutch and other colonialisms alike. By contrast, 'ethnic' frequently has a local connotation, whereby the people who define themselves, or are defined by others as being of the same group, actually do know each other, know of each other, and have some prospect of being in contact with each other.

Macro-, meso- and micro-ethnicity

We can observe ethnicity in macro-social formations, in the intermediate meso-structures of social institutions, and in the face-to-face exchanges of micro-social life. The *macro*-social formations are the major economic and political structures of the social order. When these are ethnically shaped they constitute a more or less enduring framework within which the meaning and import of ethnicity can evolve. Multi-ethnic societies vary in the manner and degree to which wealth and power are associated with a privileged ethnic elite or with an ethnic majority. In the USA there is a long-enduring association of African Americans with gross social disadvantage (Wilson 1987, O'Hare *et al.* 1991, Small 1994) among whom a great disproportion are the urban poor and socially excluded. In Malaysia, the Malays are disproportionately repre-sented as the rural peasant class who are both economically and regionally distinctive, as well as being prominent as a political and governmental elite. White supremacist America and apartheid South Africa were both societies which were politically and legally struc-tured by ethnic differentiation. In the USA social segregation was supported by law and the rule of 'separate but equal' was, until 1954, a guiding legal principle. In apartheid South Africa the whole concept of citizenship and practice of political participation was predicated on 'race' or ethnicity.

The meso-structures of society are the institutions intermediate between the individual and the state which are sometimes indepen-dent institutions and sometimes regulated by the state. Of central importance here are educational institutions since it is through schools and universities that the cultural capital for advancement is acquired and through them that cultural identities are preserved. The most decisive cultural struggles are about the dominance of languages which represent majorities, dominant cultures or elites in state-regulated education systems (Eriksen 1991, May 1999). In the past the schools have been, in Wales, the instrument of enforcing the dominance of English and are now the scene of state-sponsored efforts to revive Welsh (Williams 1994). In South Africa the state's wish to impose learning in Afrikaans on township schoolchildren was the occasion for a black student revolt and bloody repression by the apartheid state (Mare 1993). In East Malaysia, a Malay-dominated state has imposed education in Malay on Kadazan peoples and the Quebec provincial government has crucially used its control of state education to sustain the use of French and delay or roll back the encroachments of English (Khan and Loh Kok Wah 1992, Taylor 1992).

In these ways schools and universities are cultural battlegrounds where dominant cultures achieve their superiority and suppressed cultures build their resistance. Where a minority language comes to be seen as an educational and economic disadvantage, its decline may be a result of both suppression by the majority – as was Welsh by the dominant English culture – and collusion by a generation of 'minority' language speakers. A critical generation of parents decide not to pass the ancestral language on to their children whose educa-tion is in the majority language. The steep decline in Welsh speak-ing occurred in the late 19th and early 20th centuries when critical generations of Welsh-speaking bilingual parents did not pass their Welsh to their children. The language is then lost in the primary sphere – the home and family life – and while it may be revived in the educational sphere, it is an open question as to whether minority languages can thence be restored to private discourse. The same kind of process can be observed with respect to Maori speaking in New Zealand (May 1998).

In the face-to-face micro-social sphere ethnic identities, and the customs which sustain them, are negotiated in everyday life. Groups who migrate to new urban centres must eventually make decisions about what language to speak to their children, about how or whether to enforce codes of dress on possibly reluctant youngsters, and about how much latitude to permit in the marriage choices of their daughters and sons. In societies structured upon ethnic or 'racial' hierarchies, the patterns of dominance and subordination are reproduced in everyday life so that interpersonal exchanges across ethnic divides are marked by postures and manners which reinforce the hierarchy, as was the case where white Americans called black men, whatever their age, 'boy' or by their first name only.

We should not think of the macro-social dimensions of ethnicity as necessarily more important than the micro-social. It is the hallmark of highly ethnicised or racialised systems where ethnic definitions are totalised, that micro-social interactions are governed by ethnic rules just as the principal centres of economic and political power are commanded by an ethnic elite. Systems of ethnic or racial classification are 'totalised' when ethnic-relevant rules governing behaviour stretch into every imaginable corner of life. As a matter of enforced custom or law in both South Africa and the USA in the white supremacist era (Camejo 1976, Fredrickson 1981, Cell 1982), being born, going to school, making friends, making love, worshipping God, saying hello, having a drink of water, going to the lavatory, swimming in the sea, visiting parks, dying and being buried were all governed by racialised ethnic principles.

This is why the interpersonal dramas of daily life become the material of biography drama and fiction illustrating the ethnic order through the pain, irony and dilemmas of interpersonal life (Washington 1945, Douglass 1962, Baldwin 1965, Moody 1968). Frederick Douglass escaped from slavery in the old South by dressing as a sailor and boarding a ship to the north eastern seaboard of the USA. He sat for hours through the tension of suspecting that a white passenger had recognised him and speculated for the rest of his life that this German immigrant had decided to keep his mouth shut. Douglass went on to a famous career in the fight against slavery. Watson's (1970) account of passing for white in South Africa tells of individuals who successfully 'passed', and then faced the dilemma of whether to attend the funeral of a family member, knowing that their presence would have announced their ethnic identity. In societies where ethnic rules and systems of classification are not totalised, small ethnic dramas are nonetheless played out in everyday life. Black workers in British offices and factories have to decide how to respond to the insistent 'racial jokes' of their white workmates and schoolteachers have to respond to requests for absence by pupils who want to observe religious festivals or attend to family affairs. Children of migrant families balance the expectations of their parents in honouring their ancestry against the demands of the new country, demands which may appear to run against those of their parents. The sociology of ethnicity is concerned with these daily exchanges as well as the grand events and structural changes which mark the beginning and end of systems.

On the macro-social scale the US Supreme Court decision in 1954, *Brown* v. *The Board of Education of Kansas*, paved the way for the ending of segregation. A principle which lasted over half a century, that it was possible to provide separate but equal facilities, was overthrown by a mother who challenged the Kansas Board of Education's allocation procedures. On the minor face-to-face scale, in white supremacist America, a small inclination of the head, a nod or a wink, may have sustained or breached the racial etiquette by which the minutest forms of daily life were governed. A 1959 account of this etiquette describes the expectations of non-white nannies:

> If you are a non-white nurse-maid and wish to consume an ice-cream cone or soda-pop along with the white child in your custody, you are permitted by the etiquette to do so, provided you take the refreshment with you – that is you cannot sit at a table, use utensils, or have a drink of water (except in a paper cup). (Kennedy 1959)

Similar rules applied to a man rowing a boat for white men:

> Four southern white fishermen together with a non-white man found themselves in the middle of a lake at lunch-time. Before partaking of food they required the non-white to sit in the bow of the boat, and laid a fishing pole laterally across the boat to segregate him from them. (*ibid.*, p. 208)

These are forms of etiquette enforced by custom. In the matter of marriage, practice was also inscribed into the law, as a South Carolina constitutional enactment illustrates:

> It shall be unlawful for any white man to intermarry with any woman of either Indian or Negro races, or any mulatto, mestizo, or half-breed, or for any white woman to intermarry with any person other than a white man... This law prohibits white women from marrying Mongolians or Malays, but leaves white men free to do so. (Kennedy 1959, p. 69)

In these 'command' circumstances of ethnicity, where ethnic rules are regularly enforced by violence or the threat of violence, the rules must be observed, evaded by subterfuge or resisted by concerted political action. In other circumstances ethnic identities change voluntarily; the rules of, for example, language use, dress and marriage, are renegotiated in everyday life.

De facto, de jure ethnicity

These illustrations show not only that ethnicity is constituted at a macro-social, meso-social and micro-social level but also that ethnic systems of classification may be simply a matter of fact (*de facto*) or may become a matter of law (*de jure*). The illustrations from US state laws which required segregation are instances of the *de jure* representation and enforcement of ethnic boundaries. Where this kind of law is in force the customary rules of interethnic behaviour are supported by the law so that breaches are punished not only by social shaming or embarrassment but also by the full measure of legal sanctions. In the sustaining of systems of ethnic supremacy legal violence is commonly accompanied by non-legal violence. While state laws enforced segregation in the USA, the extra-legal violence of the Ku Klux Klan, founded after the American Civil War, and lynch mobs have acted to maintain white supremacy.

One of the consequences of legislating systems of ethnic classification is that everyone must be classified and, whatever identities are expressed in daily life, the law must give expression to a codification of categories. In apartheid South Africa those who were unsure of their grouping or wished to contest the one they had been assigned could appeal to a reclassification court. The logic is that, if this leisure park, this railway carriage or this beach is reserved for whites then one must be sure who is white and who is not.

Paradoxically instruments of public policy which seek to redress the historical legacy of ethnic inequalities must do the same thing; if a company is to achieve a target of 40 per cent employees from group A then it must be possible to know who is A and who is B.

Volition and constraint

The examples we have used and the conceptual distinctions we have made have begun to clarify the way in which, in Eriksen's phrase, ethnicity is the 'systematic and enduring social reproduction of basic classificatory differences between categories of people who see themselves as culturally discrete' (Eriksen 1993b). There are things here which need to be qualified and elaborated. One of the most contentious parts of this definition, plain and simple though it seems, is the phrase 'who see themselves'. This is to posit ethnicity as exclusively or principally a matter of intended and voluntary identification; many of the examples we have given do not fit this volitional model of ethnicity. Especially within systems of ethnic supremacy the categories are frankly created by some and imposed on others; even the beneficiaries of the rules can barely escape them or the behaviour the rules require. A distinction between externally imposed boundaries of exclusion and internal boundaries of inclusion as the base of a distinction between 'race' and 'ethnic' has been advocated by some but has serious weaknesses. The most important of these is that boundaries which have been unmistakably characterised as 'racial' can become the basis of a real communal and political solidarity as is exemplified by the African American embracing of the term black, above all in the wake of the black consciousness movements of the 1960s. The social exclusion known as ethnic cleansing in Yugoslavia was carried out in the 1990s by groups (Serbian, Croatian, Bosnian) who would normally be regarded as ethnic or national and, in the case of Muslims, as religious. Did these boundaries, being ethnic and cultural in the 1980s, become 'racial' in the 1990s?

We need to qualify Eriksen's use of the phrase 'see themselves', especially in the light of his equal insistence that ethnicity is expressed in relationships. Ethnicity is a game which two can play and indeed there must be two to play. Wherever these relationships are unequal they are constraining and even where they are not formally unequal the individual is subject to sets of social expectations both within his or her own group and from the 'others'.

Systems of ethnic classification are, therefore, as with all social behaviour, compounds of constraint and choice. What social history does show without doubt is that these systems are subject to change – both the ethnic ordering itself and the messages it conveys are moderated, modified and sometimes transformed, however entrenched they once may have seemed. These changes occur, we have argued, at the macro-social, meso-social and micro-social level: political struggle and reform can bring about radical redefinitions of the ethnic rules; schools, workplace and places of worship are institutional settings of ethnic change; and ethnic identities and cultures are played out, contested and renegotiated daily in interpersonal life.

The construction of categories

We have also stressed that ethnic categories, the terms which people use to describe themselves or the terms which are used by others, and what Barth (1969) has called the 'cultural stuff' contained within them, are constructed categories. They are not simply a direct product of shared ancestry, culture and language, but rather, also of the way ancestry is viewed, culture is construed and language is used in the formation and modification of ethnic identities, both as collective and individual identities. An example from Malaysia, based on Khan and Loh Kok Wah's account (1992), will illustrate the process of construction and the mixture of volition and constraint.

The state of Sabah is part of East Malaysia, has a distinctive history from the Malay peninsula but was incorporated into the newly independent Malaysia in 1963. The indigenous peoples of Sabah have regional identities, and identities based on language and dialect, and all those who are not Muslim are thus distinguished from local Malay Muslims and from the hegemonic definition of Malaysia as a predominantly Malay country. By the 1970s many of the indigenous peoples were referring to themselves as Kadazan, a term which replaced the former and less complimentary term Dusun. Those listed as Dusun in the 1960 census were categorised as Kadazan in the 1970 census, about 30 per cent of the population of Sabah. The political leaders who emphasised their Kadazan identity sought to strengthen a common Kadazan identity and to overcome regional and dialect identifications among their potential followership. 'By emphasizing the similarities among themselves and especially their common differences from the Malay Muslims and other groups' (Khan and Loh Kok Wah 1992, p. 226) they began to achieve a measure of Kadazan unity. The Kadazan leadership was in power at the point of incorporation into Malaysia as a state and sought to strengthen the Kadazan identity and conserve Kadazan language and culture.

This Kadazanisation was not complete and Malay Muslims stood to gain from consolidating their own position and from collaborating with the Muslim-dominated central government. When the early Kadazan government was replaced by a Muslim-led government in Sabah, the legislature set about reversing the cultural gains of Kadazanisation, that is by declaring Islam the official religion of Sabah and making Malay the official language of schools and courts. By the 1980s a Sabah government sympathetic to the federal government began to reclassify all people 'of Malay stock and related groups as "Pribumi"'and this term, which included Kadazan, covered over 80 per cent of the population. But the more the Sabah government worked closely with the federal government (in, for example, promoting investment and federal support) the more the Kadazan intelligentsia concluded that it was excluded, while local and pensinsular Malays benefited from the openings which development provided. Kadazan resistance to this loss of position was in part political as we have described, but was also cultural and expressed itself as the defence of the Kadazan language and the promotion of cultural activities such as the encouragement of the celebration of the Harvest Festival. At the same time the category 'Bumiputera', a federal classification of all indigenous peoples including native groups such as the Kadazan as well as Malays, being a classificatory group who can claim privileges *qua* Bumiputera, offers a basis for Kadazan to throw in their lot with Malays (Khan and Loh Kok Wah 1992).

This illustration is typical in several respects of the post-colonial world; it displays virtually all the features that we have conceptually outlined. It shows that ethnic identities are in part *grounded*, these grounded elements being represented by the regional origins of peoples within Sabah, the real differences of language and dialect, and the practice of Islamic and non-Islamic religious traditions. These grounded elements of ethnicity are reproduced in everyday life. The local languages and dialects are used in the micro-social spheres of family and friends, but are threatened with replacement by Malay in the meso-social sphere of schooling where teaching in bahasa Melayu was required. Local cultures are also at risk of being submerged as a consequence of the macro-social influence of the federal government, dominated as it is by the Islamic Malay mould. The example also shows how ethnic identities are constructed and change as a consequence of both internal and external pressures. Internally, Kadazan identity was to a considerable extent fostered by intellectual leaders who wanted to solidify a pan-Kadazan identity; externally, the pressures of the federal government ran counter to local cultural identities. The Kadazan nationalists wished to extend the meaning and the appeal of the term 'Kadazan' among a people to whom it could plausibly apply but not all of whom wholly accepted it. The changing terminology of the census shows how formal *de jure* definitions are part of the public struggle for dominance of competing definitions of groups, and the federal legislation which confers special rights on Bumiputera has the effect of making this the identity which is of greatest account in employment, business and other spheres.

Ethnicity in contexts

The last example also neatly illustrates a central element of the nature of ethnicity – the contextualisation of ethnic identities. What was once called the study of 'race relations' and 'ethnic relations' carried implications in its title. The term 'ethnic relations' suggests relations which are primarily 'ethnic' or are capable of being abstracted as such. There are social circumstances in which the consciousness of ethnicity is central or even dominant, and in racialised 'supremacist' societies, racial categories can be both all-pervasive and all-important. But there are also many circumstances in which ethnic or racial categories play a relatively minor part or where their importance varies from context to context. Even where ethnic categories are important and central they are, nonetheless, part of a wider complex of political and economic relations; to lift them from this context as ethnic relations *sui generis* is the basic error of the attempts to create 'theories of ethnic relations'. We find, therefore, in ethnicity, a double contextualisation. Ethnicity as a social phenomenon is embedded in social, political and economic structures which form an important element of both the way ethnicity is expressed and the social importance it assumes. At the same time ethnicity as an element of individual consciousness and action varies in intensity and import depending on the context of action.

Rex's 'race relations' situations

This 'structured contextuality' is well recognised and was expounded nearly three decades ago in the early work of John Rex (Rex 1973, 1983) in which he set out to distinguish 'the kinds of societies in which race relations... occur'. We may wish to set aside the term 'race relations' for the reasons cited earlier in this chapter, and replace it with race making or 'ethnic-making situations'; but the emphasis on the situations – or contexts – is classically evident. This is to say that the 'race' or 'ethnic' dimension is to be understood above all within these wider social frameworks which may be simultaneously 'typified' and historically placed. In Rex's (1983) model there are three characteristic elements in 'race relations' situations:

1. a situation of differentiation, inequality and pluralism between groups
2. the possibility of clearly distinguishing between such groups by their physical appearance, their culture or occasionally merely by their ancestry
3. the justification and explanation of this discrimination in terms of some kind of implicit or explicit theory, frequently but not always of a biological kind.

He cites, as examples of the people who may become parties to these situations, vanquished enemies, slaves, immigrants, refugees, indentured labourers and trading minorities, and he makes it clear that he sees colonial and slavery situations as classic contexts of race and ethnic making. It is this emphasis on context, type and history which guides much of what is discussed in subsequent chapters in this volume, and the choice of examples in later case studies. Ethnicity is contextualised within political and economic structures outside of whose shaping influence it is less readily understood; but the systems of ethnic classification and identification, willed and compelled, can and often do become a constituent and even defining element of the social formation taken as a whole.

The economic context

In the modern world, the world of the last 300 to 400 years, many of the new contexts of ethnicisation and racialisation have arisen from the spreading influence of the military, political and economic power of the European states. Within the economic sphere, activities have become closely identified with systems of ethnic classification in the cases of slavery, indentured labour, land dispossession and encroachment, trading minorities and migrant labour more generally. The movements of people have been both voluntary and coerced and the degree to which language and culture have survived migration has varied; in all instances where there is some continuity of culture, there have nonetheless been transformations of old forms and the creation of new ones; mosques in the cane fields of Fiji will not be quite the same as mosques in India. The recurrent feature of all these economic contexts of ethnicity is a more or less predictable and clear identification of ethnic classification with economic function. In the USA, Africans were enslaved to carry out plantation field labour, in Fiji, Indians were imported to tend the cane fields, as were Japanese, Chinese and Filipinos in Hawai'i, and in the Caribbean, parts of Indonesia and what is now Malaysia, the Chinese formed a class of traders and shopkeepers. It is these and comparable examples which are explored in Chapters 4 and 5 of this volume.

The political context

These ethnic classifications frequently come to form, as a matter of law or as a matter of fact, a constituent element of politics. Groups who are ethnically identified have differential access to political power, form the natural constituency of competing political parties, and become the bearers or the targets of ethnic and racial ideologies. In the process of the formation of states, older and more recent, there is virtually always a myth of who are 'the people' and who are the right and proper members of the national society. Nation-states, as they are commonly described, control entry into the society through immigration laws and border controls, and control access to citizenship and nationality. In these ways, ethnic categories become part of the stuff of political ideology and organization, both in creating or hardening the categories themselves, and in the fostering of stereotypes expressed in the discourse of ethnic politics. Politics are 'ethnically informed' in some characteristic settings: in the land claims and cultural restoration movements of indigenous peoples, in immigration debates and the portrayal of migrants as unwonted and alien, in political parties with ethnic names or ethnically defined support, and in the cultural politics of nation making and the racialised politics of ethnic supremacist systems.

Just how and why economic and political situations foster ethnic consciousness and action are themes throughout this book; we can sketch out some of the principal explanations and interpretations here. In the economic sphere ethnic categories are frequently mobilised in the defence of economic privilege and in the ideological rationale for suppression of the disprivileged. In such instances fall all cases of the racialised defence of slavery – where those who are enslaved are seen as being a people suited to slavery and those who are free as being naturally free. Where the division of labour matches ethnic difference, groups are often portrayed as especially fitted for their function or incapable of some higher function, and those dispossessed of their land may be portrayed as naturally idle or incapable of development. In open and competitive labour markets, groups defined by ancestry, culture and language are regarded as legitimate or illegitimate competitors, and among trading minorities the cultural familiarity and the appeal of particularistic ties become part of the lubrication of business relationships – in the right circumstances traders may have much to gain by remembering their ethnic ancestry. Those who see their fortunes diminished by the success of ethnically distinct traders may turn on them and often have, as seen in attacks in 1998 on Chinese shopkeepers in Indonesia and Korean shopkeepers in the USA.

Some of the same motives can be found in political organisations where economic interests are politically represented and ethnically defined. This would be the case where, for example, in South Africa apartheid was the expression of white economic privilege, and in contemporary Europe where xenophobic politics appeal to workers who seek to protect themselves against others they see as illegitimate competitors. Ethnicity is also expressed within the political sphere in a more generalised way since ideologies of state formation, persistence and continuity are so frequently linked to concepts of peoplehood. These themes are pursued in Chapters 6 and 7.

Contextualised ethnicity, the economic and the political

Ethnicity is, then, a sometimes pliant and sometimes compelling mode of group identity in which significance is attributed to ancestry, to culture and to language. Ethnic meanings and collective identities change in form and content as circumstances change but nonetheless ethnic meanings and allegiances are not mere constructions or inventions. Ethnicity is both socially constructed as a changing set of labels and claims and is in important respects socially grounded in forms of social organisation, extensions of kinship, and in the regularities of obligations and social bonds. Claims are made about the constitution of communities, both collectively and individually, but these claims are made in contexts of unequal power which moderate the ability of individuals and collectivities to make their claims hold, or to sustain favourable and resist unfavourable representations.

The economic settings of ethnic collectivities – through which ethnically defined populations are encompassed within specific locations in the division of labour and the class structure – are unequal in power and privilege, and so too are the political settings, with minorities appearing as both privileged elite and as relatively powerless suppressed groups. The boundaries of ethnic groups are symbolically represented – as the bearers of a specific language, religion or, more generally, 'culture'; but they are also materially constituted within the structures of power and wealth. Thus ethnicity should be regarded as materially and symbolically constituted, as a systemic feature beyond the reach of individual actors, as well as a dimension of individual action itself.

The latter part of this chapter has briefly established this contextual nature of ethnicity and suggested the economic and the political spheres as being the principal ones both within which it is played out and also within which it may be constituted. Rex's contribution, to which we referred, was clearly to acknowledge the importance of the economic contexts for the mobilisation of 'racial' or ethnic meanings, identifying these contexts and their principal features and types. The ethnically defined system of inequality, the class-situated ethnic groups and the ethnically ordered division of labour are the classic loci of what are simultaneously economically ordered ethnicities and ethnically framed economic structures. The ethnicised economic structures of colonial and post-colonial societies are important cases and Malaysia, Fiji and South Africa are classic examples. So too are the slavery and post-slavery systems of societies such as the USA, the islands of the Caribbean and Brazil. More recent in its formation is the post-colonial multi-ethnicity of the metropolitan centres of Europe such as France, Britain and the Netherlands which have received in-migrants from former colonies. These migrants have, at least in the first instance, been incorporated into characteristic low-pay and low-security niches within the urban economies. The 'ethnicised' or 'racialised' division of labour is a worldwide phenomenon. Groups who see themselves, or are seen by others, as ethnically distinct, occupy highly specific locations within the division of labour in such a way that the ethnic category and the niche within the division of labour appear to become synonymous – as with the Malay peasant producer in Malaya-Malaysia, the Chinese merchant in Jamaica or the Indian cane grower in Fiji. As well as being forms of the division of labour, these situations are also forms of inequality, of class structure and of relations or command and superordination. This is why, for example, the Hawaiian term 'haole', meaning white and European/American by ancestry, came to be coterminous with 'boss', work supervisor and manager and a social status of exclusivity and command (Kanahele 1996). Correspondingly the cultures of suppressed peoples are portrayed as inferior and backward.

Political systems too become ethnically ordered in the sense that both the actual distribution of formal power and the symbolic representations of this power come to follow the ethnic contours of a given social order. This is the case in systems of slavery, of colonial domination, and in the exercise of political power in both democratic and non-democratic orders. In the immediate post-independence elections in Sri Lanka, ethnic identities came to be actively politically salient. Tamils were seen by majority Sinhalese not merely as Tamils but as closely identified with a Colombo-based (the Sri Lankan capital city) elite whose thinking had been much influenced by the colonial elite under British rule (Geertz 1973).

In such circumstances, the legitimisation of state power, the whole domain of the state, the exercise of routine administration and, frequently, of military power, become identified with ethnicities. This is true of all those multi-ethnic societies where the composition of the military forces is ethnically distinct, as is the case in those post-colonial societies where the colonial power (for example, Britain in African societies) recruited armed forces from ethnically distinct segments of society (Horowitz 1985).

Where elite economic power and military and political power are identified with specific ethnic groups there is a real and continuing possibility that economic and political power will assume a generalised and semi-permanent ethnic frame. Similarly, there are many societies in which the contest politics of democracy take on an ethnic form. Among the most common examples are those where political parties are ethnically named – as in the United Malay National Organisation (UMNO) in Malaysia – or are parties where the majority support comes from an ethnically identified segment, as has been the case in Fiji.

In all nation-states, that is, systems of state governance which are viewed as the political expression of a 'nation', there is a politico-cultural definition of what that nation is. In this sense, in all or most societies, politics are 'ethnicised'. The explicit or implicit representations of the nation carry within them images of the ethnic majority and their supposed characteristics. In the American case the term 'WASP', meaning White Anglo-Saxon and Protestant, once reflected the dominance of European origins in the majority ethnicity; to be American was to be white, Protestant and European in origin, an assumption that is now much contested as America seeks to reframe itself as a 'multi-cultural' society. Similarly, in Malaysia, there is a continuing negotiation around Malaysia as a Malay and Muslim country marked by a Malay Muslim cultural hegemony, and a Malaysia whose hallmark is its success in making a harmonious and mutually tolerant whole out of potentially divided parts.

Summary

Examples and illustrations in this chapter have been drawn from the USA, Britain and Europe, Hawai'i and Malaysia and these four settings continue to provide the case material for the exploration of the central themes of this book. In Chapters 4 and 5 (on economy and ethnicity) and 6 and 7 (on politics and ethnicity) they are the sites of the principal case studies. In this introductory chapter we have dealt with the nature of ethnicity as both material and symbolic in its nature, as grounded in ancestry, language and culture, and as a social classificatory system which is constructed within the contexts of economic and political structures and beliefs. The historical trajectory of ethnicity, the sense in which it can be seen as a product of the modern world, is pursued in Chapter 1, along with a typology of ethnicities defined by the key features of the ethnic-making context.

Chapter 1

Ethnicity and the Modern World: Historical Trajectories

In the first part of this chapter we follow Eriksen's schema of types of ethnicity: we define urban minorities; indigenous peoples; ethnonational groups; ethnic groups in plural societies; and post-slavery minorities. We associate these with three historical trajectories of the modern world: the slavery and post-slavery world, the colonial and post-colonial, and nation-state formation in the capitalist West. In the latter part of the chapter we discuss the concepts of Universalism and particularism and the relationship of ethnicity to gender.

Historical trajectories and types of ethnicity

To take the historical and contextual nature of ethnicity seriously necessarily runs counter to any attempt to create a universal theory of ethnic relations. Attention to historical and societal context requires us to entertain the contrary thought: that, in studying 'ethnicity', we are studying collective identity and organisation which differ significantly in accordance with their historically specific origins. In the present chapter we examine this proposition and suggest that, in the modern world, there are three principal historical trajectories which have given rise to ethnicised and racialised social orders. These are the enslavement of Africans, the European colonial domination of much of Asia, Africa and the 'New World', and the development of modern capitalism and the nation-state as a political form. Within these historical processes, we suggest that the migration of workers and traders, the creation of international diasporas, the dispossession of some peoples and the marginalisation of others, have created the conditions for the emergence of different types of ethnicities. These different ethnicities are then defined in relation to labour migration, modern slavery and its aftermath, the dispossession of indigenous peoples, the post-colonial social order, and the concept of the nation and the unequal valuation of cultures. Later in the chapter we discuss some of the competing claims of an analytical emphasis on slavery, colonialism and capitalism and the implications of this for the persistence of racism. In the last section of the chapter we explore the relevance of an understanding of gender to the understanding of ethnicity, and the commonalities and divergences with respect to gender and ethnic ordering.

Ethnicity or ethnicities

In all the examples we have given of the economic and political contextualisation of ethnicity, the drawing of ethnic boundaries – a social definition of where the group 'begins and ends' – and the mobilisation of culture, language and ancestry – 'the kind of people we are' – are common features. Within this important common ground, ethnicity is not a single invariant or universal phenomenon (Fardon 1987) governed by the 'laws' of ethnic relations as earlier approaches assumed (Schermerhorn 1970, Banton 1983, Horowitz 1985; see also Fenton 1987). The economic and political circumstances in which ethnicity is activated combine to give ethnic identities a specific form in the characteristic settings we have described; ethnicity has a quite different social 'force' in its different contexts.

Under some circumstances, for example, ethnic groups become beleaguered minorities fighting for survival. Some group members leave home and migrate in the search for a better life. Such were the hopes of successive generations to European immigrants to America (Handlin 1973, Yinger 1994). If there is a long-standing pattern of economic subordination, of cultural insult, and a political arithmetic which makes democratic gains unlikely, the beleaguered minority may become the freedom fighters, terrorist movement or army of liberation (McGarry and O'Leary 1993).

In other cases, the voluntary and involuntary migration of labour and traders constitute the primary setting for the growth of ethnic identities. By describing the movement of peoples such as labourers, settlers, and traders, and the relationships of each of these to indigenous peoples – or to people making a powerful claim to indigenous status – we can begin to construct a typology of ethnic groups and ethnic-making situations.

International migrations and diasporas

The forced and voluntary movements of labour, of merchants and adventurers and colonists, have seen peoples and their languages and customs transported across the globe. Where people leave their homeland and form communities outside it, we refer to a diaspora, a word whose meaning is 'dispersion' and which is most characteristically linked to Jewish dispersion among Gentiles after captivity. It has been generalised to other populations with large communities outside the homeland, especially the African and Indian diasporas consequent upon slavery and forced and voluntary movements of labour. People from India have migrated as voluntary and coerced labour to Fiji, Trinidad, Malaysia, Mauritius, Britain, the USA and many other countries, forming an Indian diaspora of people of shared origin who have created new communities in so many diverse settings. This is why there are Hindu festivals in London and Mauritius, a Hindu revival in Trinidad, and why there are mosques scattered in the cane fields of Fiji as well as in the urban centre of Singapore (Siddique and Shotam 1982, Eriksen 1992, Vertovec 1992). In Malaysia, the imported Indian workers were almost exclusively rubber plantation workers who remained, for a long time, socially and politically orientated to their home country. Their descendants are now a class-differentiated population, conscious of their claims as citizens of the new Malaysia. In Fiji, Indian workers were imported in the 1880s under the auspices of British rule, to provide labour for the sugar plantations and many of their descendants remain engaged in sugar production in the western end of Fiji's principal island. Their political advance has been constrained by the indigenous Fijians' claim to primacy within 'their' country, a political idea which has been sharpened by the success of Indian-origin traders in the islands. Orlando Patterson's account of the way in which the Chinese migrants to Jamaica came to form a specific merchant class illustrates how their ethnic identity was implicated in their economic success and social obligations – the more the Chinese depended on each other for support and exchange within the business community, the more a collective identity was sustained (Patterson 1975).

The examples of Fiji, Malaysia and Trinidad are also cases of societies with a (British) colonial past, each of them becoming independent in the 1960s. In the cases of Malaysia and Fiji there is a strongly surviving indigenous people who have seen themselves as being in danger of being displaced by successful descendants of migrant groups. In the cases of New Zealand and Hawai'i the processes of colonisation and, of Hawai'i, US annexation, resulted in the dispossession of indigenous peoples and severely reduced their numbers. In New Zealand, as a 'white settler society' the subsequent importation of settlers and workers has been mostly from Britain (Spoonley *et al.* 1984, Pearson 1990, Walker 1990). In Hawai'i tens of thousands of labourers from the Asian continent and the Philippines have entered the islands, leaving Hawaiians a minority in their homeland, but without a simple majority of white ethnicity as is the case in New Zealand.

Ethnicity-making situations

Thomas Eriksen's (1993b) typology of groups and contexts provides a clear starting point for a classification of ethnicity-making situations. His prefatory remarks address the very question of 'universality' and 'contextuality' that we have raised in this chapter:

> There may be mechanisms of ethnic processes which are relatively uniform in every interethnic situation: to this effect we can identify certain shared formal properties in all ethnic phenomena. On the other hand, there can be no doubt that the substantial social contexts of ethnicity differ enormously, and indeed that ethnic identities and ethnic organisations themselves may have highly variable importance in different societies... Although the concept of ethnicity should always have the same meaning, [to be] useful in comparison, it is inevitable that we distinguish between the social contexts under scrutiny. (1993, p. 13)

This comes very close to the argument expressed throughout this book. To Eriksen's categories we add a fifth, the post-slavery minorities, the racialised ethnic groups of North and South America and the Caribbean, descendants of Africans brought into slavery from the 16th century onwards. In the category urban minorities we include both migrant workers and migrant merchants, the latter described by Rex as trader minorities. All these types of ethnic group are not just a system of classification but are the result of key historical trajectories which have created them.

Five types of modern ethnicity

We can, then, following Eriksen (1993b), distinguish five types of ethnic-making situations.

1. Urban minorities: examples being migrant worker populations in American and European cities and in the economies of the newly industrialising societies (for example Indonesian workers in Malaysia) and trader minorities such as Chinese merchants in the Caribbean.

2. Proto-nations or ethnonational groups: peoples who have and make a claim to be nations, and thus make a claim to some form of self-governance while being incorporated within a wider state. The French-speaking Quebecois within Canada, the Kurdish peoples of Turkey and neighbouring states and the Basques in Spain are classic examples of the claim to nationhood with repercussions for governance in the state system which 'illegitimately' rules them.

3. Ethnic groups in plural societies: these are the descendants of populations who have typically migrated as coerced, voluntary and semi-voluntary workers, and have come to form distinctive, and sometimes large (as the Chinese in Malaysia) minorities in the new context. As Eriksen observes, they rarely make a claim to separate ethnonational status but nonetheless form a relatively enduring distinct segment of a nation-state system.

4. Indigenous minorities: those peoples dispossessed by colonial settlement, key examples being aboriginal or Koori peoples of Australia, Maori of New Zealand and the island peoples of the Pacific such as the Hawaiians; and the native American peoples of North, Central and South America.

5. Post-slavery minorities: the 'black' (African) descendants of people formerly enslaved in the New World, of which black or African Americans are a classic instance. In several cases the ethnic identity of these groups has been complicated by inter-marriage so that 'mulatto' and 'mixed race' populations may form a partly distinct population – as in Jamaica (Patterson 1975). Outside the USA, Cuba and Brazil, that is, specifically in the black Caribbean societies, they do not actually form numerical minorities, although in the cases especially of Guyana and Trinidad, and the more complex case of Mauritius, (Eriksen 1992, 1993a), their social, cultural and political status is elabo-

rated and contested alongside diasporic Indian communities which typically formed after subsequent labour importations.

A closer inspection of examples of each of these five types will show how, from them, a theoretical and historical understanding of ethnicity in the modern world can begin to take shape.

Urban minorities: trader minorities

In most societies throughout the world there can be found examples of trader minorities who are distinguished by their ethnic origins, be they ethnic groups from within a multi-ethnic society or in-migrant traders and their descendants. Examples are Lebanese and Chinese traders in the Caribbean, Jewish people in much of Europe, Gujaratis in contemporary Britain, Chinese businessmen in Malaysia and Indonesia, Hausa in Nigeria, and North Africans (Moroccans, Tunisians) in Spain and Italy. As with Jewish peoples in much of Europe, the concentration in trading activities may be a result of ethnic exclusion from other economic spheres, thus giving rise to the subsequent stereotyping of these ethnic groups as having a natural taste for business. Ethnically distinct small trader groups, specialising in shopkeeping, jewellery, money lending, textiles, and in the contemporary world, computer equipment and microchips, stand the risk of being or becoming pariah groups or at least the targets of suspicion and periodic bouts of hostility. Where they manage food shops they are likely targets of hostility in periods of shortage or sharp price rises, when they are money lenders they run the risk of being seen as responsible for the financial ruin of others.

Indonesia in 1998 provides an example of a chain of connected economic events which resulted in violence and hostility towards the Chinese as a trader minority. The Indonesian economy had been one of the worst affected by the crisis in South East Asian capitalism, signalled by the steep fall in the value of regional currencies, including the Indonesian rupiah, which began in July 1997. By spring 1998 countries which were less severely but nonetheless seriously affected were reducing government expenditures and cutting back on investment and construction ventures. This meant that neighbours such as Malaysia were sending home Indonesian immigrant workers whose labour was temporarily not needed, and protecting their shores against new incursion of 'illegals'. At the same time the collapse of the Indonesian economy meant that

Indonesian workers were all the more desperate to find work outside their home country. Consequently, thousands of Indonesian workers took the risks associated with illegal immigration and Malaysian police and customs officers intensified their searches. A *Sarawak Tribune* report of 14 April 1997 quoted one of its ministers stating that there were 1.2 million legal foreign workers in Malaysia and 800,000 illegal foreign workers; with some family members added in, the total came to 2.2 million and 10 per cent of the population of Malaysia. These and other reports began to create the kind of 'anti-immigrant', and thus anti-Indonesian, climate with which observers of Britain in the 1960s and France in the 1980s and 90s would be familiar. In March 1998 there were virtually daily reports in the Malaysian press of the capture of 'Indons' in their urban hideouts or swimming ashore from the boats of the entrepreneurs of non-documented labour. In Singapore, the police unearthed a compound of illegal Indonesian workers concealed in the Singaporean jungle, living in hastily constructed shelters and in construction pipes, surviving by eating wildlife. In Malaysia, serious violence broke out in a detention camp housing illegal workers; the portrayal of Indonesians as a threat to the stability of Malaysia was reinforced daily.

The repercussions for Chinese shopkeepers in Indonesia were immediate. Food prices more than doubled within a short space of time and many Muslim Indonesians blamed the shopkeepers themselves. It was reported that national Indonesian television had not discouraged this view, even showing pictures of warehouses filled to overflowing, implying that supplies were being withheld to maintain high prices. There were reports of widespread violence against Chinese shopkeepers and looting of their stores. This chain of events in Indonesia and Malaysia stemmed from the late summer (1997) capitalist crisis in South East Asia and resulted in two familiar forms of economically situated ethnic conflict: the heightening of suspicion and fear of immigrant workers and popular violence towards an ethnically distinct *petite bourgeoisie*.

While trader minorities risk hostility from outside, their ethnic solidarity is a basis for both self-protection and business advancement. Ethnic networks become the basis of collaboration in trade and people who know each other, speak the same language, and have close or distant kinship obligations can become valuable partners in exchange (Patterson 1975).

Urban minorities: labour migration

The movement of people in search of work and a 'new life' is not exclusively a feature of the modern world but the speed and ease of travel in the period since the Second World War has made labour migration a routine global phenomenon (Castles and Miller 1993). In the 19th century it might have taken six months for Irish immigrants to reach their destination in America; today it would take six hours. At least three of the five types of ethnicity are founded on contemporary and past labour migrations – the post-slavery societies result from the massive forced migrations of people from Africa and the ethnic groups of 'plural societies' are the descendants of labourers brought to those societies in the 19th century. The urban ethnic groups of modern America are the descendants of 19th- and 20th-century migrations from Europe (for example, Germany, Scandinavia, Poland, Britain) and the cities of modern Europe have received immigrants both from internal European migrations and from sources outside Europe including Turkey, Africa, the Caribbean and India. The international labour market is made up of professional and managerial workers as well as low-paid industrial and service workers moving to the economies of the developed and developing world. And just as labour seeks out capital and looks for areas of high investment where jobs become available so too capital seeks out labour by moving, for example to low-wage zones to reduce production costs.

The movements of labour and capital consequent upon the reunification of Germany illustrate some of these points. In November 1996 the *Financial Times* reported that a German company had relocated some of its activities across the border in the Czech Republic. The company did this because it could produce its goods more cheaply and profitably in the Czech Republic where wage rates were lower. Managers, however, 'have to be on hand to ensure that the Czech employees are as productive as their German counterparts'; the manager explains that 'they have a very different rhythm in the Czech Republic' (*Financial Times* 1996). The Czech town of Husinec stands to gain 250 jobs while the parent German company's plant just across the border has seen its workforce halved in ten years. With labour costs ten times higher in Germany than in the Czech Republic, global competition has come close to home. 'People talk a lot about the competition we are facing from developing economies in Asia. We have Hong Kong on our doorstep.' (*Financial Times* 1996). The same movement is reported of other industries with machine tool industries making components in Slovakia and Bulgaria. And while Germany invests its capital funds in Husinec, many of the town's workers commute daily to work in Germany and Austria (*Financial Times 1996*).

This particular case of ethnic differences in the workforce has only just begun to take shape but we know some of the sociological expectations from prior cases of a comparable kind. Throughout Europe in the post-war period, migrant labour has been essential to the growth of the most dynamic capitalist economies, Germany being the most prominent case (Castles and Kosack 1985). The very construction of a concept of the nation – of the German folk, or of who is truly British – permits and encourages the construction of 'others' as less deserving of the rewards of a society, however meagre they may actually be. In this sense the emphasis in for example much British sociological literature on racism, in its narrower sense of a theory of a biologically deterministic nature, was misplaced. The much simpler thought – that 'these people' have no real right to be here, or that if they are here they are less fully deserving of space, benefits and services – is compelling enough on its own (Rose *et al.* 1969, Lawrence 1974). If people are viewed as not legitimately here then any gain they make is barely tolerated especially if the 'home' folk are suffering. Ethnic antagonism and divided labour markets go together as Bonacich has argued (Bonacich 1972, 1976). The traces of ethnic difference within migrant worker communities form the basis of perceived difference in the labour force.

In the Czech-Germany example, the German workers in German factories are, no doubt, already aware of the presence of Czech migrant workers competing with them for employment. Their very availability as workers affects wage rates and employment in Germany, for without them labour would have been scarcer. If, as the report suggests, German managers are relatively easily able to travel to and fro to manage the affairs of the new plant, this will mean that predominantly Czech workers within the Republic will be managed by German managers; in other words the line of authority difference is also a line of ethnic difference (Gellner 1983). The economic context here is the search for cheaper labour by an inter-national German commodity producer which sells its products (glassware, 'Europe's largest makers of specialised glass') in the world's markets. Capital is invested outside Germany enhancing employment prospects in the Czech Republic but diminishing them in Germany itself. A central dynamic of capitalist economics, the never-ending search to find ways of reducing labour costs as a component of commodity production, is played out every day on a global scale. It is a key context within which 'anti-immigrant' politics have surfaced all over western Europe, increasingly in eastern Europe, in the USA, and, as we have seen, in some of the newly industrialising countries (Husbands 1991a, b, 1997, Miles 1994a).

Parallel circumstances are known to us throughout history and certainly throughout the recent history of labour migration and ethnicity making in the global division of labour (Phizacklea 1999). We find Filipina hotel maids in London, the Gulf states and South East Asia. 'Battered slaves of the gulf' (*Observer* 1995) reported the case of a maid sentenced to death after killing her employer who had raped her. There are tens of thousands of Sri Lankan and Pakistani domestic servants in oil-rich Middle Eastern states, Korean-ancestry workers in Japan, Indian-ancestry workers in Fiji, Turkish workers in Germany or Mexican tobacco pickers in Canada. The great cities of North America throughout the 19th century and well into the 20th were able to grow as a result of mass in-migrations both from the rural areas within and countries without. At the time of the First World War more than a third of Chicago's population was born outside the USA and a growing proportion were African Americans moving from the impoverished southern states. Later in the century Toronto in Canada took on much the same character. As the second and third generation of immigrants are incorporated in American and Canadian society, Chicago and Toronto are the archetypal multi-ethnic cities of the contemporary world. Further south and west the sources of immigration are more Hispanic and Asian, a trend which has become general in much of North America. Both in Canada (Reitz and Breton 1994) and the USA (Waters 1990, Schlesinger 1991, Goldberg 1994) this has prompted debates about the multi-cultural status of these countries, a subject to which we return later.

Proto-nations or ethnonational groups

Proto-nationalist identities and movements are the political and cultural expression of populations who have been absorbed into nation-state systems which fail or are accused of failing to honour the cultural and material claims of the would-be nation-within-a nation – more accurately, within a state. These are populations or cultures which history appears to have partly swallowed up, submerged or 'left behind' in a homogenising state system. The process of homogenisation in language, culture, education, and civil administration is, as Gellner (1983) has argued, part of the project of modernisation. The state only partially completes the task of assimilation. The Basques of Northern Spain and the Catholic Irish of Northern Ireland have been 'deposited' by history in state systems whose legitimacy they do not accept – or to be more precise, whose legitimacy is not accepted by a significant segment of the population. The Kurdish peoples have found themselves enveloped by several state systems, notably Turkey and Iran and Iraq; the Sami people of Northern Europe (Paine 1992) are spread across Norway, Sweden, Finland, and Russia, all of which states are generally inhospitable to the survival of their way of life. In Britain the apparent revival of Scottish, Welsh and English sentiments of nationhood is represented in the main by peaceable constitutional movements towards devolution of political power or independence.

There are three important theoretical points with respect to proto-nations or ethno-nationalist groups. First, the ethnonationalist group is always defined in relation to a state system of which they form a part. This state system may or may not recognise their existence or their distinctiveness; the dispute may be about how much the distinctiveness is recognised, and about what are the political structures in which that distinctiveness may be recognised and preserved. Second, in all nation-state systems there is a dominant, frequently referred to as hegemonic, view of the national character of the country. If this hegemonic view excludes proto-nations then the scene is set for what Taylor (1992) has called 'the politics of recognition'. Third, the proto-nation or ethnonation differs from the ethnic group, although the distinction may sometimes seem hard to sustain. The difference lies in the fact that the ethnonation, as a nation, explicitly or by implication is making a claim to some form of self-governance, so powerful is the equation of nations and states. In other words in nationalist ideology nations are things which should have their own state and states are things which should be comprised of a nation (Gellner 1983).

Ethnic groups in plural societies

The concept plural society has historically been applied to those colonial or post-colonial societies whose multi-ethnicity was an inheritance of a colonial regime which introduced new labouring populations into the colony, as well as 'conserving' the religious and cultural differences among the population in general. Since these colonial regimes did not institute democratic institutions based on a universal franchise, there was no need to attempt to create a universal form of citizenship or to create cultural homogeneity, in the way that Weber (1976) and Gellner (1983) have argued was an impulse of modernising Western democracies. The colonial society was therefore composed of discrete groupings whose differences of custom, culture and language – as well as, usually, function within the division of labour – were conserved with no serious attempt being made towards cultural or institutional integration (see Smith 1965, Jenkins 1997, Rex 1997).

The concept of plural society has been criticised by Jenkins (1997) and others, but the cases of Malaysia, Trinidad, Fiji and Indonesia are typical plural societies fitting the characteristics we have just described. The weakness of the concept 'plural society' lies in the fact that all societies are plural in the sense of containing within them many strands of culture and social allegiance; where this is all that it means it has little to offer. There are, however, two points of distinctiveness in the concept. The societies which have been described as plural are not only composed of many cultures but also lack, or have historically lacked, any strong impulse towards social and cultural integration. This is why the early proponents of the concept (Furnivall 1948, Smith 1965) argued that the removal of an external constraining force, specifically colonial rule, would leave behind a society with no integrative mechanisms. This has proved in several instances, notably Malaysia, to be a misjudgement but in describing societies composed of segments that are largely socially and culturally separate, with no strong impulse to integration, the concept refers to something more than a plurality of cultures, a feature of any society.

The second point of distinctiveness of the concept 'plural' is simply historical. The group of societies which were indicated by the term plural were primarily Asian and Caribbean societies which had been under British, Dutch and French colonial rule throughout much of their recent history (Smith 1965) during which time coolie labour had been imported. These labourers were frequently thought of as temporary residents and many returned to their country of origin or moved further to new destinations. But many more set down roots in their new country and now form large parts of the populations of those countries, sometimes even a majority, as do Fijians of Indian descent. In some of these countries there is a large indigenous population, such as Malays who are almost 60 per cent of the population of Malaysia. In others, such as Trinidad and Mauritius, there is a large African-descent population, none or very few indigenes, plus the descendants of later imported labourers. Their forebears had usually arrived after the abolition of slavery. Such is the case in Trinidad and Guyana, while Mauritius is a singular case of a society which was uninhabited at the time of colonisation. In Singapore the earlier in-migrant Chinese form a large majority of the whole population.

In two of the instances we have referred to, there is not simply cultural separateness but also the specific problem of the 'indigenous claim' which can be summed up in the phrase 'this land is our land'. This is expressed precisely by the concept *Taukei* in Fiji which refers to the traditional disposition of land and was also the name taken by the movement which supported the 1987 coup in the name of the interests of the indigenous Fijians. Although the justification was slight (Lal 1990, Lawson 1992), those who supported the coup certainly believed that they were fighting for the cultural and political survival of the native Fijian people and way of life.

Indigenous minorities

The indigenous claim in both these cases is by populations which are either a majority (Malays almost 60 per cent and a further 1–2 per cent native peoples) or very large (native Fijian 43 per cent). By contrast there are many instances where, in the aftermath of colonisation and colonial rule, the people who claim 'this land is our land' are minorities, sometimes very small minorities in that country. In Australia, with a population of over 17 million, aboriginal peoples, or Koori, are only 1 per cent of the total. The white colonists' disregard for the aboriginal population is illustrated by the fact that they regarded the land as 'empty'. They hunted and killed many aboriginal people whom they did encounter, and pursued practices and policies leading towards the disappearance of the aboriginal population (Turnbull 1948). These policies, and the white Australia immigration policy, have now changed (Wilkie 1994) and the Australian government has apologised for the policy of taking Koori children out of their families into the families of whites, an administrative and social work practice which broke up families and disassembled a people. But the question of dealing with the consequences remains very much contested, most of all in the field of land repossession, an issue which heralded a revival of racism and threatened to divide the country (*Independent* 15 June 1998).

In New Zealand, the Maori population is about 10 per cent of the over 3.5 million total; it was only in the 1980s that white New Zealanders (*Pakeha*) began to be made aware that the land and culture they regarded as their own was viewed quite differently by people of Maori descent (Walker 1995). In Canada, American Indian and Inuit peoples make up less than 2 per cent of a total of over 26 million and indigenous peoples form a similar proportion of the USA's 250 million population. In Brazil, South American Indian peoples are less than 1 per cent of a 153 million total. Throughout the Caribbean, the Carib and Arawak peoples have not survived, neither have the aboriginal Tasmanians (Turnbull 1948); in Hawai'i the native Hawaiian people (or *Kanaka Maoli*) have survived partly in consequence of intermarrying with incoming groups; people of (part) Hawaiian ancestry now form about 18 per cent of the islands' 1.2 million population. Throughout the Pacific and the Americas, indigenous populations have often survived as intermarried groups.

In many of these cases, the period since the 1970s has seen a series of cultural revivals among these indigenous peoples in which there are a number of common features. The movements have sought to retrieve their sense of collective pride by remembering things valued and things lost and by trying to overcome the devaluing of their cultural inheritance. The very concept of 'culture' has become a self-consciously treasured and lauded symbol of dispossession. At the same time the ownership and possession of the land itself has become contested in the courts and has posed problems for real estate transactions; in the case of Hawai'i this has led to a legal contest over the land on which Honolulu International Airport is built. These indigenist movements are to be found throughout the Pacific, in North and South America and among such groups as the Sami of Norway, Sweden and Finland. The question of culture and the symbolic representations of the indigenous people and of the 'nation' within which they have become incorporated, are central to all indigenist expressions of ethnicity. This is because the process of colonisation and dispossession always entailed the economic marginalisation, impoverishment and social demoralisation of indigenous peoples, coupled with a long term deculturation. While some of the first indications of renaissance and political awareness are cultural, the most contested arena is land as is now illustrated by the Australian case.

Post-slavery minorities

About 20 million Africans were taken from the continent to the Caribbean, to Brazil and to North America. They left Africa as Mandinka, Fulani, Ibo, Hausa, Coromantee, and many other ethnic and language groups; for most purposes in the New World they were simply labour, negroes, 'niggers' and slaves. It was common for slave traffickers to mix ethnic groups to minimise the prospect of solidarity among slaves. It has been argued that where this 'mixing' was less the case, slave revolt and escape were more common. In Brazil, the scale of importation of Africans meant that there were aggregations of larger numbers of people of shared language and background, and slave revolts and escapes were more frequent. But the effect of enslavement was to erase most traces of ethnic identity and culture within a generation or so; the extent to which African culture has survived in the Americas is much contested (Huggins *et al.* 1971, Rawick 1972). From the viewpoint of the dominant European social order, the principal classificatory system became slave and free, white, coloured and black, and negro as a polite term and 'nigger' as a demeaning term and form of abuse.

In the early, mid- and late 19th centuries slavery was abolished successively in the British Caribbean, the USA, and Brazil. Since abolition the majority of former slave populations have remained economically disadvantaged and underrepresented in systems of political power. But a historical pride in African origins, which dimmed but never disappeared, was much revived in the 1960s, especially in the USA whose Black Power and African nationalist movements influenced all post-slavery societies (Marable 1984). New expressions of ethnic pride are to be found in the ethnonational labels 'African American' and 'Afro-Brazilian', with a general movement in the last two decades away from the 'racial' term black, to the national term 'African'. Since ethnic categories are elaborated within relationships with reference to others, the post-slavery sites vary in the emphasis given to cultural and ethnic markers. In countries such as Mauritius, Trinidad and Guyana, African origin is mediated by relationships to people of Indian ancestry; in the USA, the principal 'others' have been European whites although latterly joined by Asians and Hispanics. In Brazil, there has been a much more distinctive development of 'intermediate' groupings conceptualised in terms of colour differences and mediated by class and status consciousness (Degler 1971, Dzidzienyo and Casal 1979, Fontaine 1985, Marx 1998).

Typologies, history and social change

A system of classification of types of ethnicity is a static set of boxes into which examples can be placed. A typology comes to life if it is part of an understanding of social change and historical trajectory. Underlying all the five types set out above are some key social developments which are central features of the creation of the modern world – where 'modern' is understood as the last four centuries. Among modern developments are ones which are critically relevant to the creation and mobilisation of ethnic, 'racial', and national groups and identities. The key economic processes are the recruitment and migration of labour, free and unfree, and land dispossession; the key political processes are the formation of nation-states in Europe and in the post-colonial world and post-imperial world, and the creation of constitutional electoral and citizenship rights.

In the case of urban minorities, ethnic groups in plural societies, and post-slavery minorities there is a common denominator in the migration of labour and of traders. The critical difference in types of labour is freedom and unfreedom, with 'coolie labour' having aspects of both. The slave systems of North and South America and the Caribbean were built on unfree labour. In the wake of the abolition of slavery Asian 'coolie labour' was imported into many of the post-slavery sites and into some – including Hawai'i – which had not seen slavery. The minority ethnic groups of the cities of North America, South America and Europe are primarily a consequence of peoples moving voluntarily, even if constrained and in need, towards new economic opportunities in trade and employment. The industrialisation of America in the 19th and 20th centuries was achieved with the labour of migrants. In the latter part of the 19th century industrialising South American countries like Argentina imported labour from Europe.

Land dispossession is the central feature of indigenous minorities, invariably accompanied by a demeaning and devaluing of culture and language loss. In the political sphere, indigenous minorities have been informally subordinate or formally excluded; aboriginal Australians were not permitted to vote until 1962. In the case of Fiji and New Zealand, ethnic identities are politically conserved through the creation of communal rolls – where citizens are registered to vote as members of an ethnic or 'national' group (Milne 1981, Mulgan 1989, Walker 1990). On independence

Malaysia rejected the idea of communal rolls but inserted the definition of a Malay into its constitution.

The formation and mobilisation of ethnicities has therefore
occurred not simply within economic and political contexts, but in
specific historical contexts. This has happened at the local level of,
say, Indians in Fiji or Tamils in Malaysia, and at the global level in
the formation of categories of 'native', civilised–savage,
Christian–heathen, and 'black–white'. The greater part of sociological theorisation of ethnicity and racism has been precisely the
attempt to specify those historical contexts. Three historical
contexts have predominated: the enslavement of Africans and the
development of slave and post-slavery societies; European domination of much of the world through colonial settlement, economic
power and colonial rule, followed by the emergence of post-colonial
regimes; and the development of Western capitalism and the
parallel creation of nation-states

The slavery and post-slavery analytic emphasis

The central argument here has three principal points. The first is that
racial categorisation and the idea of inherently different natures –
racism in all its manifestations – became a major part of the justification of the system of slavery, especially important in a society
which declared 'all men to be equal'. For if some men and women
were to be accorded a lesser status of a fixed kind, they must therefore be men and women of a different kind. Second, this racialisation of the social order persisted into the post-slavery period partly
as a legacy of a social order predicated on 'race' and partly because
whites of all social classes sought to protect their racialised privileges. And third, this racialised social order hardened as black men
and women were confined to the least advantaged positions in the
creation of capitalist industrial society.

Looked at as an economic system, slavery, and especially the
slave plantation, was a means of controlling labour. In many
European colonial settlements, labour was in short supply for any
kind of production which required large numbers of workers, as
18th-century cash crop production did. It was not easy to get a big
enough supply from Europe, and American Indians, with their own
land and economy, had no good reason to want to labour in the plantation economy. Some Indians were enslaved but it was not to be the
answer to the need for labour.

After the first African arrivals in America in the early 17th century, there was not an immediate equation of African labour with 'slave' and of European white with 'free', but as the century progressed, an equation began to harden (Jordan 1968). Like other labourers, of whatever ethnic origin, in early industrialisation in manufacturing or in cash crop economies, black African slaves in the American south were viewed as dangerous, idle and untrustworthy. Factory workers in England were viewed in much the same way (Williams 1958). Looked at as a social system, racialised slavery – enslavement confined to Africans – was a system of racial domination. The abolition of slavery therefore entailed, in the longer run (see Chapter 4), the creation of a new racialised order, designed not to justify slavery but to protect whites of all classes from competition with Africans.

It has been argued that North American slavery was especially harsh because of its connection to the ideology and practice of an American capitalism, red in tooth and claw. The southern slave-based economy was a part of a fast-developing capitalist system and was a link in a chain of worldwide commodity production. But southern planters also behaved in ways which were at odds with unrestrained capitalism, investing in luxury and (their own) idleness and imitating the manners of a seigneurial society (Genovese 1971). Although racial domination was a constant feature of the ante-bellum (pre-Civil War) and post-bellum south, it was articulated within two quite different systems of labour.

The colonial/post-colonial analytic emphasis

Colonial settlement, trade and commercial penetration, and, in many cases, forms of imperial rule, entailed the dispossession of land and the exploitation of the labour of indigenous peoples and established a colonial political and cultural order which defined the rulers as representatives of a superior civilisation. The imperial culture was viewed as surpassing that of the ruled which accordingly defined as pagan, backward, primitive and pre-modern. In the pursuit of colonial economic and administrative interests, populations defined as ethnically different were differentially incorporated into the colonial system, forming the basis of ethnic differentiation which persisted into the post-colonial period – as it was for example in the case of Malays, Chinese and Indians in Malaya, now Malaysia. Furthermore, the ideas of inherent ethnic and racial differ-

ence were 're-imported' into the colonial homeland – for example in
the view that the British held of themselves and of others – and reemerged when peoples of former colonies were incorporated into the
economic and political systems of the colonial centre.

The colonial/post-colonial analytic emphasis is both specific to
place and time and general and global. It is specific in the sense that
each colonial or former colonial site has its own specificities of
history – for example, the widespread Christianisation of Pacific
island peoples as in Tonga, Fiji and Hawai'i, as against the persistence of Hinduism and Islam in the Indian sub-continent. But it is
general and global in the sense that in the aftermath of colonial
regimes there is cultural contest both in the countries of colonisers
and in the independent countries of those formerly colonised. In the
colonis*er* countries a colonial mentality persists in the legacy of
nation-states which see themselves as bearers of civilisation, and in
the nostalgia and resentment of 'loss of empire'. In the colonis*ed*
countries the cultural aftermath of colonial rule lies in the partial,
willed or forced, 'acceptance' of the cultural assumptions of the
rulers – frequently and most notably in the opposed claims of
indigenous and colonial languages. At the same time the post-
colonial period is marked by the revival of indigenous language and
culture – suppressed, devalued or overwhelmed in the colonial
period – coupled with debates about which cultural form is most
suited to modernity (Eriksen 1991, May 1999). The wish to restore
pride in ancestral culture may be seen to conflict with the wish to
'modernise'. In this way the cultural contest which follows the end
of a colonial system is viewed not only as a problem of decolonisation but also as a problem of modernity.

The capitalism and nation-state analytic emphasis

The principal arguments here are twofold. The first is that nation-
states have been the primary vehicle for the development of modern
capitalism, above all in western Europe and America, and that these
nation-states have been the agents for the creation of national
cultures and identities (Hobsbawm 1990). These national cultures
are seen to be pragmatically essential to modernisation – in the
widening of circles of trade, business and employment, and the state
management of education, taxation, and military conscription
(Weber 1976, Gellner 1983). They are also seen to be ideologically
important in surmounting potential social divisions, forestalling

class conflicts and in projecting a national self-image as 'energetic', 'enterprising' and 'dynamic'.

The second argument, sometimes referred to as 'capital logic', is that capitalist societies engender racialised and ethnic identities as a consequence of enduring features of capitalist formations. These endemic features of capitalist functioning and development include: the recurrent pattern of crisis, of prosperous growth and recession, the constant unplanned and revolutionary social change which gives rise to a persistent sense of social malaise and demoralisation, and the search for new sources of exploitable labour. Migrant workers, as well as women and indigenous minorities, are part of the solution to fluctuating demand for labour. Ethnic groups become part of a class structure or hierarchical division of labour which is partly, if not always dominantly, defined by ethnic categories (for example poor whites, black sharecroppers, Asian mill workers). Where there is scarcity and inequality and the competition for resources is understood as ethnic competition, the potential for conflict is greater as is the hardening of lines of division – 'we've got less because they've got more'. For both urban minorities and indigenous ethnic majorities there is a tension between the doctrines of social inclusion and equality as ideals, and patterns of actual social exclusion and inequality. Rising rates of crime and the fear of crime are aspects of 'a world changing beyond recognition' and minority ethnic groups are, in the 'common-sense' understandings of the majority, both associated with unwonted social change and blamed for it (Solomos 1988, Solomos and Back 1996).

These recurrent features of capitalist societies do not lead in any simple or 'automatic' fashion to racialised or ethnicised forms of social practice and ideas but they are a set of 'seedbeds' within which they may grow. Nation-states foster the idea of common culture identity and destiny. There is a dominant definition of common culture – what is termed a hegemonic culture. At the same time 'other' cultures, whether these are the language and customs of migrant groups or surviving minority cultures – as in the case of Celtic 'minorities' in Britain – are devalued or defined as 'backward' (Kiberd 1996). Migrant populations may be represented as competing for scarce resources in 'our' country. Classes and fractions of classes who see themselves as losing out and as having both the economic and cultural basis of their way of life undermined are vulnerable to ideological appeals which promise both to explain and to cure their malaise, the characteristic basis of racist or xenophobic politics. As Durkheim once wrote of the socially disenchanted

French men and women 'they blamed the Jews and already felt better' (Fenton 1984).

These theoretical frames – the slavery/post-slavery, colonial/ post-colonial and the nation-state/capitalist society analytic emphases – have all informed this book and the historical contexts which they indicate are reflected in the comparative examples we set out in later chapters, principally from Britain, Malaysia, the USA and Hawai'i. The USA is a post-slavery society, and both Hawai'i and Malaysia are examples of post-colonial societies. Malaysia's indigenous population is a majority, Hawai'i's is a minority; both have received large numbers of in-migrant workers. Britain is a post-colonial metropolis, an established nation-state with Celtic cultural minorities, and an advanced economy with former colonial urban minorities. The typology of ethnicity in a framework of historical trajectory is represented in Chapters 4–7, which contain case studies drawing principally on Britain (and Europe), the USA, Hawai'i (now a state of the USA) and Malaysia.

Complementary or opposing frames of reference? Capitalism, modernity and culture

The historical frames and analytic emphases we set out earlier in this chapter have been the occasion for dispute (Rex and Mason 1986) – between Marxist and non-Marxist theories of class in indus- trial societies, between the slavery/colonial/post-colonial and the capitalist/nation-state framework and between the modernist/post- modernist frames (Rattansi and Westwood 1994, Miles 1994b, Wieviorka 1994). But there is in fact a great deal of common ground within them.

Wieviorka and modernity

First, despite the persistence of periodic writings claiming scientific grounds for differential 'racial abilities' and the publications of neo- fascist groups, the older race-science theories have been largely discredited and publicly disavowed. At the same the attribution of natural-cultural attributes to ethnic groups has not receded and indeed gives periodic indications of accelerating. It is this set of conclusions which has given rise to the emphasis on 'racisms', that is to forms of attribution within systems of ethnic classification which differ in their style and import according to their context. Wieviorka, in particular, argues that racisms have emerged as different formulations prompted by a historical sequence of tensions in the creation of the modern world. They thus bear the specific marks of their historical location as well as the general form of racism. He refers to 'modernity triumphant' in the theoretical hierarchies of 'advanced and backward' races; to the attitude of the 'poor white' who fears competition and exclusion from the benefits of modern material welfare; to the revaluing of ancestral religions, nations and communities as an anti-modern reflex 'thus giving rise to a racism which attacks those who are assumed to be the vectors of a detested modernity' of which 'the Jews are often the incarnation' (Wieviorka 1994, p. 175) and to inter-communal antagonisms which are not directly traceable to modernity or anti-modernity.

Modernity triumphant is the voice of the dominant European cultures in their portrayal of others as backward. This attitude may be turned outward to subordinate nations or inward to 'marginal' cultures, in the way that Celtic language and culture was construed as 'standing in the way of progress' in Britain (Hutchinson 1987, Boyce 1991, Williams 1994, Kiberd 1996). The 'poor white' is the socially and politically disfranchised segment of the ethnic majority whose fear and loathing is reserved for minority ethnicities. And the socially disenchanted classes attribute their ill-fate to the bearers of modernity ethnically identified – the Jews. He further argues that if many of the certainties of the 'modern' world have collapsed in the 'post-modern' world, then we face new and uncertain social terrain in which racism may continue to flourish. For example, the diminution of the demand for manual factory workers in rich capitalist countries is a source of male unemployment which undermines class and gender identities in the same moment; this is an example of a social 'space' within which ethnic resentments may emerge. This theorisation merges the analytic emphasis on capitalism with the analytic emphasis on modernity.

Culture and racism

These and similar arguments carry within them another point of convergence, specifically around the concept of culture. It is clear that the concept of culture has played an increasingly central part in the debate about racism largely because the politics of exclusion (Anthias and Yuval-Davis 1992) – in, for example, the immigration laws of European countries (Gordon 1989) – have increasingly been predicated on arguments of cultural difference. This was a prominent feature of Enoch Powell's appeal to the idea of a familiar England 'we know and love' (Foot 1969) and more recently Norman Tebbit's attacks on multi-culturalism (*Daily Telegraph* 1997). Late-apartheid South Africa propounded the notion that a segregated 'plural' society was necessary both because of profound cultural difference and in order to protect those cultures. As Rex has pointed out, South Africa was one of the first societies to embrace 'multiculturalism' (Rex 1997a, b, 1986).

Although Miles (1982, 1993) has long argued for the siting of racism within the labour migration/capitalism complex, his recent work has given much more attention to the link between racism and nationalism (see also Poliakov 1974), especially with regard to the ideological construction of nations in modern Europe. Dominant national cultures portray outsiders as unwanted and devalue local minority cultures (Miles 1993). Similarly, Miles has not argued against the 'post-slavery' and 'post-colonial' frames of reference (as if these were at odds with a capitalism/migration emphasis), rather he has argued that historical determinations, which slavery and colonial frames may represent, have to be augmented by analysis of the continuation or reproduction of racialisation/ethnication in current capitalist contexts (Miles 1994b). This is well illustrated later in this book by the case of Malaysia which cannot be understood without reference both to its colonial and post-colonial setting and to the current modernisation of Malaysia as a leading South East Asian capitalist economy (Jesudason 1990).

Modernisation in western Europe and America and now in much of the rest of the world has been and is *capitalist* modernisation; the two frames may be seen to refer to many of the same processes and in this sense are convergent. One of the specific emphases within the 'modernity' debate is on the political culture developed in Western capitalist democracies, that is the elaboration of ideas of civic equality and universal human qualities and rights (Balibar and Wallerstein 1991). The contradiction here is that this philosophy is seen to be marked by its European origins in an age of European dominance and by its particularist (that is, only to the British, only to the French) application in nationalist nation-states. This contradiction in Western Universalism was illustrated in the instance of two Muslim schoolgirls in France who were forbidden to attend a state school wearing their headscarves. 'Universalist' defence of the prohibition was predicated on the principle of secular education while in the same moment it constituted an anti-Islamic ('racist') decision (Wayland 1997). The construction and valuation of cultures come to play a greater part in our understanding of racism. At the same time the concept of ethnicity, while being grounded in ideas about culture, has come to be critically viewed within a context of political contest. One of the unforeseen consequences of this culturisation of the concept of racism and the politicisation of ethnicity is the convergence of the discourse of racism and the discourse of ethnicity. The concept of ethnicity can no longer – as has so often been the case – be criticised or rejected because of its anthropological focus on simple cultural difference (Anthias and Yuval-Davis 1992, p. 7). And the understanding of racism(s) has been extended to include cultural attributions – much influenced for example by Edward Said's portrayal of the way in which the West perceived the Orient as ineffably culturally different and frequently, by implication, 'lesser' (Said 1991). Once these changes in our approaches have occurred then the understanding of ethnicity and the understanding of racism begin to occupy much of the same terrain.

A crisis in the sociology of racism?

For all these convergences and what should be regarded as signal advances in the historical and contextualised understanding of both racism and ethnicity, there remain serious difficulties, the first of which may be seen as a potential crisis in the sociology of racism. The great contribution of the insistence on placing racism within a context variously of class structure, colonial and post-colonial systems, and the aftermath of European domination, was the powerful critique of all forms of reductionism, particularly the social-psychological argument that racial discrimination, racist beliefs and ethnic loyalties were all manifestations of a kind of universal disregard for the stranger. This reductionism was not only manifested as a form of social science, but also, more persuasively, as a form of common sense – that regard for one's own group and consequent disregard for others was a natural and universal phenomenon, the only questions being how it manifested itself and how it might be moderated. The arguments from both colonialism and capitalism contained within them the tacit message that racism was not a natural universal form of social differentiation but a specific historical – and possibly specifically or predominantly

'Western/European' – product of two related systems of domination. It could therefore be transcended by the very transcendence of the historical forms which produced it, that is by the ending of colonialism and by the replacement of capitalism by a more just and rational social order. The ending of colonialism was, of course, not seen as sufficient, since post-colonial regimes would still have to struggle with the colonial legacy and with the continuation of global inequalities. Nevertheless the specific location of racism within these historical contexts held out this unspoken promise of transcendence. The pessimistic implications of this tacit understanding of the sociology of racism arise from the fact that capitalism is at least *pro tem* globally triumphant. And if capitalist modernity and post-modernity inspire racist culture and ethnic categories then where might we turn unless it is to the post-modern deconstruction of categories and classes?

Furthermore, the modernisation of the world under local and global regimes of capitalism is now much more extensive than seemed possible or even likely 20 years ago. Most of the former Soviet Union now comprises new states which see themselves modernising as market economies, Scandinavian welfarism is in crisis, socialistic experiments in South America, India, and parts of Africa and the Caribbean have either collapsed or been destabilised by the combined power of international capital and US foreign policy and been replaced by programmes of 'marketisation', while in August 1997 the new Chinese leader announced a grand programme of privatisation. For the foreseeable future modernisation can be expected to continue to take the capitalist form.

There are other difficulties in the theorisation of racism and ethnicity. Perhaps the greatest difficulty for the 'capitalism/Western European' account of racism is the evidence of the persistence of forms of racism and nationalism within the socialist regimes of the Soviet/Eastern European bloc countries (Tishkov 1997), and not only in the immediate post-collapse period. This has to be coupled with evidence of both racist ideas (Dikötter 1992) and ethnic conflicts in China (*Guardian* 1997a). In former Yugoslavia and the former Soviet Union appeals to ethnonationalist sentiments, persecution of minorities, and of national populations were evidenced *during* the socialist period and for some of the same kinds of reasons – economic crises, movements of labour, and appeals to state-national solidarity – as are cited in the case of capitalist countries (Glenny 1993). We may argue, of course, that both the former Soviet Union and China have been or are now empires and therefore exhibit the same kind of cultural imperialism as Western empires. New post-Soviet states are appealing to culture-communities whose integrity was suppressed and devalued under Soviet rule and consequently can be seen to be following some of the same arguments about language and national identity – that is, de-Russification – as can be seen in post-colonial societies once under European domination (Kupchan 1995, Tishkov 1997). This brings racism and ethnicity under a familiar analytic framework but is nonetheless politically pessimistic by contrast with the tacit optimism of the earlier capitalism/colonialism frame. A few decades into the next century we may find the 'Universalist' project engaging with forms of racism and ethnic division in quite different – non-European – zones of the world, in Indonesia, Brazil, India and China (Dikötter 1997).

Polity and economy, gender and ethnicity

The state-political and the economic tendencies which have contributed to the formation of ethnic identities and racism are also implicated in the forming of gender roles and ideologies, and the patterns of gender differentiation frequently take a form similar to ethnic differentiation. Migrant workers, identified as minority ethnicities, will commonly occupy positions within the labour force which have lower pay, poorer working conditions, less security of employment, and are concentrated in a number of industries and services. In Britain in the post-war recruitment of workers from colonies or former colonies there was a concentration in transport and the National Health Service and large numbers of migrant workers from Pakistan were subsequently employed in the textile industries of the north of England. These occupational and sectoral concentrations of ethnic populations are mirrored in the patterns of concentration of men and women, female workers being overrepresented in clerical and sales work, caring professions, and in domestic and service work (for a discussion of gender inequalities see Bradley 1996). With regard to both gender and ethnicity there is not only a pattern of occupational concentration but also of stratified inequality. Where women are represented in professions typically dominated by men, they are commonly underrepresented in the leading positions; similarly minority ethnic groups in Britain who are represented in professional, managerial and administrative work tend to be underrepresented in higher paid and senior positions (Modood *et al.* 1997).

Some of the reasons for gender and ethnic differentiation follow the same or similar lines. Because of the historical association of women with domestic responsibilities their participation in the labour force has been partial, interrupted or marginal compared to that of men. Similarly, migrant workers and ethnic groups who are discriminated against are vulnerable in ways which constrain their opportunities in employment. They may be simply excluded from whole areas of employment by either formal or non-formal means, employed on less secure terms, or constrained from asserting their rights because of their marginality; among migrant workers this marginality is a function of the insecurity of their right to stay, where employers exert pressures on workers who fear deportation (Anthias and Yuval-Davis 1992).

The economic structuring of gender- and ethnic-specific experience is matched by similar parallels in the state and political sphere. The immigration and citizenship laws of nation-states typically reinforce the marginality of migrant groups and their families affecting the lives of the migrant generation and subsequent generations. In Britain, greatly disproportionate numbers of Jamaicans are prevented from entering the country as visitors, often to attend family occasions such as weddings and funerals. For many years women entering Britain from Indian and Pakistan were assaulted on arrival at the port of entry by immigration officials who insisted on vaginal tests, on the assumption that women entering the country for purposes of marriage would be virgins (Anthias and Yuval-Davis 1992, Yuval-Davis 1997). In racialised societies where legal as well as customary constraints enforce ethnic boundaries, the state legislates to confirm the inferior position of stigmatised minorities by defining boundaries of employment, residence, education and sexual behaviour and intermarriage. In western European societies, the superordinate position of men has been confirmed in laws governing property and inheritance, and in the directly political sphere has historically been reflected in the denial of the vote to women and in a continuing pattern of overrepresentation of men in government, political parties and offices of state (Bradley 1997). This pattern is very uneven between different states and is not static; policies and legal restraints are changed in response both to organised minorities and women and to new demands in the labour market – consider the feminisation of opportunities in the labour market and the notion that the decline of manufacturing has led to the idea of surplus and marginal young men (Bradley 1997).

Women, like minorities, are the targets of both violence and the moral campaign. In the USA in the 1980s there was a political demonisation of minorities, single-parent mothers and all 'welfare-dependent' groups. These were presented as the underclass whose position was perpetuated by their own moral weakness. Similar moral campaigns were pursued in Britain (Levitas 1986). The subordinate position of women and minorities is frequently enforced by violence: 'Violence is often employed to reproduce this system of domination; women like members of other minorities, are harassed, beaten, raped, maimed and murdered because they are women' (Guillaumin 1995).

Beyond similarities: the intersection of gender and ethnicity

There are parallels in both the state structuring and the economy structuring of gender and ethnicity. They are not, either in theory or in practice, perfect parallels or unchanging, but share important similarities and continuities. A rather different question, and historically underexplored (but see Anthias and Yuval-Davis 1992, Guillaumin 1995, Bradley 1996, Barot *et al.* 1999), is that of the relationship between gender and ethnicity, how they intersect and how both intersect with class experience. In subordinated ethnic groups, women and men are treated differently within the sexual mores, subordinate men being regarded as a threat from whom superordinate women must be protected, while subordinate women are regarded as being available to superordinate men. This is true both of racialised slavery/post-slavery societies, and of war waged under the influence of a powerful ethnic ideology, as in the civil war in Yugoslavia where the women of opposed ethnic groups were raped and murdered. One of the striking features of migrant labour in Europe and other zones of the world has been the feminisation of labour 'opportunities' in which women as sex workers and maids are regarded simultaneously in gender and ethnic terms (Phizacklea 1999). In these and other ways, interethnic imagery and behaviour is frequently sexually expressed and sexual behaviour is ethnically structured.

The class and sector concentrations which we have described with respect to gender and ethnicity are frequently found to be gender-ethnic concentrations. In Caribbean post-war migration to Britain, women migrated independently of men and a high proportion of them worked in nursing, and in those South Asian populations where women entered the labour market in large numbers, a majority were in superexploited service and industrial occupations often working alongside other South Asian women (Phizacklea and Wolkowitz 1995). Where minority men entered business as, for example, small and medium-size manufacturers in the clothing industries, they typically recruited labour 'within the ethnic community' depending on word of mouth recommendation and fear of social shaming as a mode of control in the workplace (Hoel 1982). On a global scale there is a gender-defined labour market for domestic labour and sexual services, where women from poor countries – Pakistan, the Philippines, Sri Lanka and others – become the maids of families in rich countries, sometimes thereby making it possible for the women as well as the men in these rich countries to pursue independent lives and careers. Their incomes are important to the countries from which they migrate:

> An estimated four million Filipinas earn their living abroad, at least half of them working as domestic servants in the Middle East, Hong Kong, Japan and the rest of South East Asia. The Philippines government is pressed to ban the export of labour to various countries, notably the Gulf Arab states [but] finds itself in a quandary. The estimated $4 billion sent home annually in remittances has kept the Philippines in a balance of payments surplus for years. The average Philippine teacher is paid $120 per month less than a semi-literate maid in Kuwait. (*Observer* 1 October 1995)

In these examples we see gender inequalities within ethnically defined communities, ethnic-specific sex rules and patterns of exploitation, and global inequalities underlying the international market for female labour.

One of the key intersections of ethnicity and gender is the fact that, in so many instances of the maintenance of ethnic boundaries, women are assigned the leading role in ensuring the cultural reproduction which is seen as essential to the real and symbolic survival of the ethnic community. This, of course, reflects the role which generally women have or are expected to have in the sustaining of social networks and cultural goods. In Anthias and Yuval-Davis' words women are 'the biological reproducers of ethnic collectivities, and the central participants in the ideological reproduction of the collectivity and as transmitters of its culture' (1992, p. 115). For example, among Catalan women in southern France they are responsible as young mothers for preparing their children for participation in French society and as older women for the reproduction of Catalan culture:

> In St Llorenc de Cerdans mothers reproduce French culture and language and grandmothers reproduce Catalan culture and language. This is a reflection of the changes women go through in their own life cycles whereby they become progressively incorporated into a Catalan ethnic identity from a French ethnic identity. Young people confirmed that their grandmothers were a source of knowledge about language, customs, cooking, music and the past. These same grandmothers often had only spoken French as young women. Grandmothers are seen as reservoirs of Catalan culture and customs as a result of the changes a woman goes through during her life cycle. (O'Brien in Goddard *et al.* 1994)

Catalan women in southern France thus play a key part in reproducing Catalan culture and in managing the point of balance between French and Catalan society.

Just as women play a leading role in maintaining ethnic cultures and boundaries, so too rules *about* gender have a key place among those customs and expectations which are seen as defining the community. Again in the words of Anthias and Yuval-Davis:

> The boundary of the ethnic is often dependent on gender and there is a reliance on gender attributes for specifying ethnic identity; much of ethnic culture is organised around rules relating to sexuality, marriage and the family, and a true member will perform these roles properly. (Anthias and Yuval-Davis 1992, p. 113)

Among South Asian populations in Britain, traditions of arranged marriage are a salutary index of this point. The collective concern of the wider family network in the making of a suitable marriage is directly contrasted to the individualism of the marriage ideology of choice and romantic love and is one indication of the way in which individualism in its widest connotations is seen as antagonistic to the integrity of culture communities. In the social management of marriage, the cultural definition of gender relationships can be seen to stand at a critical point of conservation, adaptation and change among ethnic groups formed out of urban migrations.

Universalism and particularist principles

Gender and ethnicity can both be viewed in their relation to Universalism, discussed in Chapter 2 in the context of racism. Gender and ethnic discriminations both run counter to Universalist principles of access to jobs and resources on merit and to principles of bureaucratic neutrality. Wallerstein has accordingly argued that in both cases capitalist democracies engender a constant tension between Universalist and particularist – racism, sexism – principles. The 'two ideological principles of the capitalist world-economy stand in open contradiction to each other' (Balibar and Wallerstein 1991, p. 35). Racism–sexism underpins forms of super-exploitation in a gender and ethnic-differentiated division of labour. In his view, they are resisted both by their victims and by the capitalist order when they reach a point of 'irrationality', thus producing a series of zigzags in Universalism–racism (and sexism). The resistances to racism and sexism also face the same dilemmas in which reform is counterposed to radical change, cultural change counterposed to structural reordering and equality of opportunity to equality of outcome. Finally, ethnicisation and gendering as dimensions of social action and social organisation are not limited to the areas – for example labour markets – in which they may be primarily contextualised, but are typically generalised to all or many spheres of social action. This is a cardinal reason why gender and ethnic differentiation respond to political-economic tendencies but cannot be seen as mere products of them.

Summary

In the early part of this chapter we addressed the question of 'ethnicity' or 'ethnicities'. The term ethnic group is now widely used both within and without academic discourse but we should not assume that what is termed ethnicity in different sites and settings is the same phenomenon. There are features which are common to many of the examples we have cited. Symbolic importance is attached to ancestry and to all the emblems of identity; language is universally a marker of social difference, and culture becomes reflexively understood as a possession of the collectivity. The significance which this ordering of identity and culture takes on, however, has to be placed within specific historical and social contexts and these can be quite different in both structure and meaning.

In the introduction we had argued that ethnicity is both grounded and constructed. The social uses of ethnic classifications change, sometimes rapidly, as a consequence of political decisions – such as the abolition of apartheid in South Africa – and as a consequence of incremental shifts in the representations and behaviour of individuals. The classifications change as does the cultural content which is expressed in what people say about themselves; people restate who they are and what kind of people they are.

But these ethnic identities are not 'mere' constructions. They are sociologically grounded in a double sense. In the first instance, the defining features of ethnicity are sociologically grounded: as we argued, people really do participate in collective memories, do share a language through which sentiment and shades of meaning are expressed and music and love are made, and learn within families the custom and practice of a wider community. And in the second instance, the contextual features of ethnicity are grounded in the social and material experience of people who reproduce a collective identity. These contextual features are the enduring – persistent although changing – political and economic circumstances of ethnic groups. In the USA, the persistent economic disadvantage of African Americans is an enduring contextual feature of African American ethnicity. In Malaysia, the politico-cultural hegemony of Malay ethnicity is an enduring political circumstance.

In this chapter we have argued that these contextual features are critical to an understanding of the differences between variable manifestations of ethnicity. Drawing on Eriksen's discussion of ethnicity-making situations and of types of ethnic groups, we suggested a fivefold typology: urban minorities, indigenous peoples, proto-nations or ethnonational groups, ethnic groups in plural societies and post-slavery minorities. Enforced and voluntary migration of labour is a feature of three of these five types of ethnicity. People from Africa were transported and enslaved in the Americas, the plural societies of, for example, the Caribbean and South East Asia are home to the descendants of indigenes and the descendants of 19th-century migrants; urban minorities are the ethnic groups characteristic of the cities of the advanced and developing capitalist economies.

Alongside this typology of ethnic groups we described three historical trajectories which have been part of the context of ethnicity making and have been central to theorisations of contemporary ethnicity. We referred to three analytic emphases: the slavery/post-slavery; the colonial/post-colonial; and the capitalism and nation-state complexes. In discussing the theoretical emphases allied to each of these points of departure, we suggested that there were some convergences in apparently opposed viewpoints. In particular, the 'structural argument' from capitalism and the 'culturalist' argument grounded in the construction of 'nations' and in the key features of modernity were seen to be reconcilable and complementary.

In the development of modernity and the ideals of democracy in the modern nation-state, Universalism is a central and pervasive principle. The idea of common humanity replaces particularisms while the concept of particularism requires its binary opposite, Universalism. In the last part of the chapter we discussed how Universalism and particularism are opposing principles in contemporary societies and on a global scale. Racism and sexism were discussed as classical particularist principles. We compared ethnic minority status and gender ordering as similar but not identical modes of particularism. In the next chapter we turn our attention to racism.

Chapter 2

Ethnicity and Racism

We turn in this chapter to the questions posed by the existence of two discourses: one of race and racism, and one of ethnicity. These two discourses are represented in academic writings and traditions, and in public and popular modes of thought and speech. We shall see that there is very considerable common terrain occupied by the terms 'racial' and 'ethnic' while each has its own specific connotations. But the word 'race' and the ideas associated with it have a profound historical association with modern racialised slavery, colonial domination, and political and economic oppression, in a way that 'ethnic' does not. The ideas and practices linked to slavery and colonial domination in post-slavery societies became global in their reach and part of a binary black–white opposition which is conventionally referred to as 'racial'.

A discourse of race and racism survives even though the central term 'race' is discredited, as are the ideas associated with it. It survives most potently in those societies where the racialisation of attitudes, beliefs, practices and social institutions became and remain most firmly embedded – above all South Africa and the USA. In the USA 'race' and 'colour' not only remain part of popular and public discourse, and of official systems of classification as in the census, but also remain part of the academic social science discourse (Omi and Winant 1986).

In the second half of this chapter we shall show that the discourse of 'race' has some very particular roots in the disposition of power and economic dominance within the modern world. Like other ideologies, racist doctrines involve the creation of categories and the implication that those within the category have certain natural and inherent characteristics. The central features of racist thought are then, the construction of categories, and the attribution of inherent qualities. Other categories with similar roots in slavery and colonial domination are the terms 'native', 'heathen', 'savage' and 'pagan'. The latter part of this chapter explores some of the ways in which these terms have been used. First we discuss the discourse of ethnicity via examples from Malaysia and through a discussion of the political significance of French-Canadian and Quebecois as ethnic or ethno-national categories in Canada. We will suggest that while ethnicity may be 'constructed' out of cultural difference, these ethnicities are not *merely* constructed, they are also grounded in historical accumulations of experience and memory conveyed by a common language In this sense the distinguishing feature of 'race' as a term is its link to scientific error.

Turning our attention to racism we examine the historical contexts in which categorical views of 'others' have emerged. The colonial encounter of Europeans with the Americas from the turn of the 16th century posed the question – in European minds – 'what are other men like?' Although it was sharply contested, the European view of the peoples they encountered as pagan, less worthy of life itself and as lower creatures began to take shape. By then interposing excerpts from a late 19th-century English novel we can see how the European view of the other has taken root. Turning then to slavery as the historical context and to science as the ideological frame, we give examples of how enslavement of Africans formed a critical backdrop to the spread of a conception of a universal hierarchy of races. Next we look in detail at a missionary view of Malays conveyed in the memoirs of an American visitor, from which we can detect the contradictions in the portrayal of a colonised people. In the last part of this chapter we consider an important study of race-thinking in China which raises the question of the European specificity of racism.

Ethnicity and racism

Ethnicity and racism are not, on first inspection, the same order of sociological concepts. The concept of ethnicity refers to the way in which social and cultural difference, language and ancestry combine as a dimension of social action and social organisation, and form a socially reproduced system of classification. The term racism refers to ideas which claim to classify different races and view these races as fundamentally different and unequal; and it refers to the reproduction of a racialised system of inequality itself (Fredrickson 1988, Miles 1989). In its concrete form ethnicity refers to the social mobilisation of ethnic ties and the social significance of ancestry, language and culture. We may speak of ethnic groups – identifiable groups whose 'actual' or 'claimed' shared ethnic attributes mark them off within a social system. But we should not think of these groups too concretely; they are not discrete, permanent or fixed.

As we have argued, the 'cultural stuff' of ethnicity is grounded in social relationships. In a more or less conscious way, it is a feature of daily practice. This cultural content – the shared ancestry, the claims to a shared inheritance, the common customs and language – is also used or 'drawn upon' by ethnic group members, to give substance to an ethnic label. It may be drawn upon, too, by those who do not belong and do not share the cultural inheritance – that is, to mark them off from us. In Malaysia, the 'cultural stuff' of ethnic difference is grounded in social relationships, in the sense that there are differences of custom and practice between Malays and Chinese and Indians which are reproduced in everyday life. The majority of Malays speak Malay and many of them also speak English; relatively few speak Chinese or Indian languages. The Malay Islamic practice of eating only halal meat restricts the possibilities of shared eating and, as Nash (1989) suggests, the shared table – commensality – is the basis of much social exchange and solidarity. Modes of dress are characteristically different, social circles are often intra-ethnic, and intermarriages are uncommon. These differences are what we may regard as 'grounded' cultural differences, routine patterns of behaviour and preference reproduced in the day-to-day social practice of Malaysia. Differences of personal style, marriage preference and of food and dining customs combine to define ethnicity at this micro-social level:

> In addition to Melayu as a mother tongue, a style of comportment, called *halus* (refined) is alleged to be Malay. This *halus* style is seen in polite social interaction, a consciousness of deference to age, status, piety, and other socially valued personal characteristics. (Nash 1989, p. 33)

Islam and Malay ethnicity correspond directly; being Muslim is part of the definition of being Malay. However the nature of being Muslim is contested – between more and less 'fundamentalist' for example – and there are Muslims in Malaysia who are not Malays, being Arab, Pathan, Indian or Pakistani (Nash 1989). Although some of these Muslims may intermarry, for the most part Islam forms a hard boundary between Malay and Malaysian Chinese and Indian. Religious food codes also serve to harden social lines of demarcation:

> Along with the boundary mechanism of endogamy among categories is the virtual bar to commensality. Eating together is the closest form of interpersonal intimacy, and is often a metaphor for connubium, common substance and common origin. The Muslim code of halal-haram separates Chinese from Malay [and] this code prohibits so many of the ordinary foods of the Chinese that Malays cannot dine in a Chinese home or

restaurant. Chinese restaurants must post halal signs if they seek Malay custom. (Nash 1989, p. 36)

At the same time as forming organising principles of everyday life, these cultural preferences are mobilised as ethnic markers. In Malaysia, the Malay language, the religion of Islam, and indigenousness, claimed by Malays as against Chinese and Indians who are portrayed as in-migrants despite their long presence in the country, have all been used to signify the distinctiveness of Malays and to underline their political claims.

Ethnicity as 'invented', ethnicity as 'grounded': the French-Canadian example

The social process of making ethnicity significant is part of a constant interplay. This is an interplay between those who belong, 'us', and those who look on, 'them'. Historically, the basis of claims made about ethnicity in 20th-century Canada lies in over 200 years of the French presence in what is now Canada. The 'cultural stuff' of modern ethnicity resides in the customs, the social styles, the language and the loose though plausible claim to be descendants of a common stock – the earliest French settlers in Canada (Handler 1988).

A grounded historical accretion of culture, language and ancestry is to be found in the long experience of French speakers in Canada. This experience has been shaped by the influence of the Catholic Church, and until recently the largely rural and small town context of French Canadian life, and by the close proximity of the border with the USA (Handler 1988).

In the historical resolution of the French-English struggle for control of Canada, the victorious British made provision for the social and cultural autonomy of the French in Canada. This autonomy was always hedged about by the actual economic and political and, for the most part, numerical superiority of the British in Canada. For a long period the French were on the one hand 'permitted' to retain their 'Frenchness within Canada' but were in a broad sense subordinated to Anglo-British (Protestant) domination of Canada. As French Canadian political awareness grew in the 1960s and thereafter, a struggle has ensued about the place of French Canadians in Canadian society. In this process the French Canadians make claims about themselves (that is about 'us') and these claims are made to at least two audiences – French Canadians or 'potential' French Canadians, those likely to identify with Frenchness, and English-speaking Canadians. Meanwhile, English-speaking Canadians make 'defining statements' about French Canadians (Vallieres 1971).

Ethnicity requires this team collaboration even if the co-players are not so friendly. In Eriksen's phrase (1993b), to think of ethnicity as anything other than a relationship is like 'thinking of one hand clapping'. The English speakers also have at least two audiences: themselves ('this is who we are and this is what we are like') and the French Canadians ('that is who *you* are' and so on). The cultural stuff, the shared language, ancestry and customs, is given a certain significance, it is shaped, it is selectively drawn upon – but it is not entirely 'made up' or invented. There is a real historical social process from which French-Canadian ethnicity derives; at the same time it is always being constructed and reconstructed in its contemporary social significance. In the last three decades this French Canadianness has increasingly found expression in the pursuit of a large measure of autonomy for the province of Quebec. What was once 'French Canadian' is now politically 'Quebecois'; the search for recognition of French culture and language within Canada has moved towards autonomy or independence for the province of Quebec as a nation or as a 'distinct society' (Taylor 1992).

As 'French Canadianness' or 'being Quebecois' is politically constructed, the historical and contemporary materials are drawn upon to 'colour in' the picture of ethnicity. The threat to the purity and survival of the French language, the portrayal of Quebecois or French-Canadian culture as less selfish and materialistic than English culture, the determined promotion of music, dance and custom (Handler 1988) are all part of a picture of a French-Canadian culture threatened with submersion in a surrounding Anglophone sea. Provincial Quebec influence over education within the province and the ability to pass laws intended to preserve the use of the French language demonstrate how a state-like bureaucracy can use its powers to shape the meso-institutions of a society – the schools and universities which are important reproducers of culture.

Thus French-Canadian identity is both constructed in the sense of being politically reshaped and historically grounded. French Canadianness is constantly being invented and reinvented, but it is not simply an invented ethnicity; it is grounded in the historical and present experience of a population who have some basis on which to call themselves a people. In this sense, ethnicity diverges from 'race' in that the very logic which the concept race refers to is a discredited race science. This is represented by the claim of natural biological divisions of humankind which were believed to be the basis of differences of culture and civilisation (Kuper 1975). There is no parallel in the concept of ethnicity to the 'error' basis of the concept of race.

'Race' as mistaken science

Race has been described as the phlogiston of social science, phlogiston being the substance invented in the minds of scientists prior to a proven understanding of combustion. The error base of the concept of race lies in the fact that for much of the 19th and 20th centuries the term race was taken to mean discrete divisions of humankind with visible characteristics marking those divisions. This classification was combined with the idea that races had characteristics of temperament, ability, and moral nature, which constituted a racial inheritance. Race was seen to be a 'natural' – in scientific terms 'biological' – grouping of human populations and the primary determinant of civilisation.

Theories of the inheritance of character and moral stature as a set of racial traits were entirely speculative and most race thinking was produced before our present understandings of genetic transmission. Indeed much race science preceded Darwin's theories of evolutionary development which in principle undermined the idea of fixed racial types (Banton and Harwood 1975, Banton 1977). To a large extent in biological science and in sociology the term race has fallen into disuse or is surrounded by quotation marks to show that it is not something real, one notable exception being academic – and political – discourse in the USA.

The physical signs, of skin colour and other physical features, which were used by race scientists – and by race thinkers of many kinds – are visible and real. There are, unevenly spread over the globe, clusters of populations with notable differences of skin colour, hair form, eye form and other facial features. What is erroneous is the assertion that these are the bases of discrete races of humankind with social and moral characteristics which are grounded in their biological difference (Kuper 1975).

Racialisation is the social process of conferring social significance on these visible markers. Racialisation is the process of making physical differences into social markers and, typically, enforcing them in a regime of oppression.

The falsity lies in the unambiguous description of physical types as 'races' which are then viewed as having common attributes as a consequence of their shared race. But it is clearly not false to say that there are characteristic differences in appearance loosely clustered in populations spread over the globe. And it is clear that these appearance characteristics are one of the bases on which people socially distinguish themselves from others, whether voluntarily or by compulsion of others. People who are designated as being of this or that 'group' on the basis of physical distinctiveness come to share a common social experience: complex though it is, there is a social reality underlying what it means to be white or black in America. None of these social realities runs counter to the view that race as understood for most of the concept's recent history comprises a significant falsehood, which means that the term race cannot be brought into play as an analytic or descriptive sociological term.

In Miles' summation:

> It was generally concluded after the Second World War that the scientific conception of 'race' grounded in the idea of fixed typologies and based upon certain phenotypical features such as skin colour and skull shape does not have any significant scientific meaning or utility. Moreover it was concluded that there is no causal relationship between physical or genetic characteristics and cultural characteristics. (Miles 1989, p. 37)

People who are designated as belonging to a 'race' come, as we suggested earlier, to share experiences as a consequence of this social process of designation. In many respects, the USA invented the category 'black' as a social marker of primary significance and Americans constructed a whole social edifice around the binary divide of white and black (Fredrickson 1981, 1988). This lasted in one form – racialised slavery – through slavery to its end in 1865, in another form – racial segregation and oppression – up to 1954 and the beginnings of the dismantling of a system of social segregation, and in a third form in present day America where racial categories are highly contested and embraced by those who have been disadvantaged in racialised America. In America, the idea of race became the leading social marker, almost the defining feature of American social structure (Kymlicka 1989). Over centuries of shared experience, communities of black people in the USA gave rise to a new ethnicity or series of ethnic claims and cultures. As Goldberg has argued, the idea of race became an element of American culture, first mobilised by whites as an instrument of oppression, and subsequently claimed by many black African Americans as a counter-hegemonic symbol of unity and peoplehood (Goldberg 1993).

Despite the overwhelming power of whiteness in America, enforced against black Americans by violence and coercion as well as by the routines of a racialised society, black African American ethnicity has been expressed as a voluntary social and political project, and in many ways. The terms African and black have been embraced, black as an expression of unity and pride, African as an expression of peoplehood. This shift from an unmistakably imposed racialised system to an expression of ethnic communality suggests that processes typically described as racialisation and processes typically described as 'ethnicity' or 'ethnicisation' have much in common. There is reference to 'them' (or 'us') as a distinct people, reference to ideas of ancestry and 'inheritance' and the use of social markers as setting the limits and styles of relationships between groups or between individuals viewed as group members.

'Ethnic' as the generic term

Since the term 'race' suffers from its history of mistaken science, there are good arguments for making 'ethnic' the generic term of which ideas about 'race' may be taken as a sub-set. Gellner (1983) and Eriksen (1993b) treat it in this way. In Gellner's case he is discussing how ideologies are developed in the demarcation of 'rulers and ruled, privileged and underprivileged' and the way in which ethnic elites 'justify' their dominant position. An ideology of dominance which supports an ethnic elite, he argues 'may seize on language, on genetically transmitted traits (racism), or on culture alone' (Gellner 1983). Similarly Eriksen suggests that 'since ethnic ideologies tend to stress common descent among their members, the distinction between race and ethnicity is a problematic one. Ideas of "race" may or may not form part of ethnic ideologies' (Eriksen 1993b). In many, maybe most, instances the ideas of racial and ethnic difference are found side by side. In the American case, the concept of the WASP, as the dominant ethnic group in America's recent history, expresses both themes. In the term White Anglo-Saxon Protestant there are racial (white), ancestral (Anglo-Saxon) and cultural or religious (Protestant) components which are juxtaposed. In trying to sustain an analytic distinction we are prisoners of conventional or customary usage. In academic discourse (see Rex and Mason 1986, Barot 1996), 'racism' is more common than 'ethnic ideology'; in popular and newspaper usage the terms race and ethnic are often used interchangeably even in the same sentence (see the *Guardian* report on the British Census, 1997a).

Just as terms which are part of a racist categorisation (black) may be embraced in a movement of liberation from oppression, so a term which is ethnic or ancestral in its reference to country of origin may take on the characteristics of a racist categorisation. In Britain, the term 'Pakistani' has its origins in migration, it has cultural connotations in the close association with Islam, and is willingly adopted by community leaders. But at the same time the word Pakistani and, more so, 'Paki' is used as a derogatory term by whites and in a way that has little connection with the meaning of Pakistani for those who willingly claim it.

If it is difficult to give a final meaning to these related terms it is certainly possible to be clear about connotations which are relatively enduring. The term race is associated with mistaken science, it connotes physical difference and, frequently, colour. It is typically seen as malign, and racial ideologies have been associated with compulsion and regimes of oppression. By contrast, ethnic can be taken as an analytic term in social science, is often seen as the voluntary identification of peoples, and as (at least potentially) benign. The malign–benign distinction has been most clearly transgressed in the use of the term 'ethnic cleansing' in the Yugoslavian civil war and this term has come into general usage in contexts where 'racial discrimination or segregation' might have been used.

Political domination and economic exploitation: Universalism and racism

The discourse of race, race thinking, and more specifically racism, has developed within a context of political domination and economic exploitation (Wolf 1982, Stannard 1992), within which one people, or grouping of peoples, have set themselves over others and have expressed their actual superiority through a doctrine of inherent difference. One of the forms which this race thinking took was 'scientific racism' although neither scientific racism nor racism more generally was the only form of expression of inherent difference. But an important and significant aspect of a dominant 19th- and 20th-century racist discourse' was that it found its legitimacy in an appeal to the authority of science.

The development of science was a key element of the language of humanism; 'man' was the agent of scientific discovery and 'man' was at the same time one of the subjects of inquiry. Biology, life sciences, human sciences, social sciences, and medicine were all expressions of the devotion to the aim of making man the centre of enquiry. So the same revolution of thought which proclaimed that humankind was endowed with the capacity for independent rational thought, that each person had human rights encompassing participation in their own governance and the recognition of individual human dignity, this same revolution produced the mode of thought we refer to as science which was to replace superstition, mere speculation, and religious authority. So it is no accident that the same period of history – above all the last 250 years – that has produced humanist rationalist thought as the basis of liberation from God-given authority and from the concomitant pre-modern systems of hierarchical domination, has also produced racism as the antithesis of humanist Universalism. Science was thus a feature both of the doctrine that men (and it was virtually always stated as men) were created equal and had equal human dignity and worth and as such was an ally of a universalistic humanism, and was a feature of race science, of the doctrine that 'men' were inherently unequal.

This was not, or not only, a corollary of an argument that social orders were necessarily unequal (that is, were class, caste and estate societies), but as a proposition that humankind was divided into inherently unequal parts – races. Religious ideas had supported the belief that society was composed of 'the rich man in his castle and the poor man at his gate/God made them high and lowly and founded their estate' – as the hymn told us – and gave religious authority to a natural hierarchy. It also allied itself to the doctrine that all men were created equal – in the eyes of God, in his image. Thus was science brought to the defence of slavery and Christian principle to its denunciation; and Christian principle was called into service to defend racial slavery and science to denounce it (Curtin 1964, Montagu 1964, Gossett 1965, Balibar and Wallerstein 1991). Anthropology, emerging in the 19th century as the science of 'man', has embodied all the aspects of these contradictions: the alliance of anthropology with the science of races, the critique of race science through the emphasis on culture and environment (Boas 1982), the use of culture as emphasising ultimate plasticity, and the representation of cultural difference as profound and fixed (see Balibar and Wallerstein 1991).

Universalism and racism

Balibar speaks of the two opposing principles, Universalism and racism whose assumptions are threaded through the global social changes of the last three centuries. These last three centuries have been characterised by the material, political and economic domination of a greater part of the world by what we typically call 'the West'. This period has seen the domination of Middle Eastern, Far Eastern, Malaysian, Indonesian, North, Central and South American, Caribbean, Pacific and African societies by the agents direct and indirect of European states, in particular by Portugal, Spain, Britain, Holland, France, Belgium, Germany and Italy. If the history of the world were pictured as now reaching 'midnight', this western European domination might only have lasted since five minutes to twelve but in that brief period the impact has been very great (Lévi-Strauss 1975).

While the most direct and imperial forms of domination are more recent, the beginnings of European incursions into the new worlds began well before the 18th century. In the earliest periods of Portuguese, Spanish, and later British expansion from the late 15th century onwards, there were great voyages of 'discovery', expeditions in search of the treasures of the earth, and the establishment of trading posts and trading companies. Some of this trade was in slaves and as the Portuguese sailed down the west coast of Africa they began to establish a special kind of trading post – the shoreside fortresses in which captured African villagers were held prior to sale and enslavement in the New World (Walvin 1983). From 1526 to 1870 about twenty million Africans were enslaved and sold into the New World, Brazil alone accounting for over three and half million of them. In the same period not just hundreds of thousands, but millions of people native to North, Central and South America, the Caribbean and the Pacific were swept away by a triple onslaught of disease, demoralisation and slaughter in the wake of the fateful encounter with the West.

It has often been argued that the systematisation of colonial adventures, the harnessing of indigenous, slave, indentured or imported wage labour in the service of plantation production, extractive industries and other economies which became part of a worldwide trade in commodities, provided the stimulus for racism. Fryer distinguishes race prejudice from racism, the latter being a coherent doctrine rather than mere 'scraps' of irrationality:

> It was their drive for profit that led English mechant capitalists to traffic in Africans. There was big money in it. The theory came later. Once the English slave trade, English sugar-producing plantation slavery, and English manufaturing industry had begun to operate as a trebly profitable interlocking system, the economic basis had been laid for all those ancient scraps of myth and prejudice to be woven into a more or less coherent racist ideology: a mythology of race. (Fryer 1984, p. 134)

In short, the development of world capitalism provided the occasion for the development of world racism.

We should regard this as a historically situated guiding argument, rather than as a single postulate which accounts for race thinking. To stick too closely to such an argument can look like a search for a once-and-for-all answer to the question 'where does racism come from?' Not only does the search for the answer lead in many different directions but in the end we must regard the question as flawed, not least because of the implication that we can define a single essential 'thing' in human history as racism. What we find, at least over the period described, is a wide range of forms of categorical thinking in which others are regarded as inherently different and usually as inferior – a prominent and repeated ideological feature of the European encounter with the non-European world. The growth of capitalism within Europe and the spread of capitalism across the world chiefly under European auspices prompted the hardening of racist ideas and ideologies; and the management and political defence of slave labour as one phase of this expansion played a particularly crucial part.

What are other men like?

In the 16th and 17th centuries, as Spanish, Portuguese, Dutch and British adventurers and would-be colonists sailed into the 'New World' the ideological battles commenced about those who were, to the Europeans, the 'new' peoples and the kind of people they were seen to be. The brutality of the way in which Spaniards treated the Indians whom they met was a matter not only of a brutal philosophy – to the extent that such had taken shape – but also of the cold brutality of the sword. Men and women were pursued and massacred, their hands severed, their entrails spilled out, they were burnt, they were speared together with their offspring, they were hunted and they had their heads dashed against rocks (Stannard 1992).

Stannard has collected accounts of the 15th- and 16th-century Spanish incursions into Central and South America:

> In Cuba a troop of a hundred or more Spaniards stopped by the banks of a dry river and sharpened their swords on the whetstones in its bed. They drew their weapons and began to rip open the bellies, to cut and kill... the men women, children and old folk... This particular slaughter began at the village of Zucayo, where the townsfolk earlier had provided for the conqistadors a feast of cassava, fruit and fish. Las Casas puts the number of Indians killed at 20,000 (Stannard 1992, p. 71).

And in a further account:

Some Christians encounter an Indian woman, who was carrying in her arms a child at suck; and since the dog they had with them was hungry, they tore the child from the mother's arms and flung it still living it to the dog, who proceeded to devour it before the mother's eyes. (Stannard 1992, pp. 71–2)

The Spanish adventures in the New World eventually provided the occasion, in 1550, for a famous dispute about the 'nature' of Indians as they so regularly termed the people they met. The Roman Catholic missionary Bartolomé Las Casas not only chronicled these brutalities but also engaged in a formal debate with Juan Gines de Sepulveda as to whether Indians were men capable of rational thought or mere brutes who were naturally fit for enslavement or worse. This was a *locum classicum* for the creation of categories and the attribution of inherent qualities. Men and women were assigned to a category and debate ensued as to what their inherent characteristics were. Las Casas argued that they should be regarded as rational men; they should not be seen as naturally fit only for slavery. Even more did he protest against the maiming and massacre of thousands and against their being hunted like animals, something of which others returned and boasted.

At around the same time other Spanish travellers wrote of the Indians as 'naturally lazy and vicious, melancholic, cowardly, and in general a lying shiftless people' (Stannard 1992). Sepulveda argued against Las Casas to the effect that Indians were lesser men, barbaric and beyond humanity. As Stannard records, Sepulveda regarded himself as having won the argument, that he had the support of the majority of his countrymen in contending that Indians existed to serve their conquerors. These arguments were conducted within a framework of Christian belief, at least 200 years before scientists set themselves the task of classifying the divisions of humankind as the Swedish scientist Linnaeus did in the mid-18th century. As people guided by Christian principles they had somehow to persuade themselves that what Stannard calls the American Holocaust – the dispossession and massacre of whole peoples across the American continent – was consonant with the will of God. Many Christians were not persuaded, Las Casas being the most famous dissenting voice of the time.

Two hundred years later in a quite different context – the English debate about slavery – a certain Reverend James Ramsay produced his essay on slaves in the British sugar colonies, a work which Curtin has described as the best anti-racist tract of the 18th century. Ramsay (Curtin 1964) questioned the very use of the category itself, arguing that one could not speak simply of the 'Negro' or of the 'African';

and he questioned the assumption of inherence, the unproven connection between the physical and the temperamental and intellectual. As religious and, subsequently, scientific thought were brought into the search for a proper view of the peoples encountered by adventurers, colonists, missionaries, slaver traders and slave owners, they reached contradictory conclusions, and, as in so many spheres, the religious and the scientific came into conflict with each other. So the belief among later scientists that there had been a multiple creation of races (what was termed polygenesis) ran quite counter to the conventional Christian belief that God had created men and women from a single source. Christians persuaded of the superiority of white Christian peoples were nonetheless loathe to accept a 'scientific' view of races which contradicted the story of Adam and Eve (Stanton 1960). Others viewed the races of the world as descendants of 'Ham, Shem and Japhet' and in this way racial classifications were in tune with the Bible.

The Spanish and Portuguese, having initiated the plunder of the Americas, also laid the foundations of the trade in people who were enslaved along the west coast of Africa. Agents of other countries – including the British, French and Dutch – soon joined them and pursued the trade to new heights in the 18th century. The trade was officially abolished at the beginning of the 19th century, but slavery itself was not abolished until 1833 in British colonies, 1863 in the USA and 1888 in Brazil.

The debates about the nature of the peoples of the world were conducted throughout this period, that is the period of the earliest Hispanic ventures into the Americas and through the high points of the slave trade in the middle and late 18th century. And this era witnessed the acquisition through colonial settlement, warfare, deceit, treaty, purchase and simple superior force of the great tracts of earth we now know as North, South and Central America, Australia, New Zealand and most of the Pacific, Malaysia and much of the Far East, and Africa, including what was called 'the scramble for Africa' in the latter part of the 19th century. The Christian and scientific arguments about slavery, race and civilisation were the most prominent but 'race' thinking spread to many fields. By the 19th century when slavery was open to debate but colonial rule was at its most confident, race infused almost every imaginable field of inquiry, including linguistics (Gossett 1965), anthropology (Lorimer 1978), history and medicine. Few people read the annals of the ethnological societies; many more read novels in Victorian England.

A Victorian novel: an Englishman abroad

The form of thinking which became characteristic of social science and history and the study of language can be found in the novels of the period, a fine example being Trollope's *The Bertrams* in which the Victorian writer has the central *personae* visit the Middle East. Published in 1859, a year after Trollope himself had visited the Middle East as a representative of the British Mail service, the main characters' comportment in Cairo and Jerusalem illustrate the attitudes of English folk abroad, largely from the middle and upper middle class, towards the 'Oriental Other' of Edward Said's (1985) account. In the brief excerpts that follow it is possible to see displayed almost every imaginable mode of 'perceiving the other': there are portrayals of what it is to be English in sheer contrast to orientals, differences between Muslim, Christian and Jew, differences attributed to nature and culture, and images of men and women within the ethnic categories.

In the early part of the book Miss Todd, on a visit to Jerusalem, has lost her parasol:

> Mamma, I lost my parasol coming down the Mount of Offence. Those nasty Arab children must have stolen it.

Almost as disturbing for our English heroes was the utter disregard for proper English food at the evening meal:

> What no potatoes! There were potatoes yesterday. Waiter, waiter, who ever heard of setting people down to dinner without potatoes.

In mingling as tourists in the crowded streets of Jerusalem, the crowd takes on, in Trollope's description, a more sinister appearance:

> Those who were around him seemed to be the outcasts of the world... cut-throat wretches with close shaven heads, dirty beards, and angry eyes; men clothed in skins, or huge skin-like looking cloaks, filthy, foul, alive with vermin, reeking with garlic – abominable to an Englishman.

When Bertram visits a Christian site he is:

> Mainly occupied with watching the devotions of a single woman. She was a female of one of those strange nations, decently clad, about thirty years of age, pleasant to the eye were she not so dirty, and had she not that wild look, halfway between the sallow sublime and the dangerously murderous, which seems so common to Oriental Christians, whether men or women.

So much for oriental Christians, but Jews and in particular Jewesses shone in comparison with Muslims:

> It was wonderful that the same land should produce women so different as were these close neighbours. The Mahomedans were ape-like: but the Jewesses were glorious specimens of feminine creation.

As the story moves to Cairo, Trollope is intent on warning his readers about a visit to the pyramids:

> Oh those pyramid guides! foul, false, cowardly, bullying thieves! A man who goes to Cairo must see the Pyramids... But let no man and, above all, no woman, assume that the excursion will be in any way pleasurable. I have promised that I will not describe such a visit, but I must enter a loud screeching protest against the Arab brutes – the sheikhs being the very worst of the brutes – who have these monuments in their hands. Their numbers, the filthiness of their dress – or one might say no dress – their stench, their obscene indecency, their clattering noise, their rapacity.

The European view of the 'Other' is in this account wonderfully particular – it is the Englishman and woman, with some trepidation and much irritation, picking their way through being abroad. In this manner the representations of foreigners, others, heathens are captured in the daily concerns of the traveller and it was Europeans as travellers who told these tales to audiences at home with a great appetite for the 'exotic'.

Africans, slavery and hierarchy

This combination of travellers' tales, anthropologists' observations, and philosophers' speculations is assembled in Curtin's classic account of the way white Europeans apprehended Africa (Curtin 1964). In his history of European images of Africa he shows how Enlightenment philosophers either helped to confirm or simply shared the view of racial hierarchies which were taking shape through the 18th and 19th centuries. Voltaire and Rousseau regarded 'Negroes as naturally inferior' – a confirmation of Balibar's argument that Enlightenment and racist thought occupied the same space. Balibar instances the philosopher David Hume's view that 'there never was a civilised nation of any other complexion than white' (Balibar and Wallerstein 1991). Hume could find no other reason than that nature had fashioned this 'original distinction betwixt these breeds of men'. But it was later in the 18th century that one of the most frequently quoted inspirations of racial theory – Edward Long – wrote his *History of Jamaica* and testified to the 'brutish ignorant idle crafty treacherous bloody thievish mistrustful and superstitious' nature of the people. Although not a scientist by training, Long's views were cited as scientific evidence in support of slavery and a racial hierarchy. Frequently quoted in England his work was published in America in support of the pro-slavery cause (Curtin 1964, Fryer 1984).

We cannot assume a simple equation between abolitionism and a Universalist–humanist perspective, the view that men were naturally equal, or Universalist–Christian, the view that men were created equal and were equal in the eyes of God. Some believed that slavery was evil at the same time as believing that Africans were inferior; if Africans were childlike, primitive, lesser in abilities, all the more reason why they should not be further degraded by slavery. In the USA Abraham Lincoln is remembered as the Great Liberator whose party, government and army effected the abolition of slavery in 1863. But his reasons were economic and political, his wish to see the bourgeois industrialising north overwhelm the stagnating 'seigneurial' society of the south, and the wish to preserve the Union. His motives and reasoning were not primarily humanitarian; indeed, he looked with some apprehension on the possibility of a 'white and black' society which abolition would bring, expecting that freedom would make it possible for most ex-slaves to quit America (Fredrickson 1988).

It is important too to remember that 'race' was not the only or even the principal ground for the defence of slavery. The 'peculiar institution' was defended as economically necessary, as more beneficial to its labourers than manufacturing capitalism in the dreary cities of industrialising England, or as an instance of the solidity of property, the prerogatives of the propertied classes, and of an inevitably unequal world.

Fredrickson has argued that all these pleas were made on behalf of slavery in the period when abolitionists brought it under attack – much of the first half of the 19th century in the USA. Most interestingly, he suggests that the last argument – that societies were naturally unequal orders and slavery only an instance of this fact – was the least appealing to the white labouring classes and unpropertied men of the pre-war south. The majority of people in the old south were neither slaves themselves, nor did they own them, yet as democratic government took shape in the southern states, their views could not be ignored and would preferably be brought to support slavery as much as slave owners did (Fredrickson 1972). They could be persuaded that the wealth of the south depended on slavery, or that they as white farmers and farm labourers were threatened by competition with freed men and women, or that the whole abolitionist enterprise was a northern states' plot to conquer the south; or they could be persuaded that white men and women were a superior breed whose status was protected by the institution of slavery.

The last was not the only argument but it was, Fredrickson argues, the one which held most sway in the end. This laid the foundations of a 'herrenvolk democracy' – a democracy from which a subject people are excluded, a master race democracy – and of the idea that white and black could not live side by side unless the whites were protected by institutions which preserved their status.

Scientists: rational men with malign thoughts?

Alongside the political protagonists and the ministers of religion were those serious minded men who saw themselves as scientists dedicated to the perfection of the cephalic index – a measure of the skull – and busying themselves filling skulls with mustard seeds and enumerating the hat sizes purchased in different regions of America (Gossett 1965). The study of the head or the skull was seen as crucial to race science on the simple proposition with three parts to it: that skulls or heads varied in average size within apparently distinct populations; that bigger skulls must have contained bigger brains; and that bigger brains meant better brains.

The fact that all three of these propositions were extremely doubtful was not apparent to men who were convinced that racial difference held the key to understanding human achievement, capacity for civilisation and virtually every known human tendency. There were some who knew that what they claimed to prove – racial inequality – would lend support to politicians and ideologues who sought to keep categories of men apart and the one in subjection to the other. Others – probably most – battled on in pursuit of the knowledge which they were sure held the key to all understanding of civilisations. There is little to be gained from arguing about the motives of individual scientists, to discern whether race science was the great conspiracy or the great error, for it was both.

Before collapsing under the weight of scientific evidence in the 20th century, and declining in the face of the social anthropological contention that men and women became as they were principally through socio-cultural learning in their natal and adult milieu, race science had a period of clear ascendancy in Western thought. It was not an unquestioned ascendancy, as Michael Biddiss (1979) and others have shown; and the idea went through a series of twists and turns which Michael Banton has amply demonstrated (1977). There were debates about how durable the differences were and whether learning and development could make it possible for 'lesser' groups to catch up with their gifted cousins. Even where this was conceded it may make little practical difference in political policy if the process was seen as long and slow. The idea that populations were different in type was not the same as the idea that populations stood at different stages of a process of civilisation. As ideas they stood on different grounds; in practice the difference may have mattered little.

Scientists usually stood at some remove from the affairs of everyday life and we can be sure that the average slave owner in the American south or sugar planter in the Caribbean, and even more so the poor whites of the American south, did not have their heads filled with science – or mustard seeds. Categorical attributions of inherent qualities did not stem from science alone. Men whose job it was to subordinate slaves, to dispossess indigenous peoples, to rule subject peoples, soon convinced themselves that their subordinates were dangerous, idle, treacherous, compliant, dull, cunning, carefree and lacking in moral restraint.

Accounts of plantation life (Blassingame 1979) in America have shown how masters had varying and contrary stereotypes of their slaves – as hard-working, as rebellious, and as carefree. The contradictions were no matter; people show an enduring capacity to hold in their minds ideas which, if coldly set out in an analytic frame, would evidently contradict each other. Most people do not lead their daily lives in 'analytic frame'. Everyday 'common sense' will do and 'common sense' told masters that they had better watch those whose freedom they daily curtailed, whose land they stole, or whose patrimony they destroyed.

Categorical thinking and the attribution of inherent characteristics were thus organised around not one but many principles and found their inspiration not just from science and ideology but also from everyday life. The theories of domination found their confirmation in the practice of domination.

Exploration, colonies and the appropriation of the Other

The history of Western appropriation of the Other over at least 400 years may be seen as conveying in ideas what it also conveyed in firearms, dispossession, and in appropriation of the plainer economic, military and political kind. The sciences of navigation, botany and anthropology went hand in hand with the journeys of exploration and colonial adventures. From the early days of the exploration of the Pacific the ship's company was charged with exploring flora and fauna, perfecting geography and cartography, and was expected to act as anthropologists of the peoples it encountered. Scientific illustrators and botanists were much valued; plants discovered might provide cheap food for slaves; navigation routes charted might give the British an advantage over their French or Dutch colonial competitors; the peoples met, counted and observed also became souls to be won.

The recorded views were sometimes crudely demeaning, at other times were ambiguous and uncertain. Bernard Smith, in his study of European art in the Pacific (Smith, 1985) has shown how the same people were drawn and painted as 'noble savages', as brutes, and as divine inhabitants of a heaven on earth. Christian missionaries would portray the 'natives' as savage heathens but had, nonetheless, to hold to the principle that they were capable of attaining the same state of grace as themselves – in the long run.

Towards the end of the 19th century we find an American missionary to Malaysia summarising his view of Malays and in it we find most of the tendencies and ambiguities of which we have spoken:

> It is not easy to write confidently of the Malay character. For centuries they have been represented as treacherous, vindictive and cruel, and not many apologists have come forward to speak in their favour. It is more than probable, however, that they are a much better people than the outer world has given them credit for. It is not to be expected that a people who have been known to the world chiefly as a race of pirates will be spoken of very highly, and it is easy to understand how their character has been painted in too black colours. (Thoburn 1892)

But he later concludes:

> It may generally be taken for granted that indiscriminate denunciations of a whole people are exaggerated, if not groundless; and it may be assumed at once that the Malays have not a monopoly of all the bad and base qualities that are claimed for them. (Thoburn 1892)

The caution about 'indiscriminate denunciations of a whole people' represents a welcome sign of liberality. The missionary knows what others think and that the 'reputation' of Malays is poor, but is willing to balance this with acknowledgement of the sins of other races:

The Anglo-Saxon has inherited enough treachery and cruelty to sink a dozen nations; and we are the last people to take up stones against tribes and nations which have never enjoyed a tithe of our advantages. (Thoburn 1892)

We see the willingness to see good and evil in all races at the same time as the existence of distinct races is taken for granted. But he also introduces the idea of different 'advantages', the idea that people may be as they are in consequence of their circumstances:

It is more than probable that the Malays, under a settled government and controlled by a firm hand, will rapidly settle down into a quiet and peaceable people, and quickly forget the bloody practices by which, in darker days, they earned their evil reputation. In many regions they are even now as orderly and peaceable, if not as industrious, as the inoffensive people of North India, who, less than a generation ago, went armed like so many assassins. (Thoburn 1892)

Different circumstances may lead to different and better behaviour – but note the need for a 'firm hand':

Moral delinquencies, however, are not the only accusations laid to the charge of the Malays. They are averse to hard labour and industrious habits; are improvident and indolent in disposition; fond of cock-fighting and childish sports; are inveterately addicted to gambling; and altogether lack those qualities which are absolutely indispensable to a people who would rise in the scale of civilization to a place of respectability among the great family of nations. (Thoburn 1892)

Now the catalogue of weaknesses of character is lengthening. It may have been the passage which most caught his readers' attention. But he ends by wondering whether the cause of these deficiencies is not racial character but the indolence induced by an easy life, a common theme of commentary on tropical countries. He cites an authority:

Dr W.F. Oldham says:

'The Malay is lethargic because of the condition in which he finds himself. Life under the equator does not tend to activity. The sea is full of fish, the shores covered with coconut groves, the rice fields easily produce their crops. You talk to him concerning the civilised life of other men, and the unceasing activity and tireless energy of the West, and he looks at you through his large soft eyes, shrugs his shoulders and says a single word – Susa – "it is difficult".' (Thoburn 1892)

The 'indolent Malay' will have to beware the competition from a more vigorous race. The Chinese are seen as having a quite different 'racial character' and they may have come to stay – and dominate:

> During recent years a new race-factor has been introduced into these islands and one which is destined not only to be permanent but to exercise a most important influence upon the future of the country and the race. The Chinaman has made his advent in Malaysia and has come to stay. He is the Anglo-Saxon of the tropics, and will push his way wherever land awaits cultivation or mines invite exploration. (Thoburn 1892)

The Malay is seen as maligned by others insensitive to their virtues, as having among them, as in all peoples, good and bad in customary proportions. They are seen as capable of peaceable living – but, significantly enough, only when 'firmly' ruled by others. The Anglo-Saxons are the vigorous people and the bearers of civilisation; but it was not always so. The Chinese are the 'Anglo-Saxons of the tropics', an idea of racial or national character determining future progress. The Malays are commended for their generosity but they too, are idle, improvident and inveterate gamblers and seemingly unlikely to rise above a lowly level in the scale of civilisation. The indolence is, so our writer suggests, a product of the easy life of the tropics where fruit drops from the trees and fish leap obligingly from the deep.

Examples of this kind show that the way in which Western commentators viewed the 'natives' whom they encountered throughout the world and who became subject to colonial and imperial rule could take many forms. The construction of other peoples varied from one in which these Others were seen as scarcely partaking in the same common humanity to one in which they were different and maybe 'lesser' but in some way which could be, in however long a run, surmounted. But even where this long run held out the possibility of peoples living side by side in equal regard the short and medium term still required a relationship of subordination, a slow evolution of custom and development, a relationship of children to kind and firm parents, a paternalistic burden of care in which strong unyielding governance was mixed with instruction and uplift.

Racism, class and history

The attempts to work with an unhistorical concept of racism founder on the fact that the word 'race' has changed its emphasis over recent centuries and on the fact that fundamental assumptions about the nature of men, women and society change significantly from one period to another. The early 19th century, for example, was a period in which the ideas of democracy were highly contested in a way that is not true or is very much less true today. This means that, in thinking about 'racism' then and now, we are comparing two periods in which ideas about governance and 'natural' rulers differ dramatically. For the idea that there were people who were of superior quality, by dint of birth and property, for whom the exercise of political power was natural and proper – and others whose admission to power was dangerous, was a common theme of 19th-century thought (Williams 1958). Such class-formed views paralleled racialised views in seeing a people as naturally subordinate, dangerous and inherently of lesser quality.

The inclination to try to trace racism to a single cause founders both on the problems of historically specific racisms and on the fact that ideologies and popular cultures which incorporate racial or ethnic hierarchies are to be found in not one but a series of historical contexts. The association of racism with colonialism has to be understood alongside the fact that racial characterisations of those fit to govern and those fit to be ruled were common within western European societies in ideologies of dominance which were formed in response to domestic class structures. The themes of racial difference were paralleled by class ideologies in industrialising European societies.

The linkage of racism and capitalism must also contend with the evidence of racist ideologies in non-capitalist societies; it is clear for example that ethnic conflict and nationalist politics in the former Soviet Union and eastern Europe are not 'simply' a product of the collapse of empire (Bennett 1995, Tishkov 1997). The portrayal of racism as a peculiarly Western invention has to be tempered by the evidence of apparently similar ideologies in non-western societies. The most challenging research in this respect is to be found in Dikötter's account of the 'discourse of race in China' (1992, 1997).

Dikötter: China and ideologies of ancestry

It may be that there is a curious and ironic ethnocentrism in the tendency of Western scholars to see the 'modern world' as a world they have created, and to see racism as one of the West's inventions. As Dikötter argues:

Attitudes about skin colour and physical characteristics are of great antiquity in China... significant parts of the Confucian universe predisposed the Chinese to perceive the new world order created by Western expansion in terms of race; and successive periods of contact with frontier peoples fostered proto-nationalist feelings and generated a strong sense of biological continuity. (1992, p. 1)

In the 13th century the Chinese were conquered by Mongols and later by Manchus, and the closer we come to the present the more the Chinese can be found responding to the presence of Europeans, notably the Portuguese and the British. But the evidence of a kind of race thinking which saw non-Chinese as Barbarians and linked culture to physical type dates well before these contacts. A 4th-century mythological-cum-ethnological work portrayed 'dehumanised Barbarians living beyond the realm of Chinese civilisation' (Dikötter 1992, p. 6) including one-eyed people, three-headed barbarians and one-armed tribes with three eyes. Only the Chinese were described as *ren*, 'man', or 'human being', thus implicitly degrading alien groups to bestiality.

As early as the 8th century there were references to 'physically defective Europeans comparable to albinos in the European mind'. Dikötter claims that Chinese variously described themselves as yellow and as white. As yellow they fixed this colour as representing the good, as white they contrasted themselves with white Europeans who were 'ash-white, deathly white' (Dikötter 1992, pp. 13–14). Although the antipathy to the Buddhism which they encountered was 'cultural' they also portrayed Buddhists as 'violent and without manners, not different from birds and beasts... coarse and uncivilised'. And from an early date, Dikötter suggests, the Chinese equated black with slave and associated darker skin with lower status 'well before Westerners established themselves at the frontiers of the empire' (1992, p. 16).

The emergence in Europe of what Banton has called 'race as lineage' is paralleled in China by the word *zu* which could be translated as family or people, lineage and race. Although the sources are the products of scholarly elites, Dikötter suggests that by the time we have some evidence of popular views, elements of race thinking can be found in attitudes towards Europeans. The British were white devils and their Indian troops black devils, and the white devils had the bodily enormities of people less than human – one straight leg bone (1992, p. 40) or 'four testicles' (1992, p. 43) which might explain their unsavoury sexual behaviour. By the 19th century writers influenced by English studies were constructing ideas deriving from Darwin and Spencer, tailored to a Chinese view and in the

1930s a Chinese scholar drew up a programme of eugenics, warning of the dangers of miscegenation.

By linking people to places and drawing boundaries between outsiders and 'us', Dikötter concludes 'every civilization has an ethnocentric world image in which outsiders are reduced to manageable spatial units' (1992, p. 5). This is reminiscent of Lévi-Strauss's argument that the conception of a universal humankind is a recent cultural creation. Most peoples in most of human history have constructed ethnocentric views of themselves and of others which have relegated others to below human status (Lévi-Strauss 1975). Whether the Chinese text and myth can be termed racism in the same sense as the European constructions which we have discussed, is not so much difficult to answer as the wrong question. It is clear that some of the same lines of thought can be detected and that there is an elision of physical type and cultural status. Other strands in Chinese thought may support an interpretation that the linkage between the racial and the cultural is not fixed. People, on such a view, may properly be or become 'Chinese' through an adoption of the standards of culture and civilisation (Dikötter, p. 3).

And the evidence that ideas parallel to European racism are formed in a quite different context does not *per se* undermine the tracing of modern racism to a historically specific Western context. But it does serve as a reminder that the ideological construction of a civilisation centre, with barbarians beyond its limits, is not the sole prerogative of Europeans. Furthermore the idea of racism depends crucially on the idea of Universalism, because to think of one set of ideas as 'particularistic' requires a conception of Universalism. Racism had a contradictory relationship to Universalism. On the one hand, race science was part of the universalistic scientific project; on the other hand, racism confounded Universalism by positing unequal orders of humankind and undermining the idea of common humanity. Partly because Western thought harboured both Universalism and racism, the 'Universalist project' has itself been seen as Eurocentric (Sayyid 1997).

Racism may take many forms, betraying the influence of its historical and regional contexts; in each instance there is a structure of ideas which we have termed 'the attribution of inherent qualities'. The systematic creation of categories and the attribution of natural character to those categorised is particularly but not exclusively a feature of the modern world in which peoples have subjugated other peoples within and without their national boundaries. If racism, and ideologies with strong resemblances, have more than one origin, this does not mean that the specifying of origin in a historical case is any less compelling. If Englishmen and Americans had conceptions of Africans prior to the institution of slavery in the New World colonies (Curtin 1964, Jordan 1968), there can be little doubt that the practice of the institution had an overwhelming and powerful persuasive effect. Not only the political defence of the institution under challenge, but also the very practice of subjugation provided the grounds in which one category of men and women feared, belittled, and demonised others. In treating them as children needing a firm hand – a mild term for brutal coercion – white masters consoled themselves that their slaves were children by nature; white colonists assured themselves that the 'natives' were children in need of correction.

Summary

In this chapter we have seen that religion and science played vital parts in the West's view of others; these were the two systems of ideas which were generally central to social and philosophical thought in the Western world. The ideas were replete with contradictions, as the arguments about God's children illustrate, but the central messages of superordination are constant. And the very ideas themselves have persisted with remarkable tenacity. However removed we are from missionaries to Hawai'i in 1820 or to Malaya in the late 19th century, or from planters in Virginia in 1840, or from Democrats in America in the 1880s, the ideas of 'native', 'heathen' and 'pagan' are still with us, as are ideas about sexual threat, fitness to govern, indolence and weakness of character.

The examples from the early ventures of the Spanish and Portuguese illustrate how the initial colonial encounters posed a question of the worth of others. Several centuries later a novel about English people 'abroad' illustrates how representatives of a powerful country depict the peoples they meet. The enslavement of Africans and the creation of slave-based societies in the colonies of the New World eventually brought together diffuse ideas of otherness and of 'lesser peoples' with the seeming precision of a science of races. Each of these strands has fed into what the 20th century has identified as racism. Paradoxically it is the Western notion of Universalism which gave force to the idea of racism. Universalism had roots in both science and Christianity as ideologies which allowed a view of universal humankind. Equally, science and religion were vehicles for the transmission of the idea of fundamental divisions of humankind. In alliance with romantic ideas of 'folk' and of nations as 'natural communities', the 20th century saw the fusion of ideas of racial and cultural difference in the ideology and practice of racism in its most terrifying modern form – the theory and practice of anti-Semitism in pre-war and wartime Germany.

In the genocide of Jews and Romanies in the 1930s and 40s in Germany and other countries we see the brutal and systematic convergence of many of the cultural dimensions of racist ideologies. The presence of three strands can be schematically identified: that of race, nation and science. And each of these coalesced in the late 1920s within a context of bitterness in the aftermath of defeat in the First World War and a context of a crisis of capitalism. The ideology of a super-race and the vision of a white 'Aryan' people as the pinnacle of a racial hierarchy was continuous with themes of racial hierarchy which were commonly espoused throughout the Western world in the latter half of the 19th century and the first half of the 20th century. Hitler and his ideological lieutenants drew on these theories and created a special place within them for the doctrine of the Jews as a lower people and as a threat to 'higher beings'. At the same time the idea of a nation as a 'folk', as a culturally and spiritually unitary community, found its highest expression in German fascism. The idea of 'race' drew some of its inspiration from 19th century science, while that of 'folk' or nation drew on a mystical nationalism which in the end was expressed as requiring the extermination of the 'non-folk'. The scientific dimension of fascism was not only an elaboration of race-science as a theory of racial hierarchy but was also embodied within the application of eugenics to the 'purification' of the race. In Germany all three elements eventually came together in a single genocidal project – the extermination of Jews and other minorities in Europe. But each of these elements was to be found in some measure in all other European and Western societies: anti-Semitism as a specific identification of Jews as targets of discrimination was common throughout Eastern Europe, Russia, France and Britain; race-science positing white Europeans as the apex of a racial hierarchy was common throughout the West as were more or less fanatical versions of nationalist ideology; and eugenics as the basis of a theory of social improvement was to be found throughout Western societies – on the political left as well as the right – and forms of eugenics were preached or practised in many countries including Sweden and the USA. The revulsion prompted by the evidence of the Holocaust was a key factor in placing the question of race and racism on the immediate post-war political and scientific agenda (see Poliakov 1974, Kuper 1975, Bauman 1989, Miles 1994b).

Chapter 3

Hot and Cold Ethnicity: Theories of Origin and Intensity

The variations in the economic and political contexts of ethnicity provide a basis for a typology of ethnic groups. What we have called 'historical trajectories' of ethnicity contribute to an explanation of the origins of ethnicity in the modern world. These socio-historical frameworks explain why there is a Malaysian Chinese Association in the alliance of political parties which governs Malaysia, why contemporary Maori movements re-form the national culture, and contest the politics of participation, social advantage and land ownership in Aotearoa/New Zealand, why Quebec provincial language police require that business outlets advertise themselves in French, and why tens of thousands of Americans have embraced Islam. In this way a historical understanding is always part of a theory of origin, and a structural account establishes the probable limits of action within a given social system. These must be combined with motivational and meaningful accounts of how and why ethnic identities persist, acquire greater or lesser intensity, and lead to greater or lesser degrees of conflict. In this chapter we discuss the nature of the link of ethnicity to kinship and the 'intensity' of the ethnic bond. This entails a discussion of primordial, instrumental and situational concepts of ethnicity. We also discuss the view of modernity as antipathetic to ethnic ties.

Contexts of ethnicity: structure and action

Ethnicity has a structure context and an action context. The structure context is constituted by the political and economic conditions

88

of a social system insofar as they are racialised and ethnicised. Such, economically, is the persistent overrepresentation of black Americans among the urban poor (Small 1994), and, politically, the family-origin principle for determining citizenship in Germany and other countries (Miles 1993). These are material and constitutional conditions that constitute the framework of action and are largely beyond the control of individual actors. The action context is the world looked at from the point of view of the individual actor in daily exchanges in the private sphere, the circle of friends acquaintances and family, and in the meso-institutional spheres of work, education and formal associations. To be comprehensively understood we need to examine ethnicity in its local, regional, societal and global frames, and in the grounded experience of individuals, seen as actors in a series of face-to-face contexts.

The structure context of ethnicity sets the macro-scene within which individuals act out their daily lives. Accounts at the level of meaning and motive take explanation a few steps further by linking the political and economic contexts to the exchanges, negotiations and sentiments which are the stuff of everyday life; both levels of explanation are required. Structural accounts typically understate the room for maneouvre within a system of action; accounts which highlight choice and interest understate the complexity of the tension between choice and constraint.

Motive and meaning

In this chapter we pay particular attention to ideas about the origin of ethnic sentiments and bonds; to the place which ethnicity has had in classical theories of the modern world; to the primordial and the instrumental character of ethnicity, and to the relationship of ethnicity to the problem of integration. The cases cited in this and subsequent chapters will give many illustrations of the characteristic motive and meaning complexes associated with ethnicity. By way of preface we briefly consider some typical examples here.

In many instances of ethnic mobilisation we find a pattern of resentment/disenchantment expressed in a language of ethnicity. It is one step from 'the world has changed for the worse' to the 'world has changed since they came'. Those who see their world undermined and devalued are inclined to see their loss as caused by ethnic competitors or 'invaders'. Similarly, where competitors are seen not only in ethnic terms but also as non-legitimate competitors, then conditions of market competition in labour, education, housing or other social goods, can be converted into individual and collective ethnic self-interest. Ethnic collaboration may be a means of overcoming barriers 'in front' as well as a means of achieving closure – by closing the door 'behind' (Parkin 1971, Steinberg 1981). Collective ethnic action can be in defence of group and individual interests, as in the ideologies of dominance of a majority or an elite, or in the aspirations of a suppressed people; action and ideology may also be in defence of dignity and in the search for recognition (Nagel and Snipp 1993).

The politics of recognition (Taylor 1992, Fraser 1995) will often be allied to the politics of redistribution; where a group wants to make sure that it is not overlooked in the distribution of social goods, it will also want to be sure that it is not overlooked as a group of people. So where a minority's religious sensibilities, customs or language are disregarded by the majority there comes a point where the minority says, in effect, 'if they can treat us like that – with such indignity – what hope is there for us?' To a greater or lesser degree the individual will see his or her own fate as tied to the collective fate of a wider ethnic community. The more individuals see their fate bound to the collective fate, the more anxious is the defence of collective pride. *In extremis*, where for example the political or economic order is on the verge of collapse, anxious defence of collective pride may turn to desperation. The sole thread of survival hangs by ethnic identification. To explore further these complexes of motive and meaning we shall look at the nexus between ethnicity and kinship.

Kinship and ancestry: hot and cold ethnicity

Part of the rhetoric of public and political ethnicity, as of nationalism, is the language of family and kindred. This may be the 'hot' ethnicity of appeals to blood and passion or the 'cold' ethnicity of calculation and instrumentality. Where people seek support for an ethnic or national cause they make an appeal to 'people like us' – the assumption of the ethnic politician in Chicago or New York, in Serbia, or in Trinidad is that the audience will recognise the appeal and the implicit collective identity (Glazer and Moynihan 1963, Eriksen 1992, Bennett 1995). As Walker Connor (1993) has argued, the language of ethnonationalism is the language of 'blood, family, brothers, sisters, mothers, forefathers, home'. Connor provides the telling example of Mao appealing to 'family ties deriving from a common ancestor' when he exhorted his 'Compatriots!... all fathers, brothers, aunts and sisters throughout the country... transform this glorious future into a New China... all our fellow countrymen, every single zealous descendant of Huang-ti'. And Connor cites Ho Chi Minh calling on all the people of Vietnam (North and South) to remember that 'we have the same ancestors, we are of the same family, we are all brothers and sisters... no-one can divide the children of the same family' (Connor 1993, p. 379).

The appeal to family likeness is not the same thing as real shared ancestry. As the same writer observes, 'the sense of unique descent need not, and in nearly all cases will not, accord with factual history' (Connor 1993, p. 382).

This ideological sense of family and ancestry is characteristic of many instances of nationalism and ethnonationalism. Evidently the claim is more or less fictive but nonetheless the sentiment of family is intoned because it is seen to be powerful and emotive. At the micro-social level, however, relationships within the circle of kin may be the crucial social supports of ethnicity, reproduced in the sentiments and mentalities of the individual.

There are many instances of this: the urban migrants in industrialised societies who pass on the language of home to their children and set expectations about dress, marriage and family obligations; in-migrants in African cities who reproduce some of the obligations of kin in the urban neighbourhood as well as maintaining links with the home village (Cohen 1974, Epstein 1978, Werbner and Ranger 1996). Some of these acknowledgements of ethnicity at the interpersonal and individual level have a formal and *de jure* component. In Hawai'i there is an informal social recognition of people as Hawaiian but 'real' ancestry is necessary to claim rights (MacKenzie 1991). The Hawaiian Homelands Act of 1925 restricted the right to apply for a home and a small parcel of land to those who could demonstrate that they had at least 50 per cent Hawaiian ancestry – meaning that they had to show either one 'full' Hawaiian parent or both parents themselves being 50 per cent Hawaiian ancestry, a rule described as 'racist' by its strongest – Hawaiian – critics (Hasager and Friedman 1994).

Under Malaysian legislation designed to improve the economic position of Malays, a person must be Malay to qualify for the benefits and a Malay is defined in quite precise terms by the constitution. By contrast it would be possible in Britain for a person making a census return to choose, in theory if rarely in practice, any ethnic category they fancied. On the other hand for a person to 'qualify' under the provisions of legislation forbidding discrimination on grounds of racial or ethnic origin, that person would have to show that they belonged to an ethnic group under the meaning of the Act. Similarly any system of administering public policy designed to reduce discrimination will have to create ethnic categories and apply them to individuals – how else would it possible to count what proportion of a hospital's nurses are of one group or another? This is an abiding paradox of any policy which seeks to reduce ethnic or racial discrimination (aiming in principle at an ethnic-blind pattern of recruitment) – the system must first create and institutionalise the categories.

By contrast in many of the informal and routine exchanges of daily life, ethnicity is mobilised or suppressed in subtle and changing ways. The informal transmission of ethnicity allows social space – sometimes to a very great degree – within which the individual can control the transmission of ethnocultural difference. But informality is no guarantee of a lack of constraint – individuals may find it difficult to escape (if they wish to) the ethnic definitions of either their friends or their enemies. This is a partial answer to the question of the depth of hold which ethnic identities have; a clue to understanding 'intensity'.

Theories of intensity

Much of the sociological commentary – and not a little of the public and political commentary – on ethnicity, suggest that it represents a set of ties and obligations, of symbolic representations of belonging, and of personal identity in such a way that this kind of obligation and identity has a firm emotional grip on individuals and groups. Horowitz's (1985) sociology of ethnic groups and conflict portrays ethnic sentiments as not just fictive but as real extensions of kinship attachment and commitment, the implication being that they are thus deeply rooted and intensely felt. Press, radio and television comment routinely refers to causes of conflict as ancient ethnic enmities – the Serb–Croat enmity in the Yugoslavian civil war is a classic instance of this assumption of the depth and intensity of ethnic sentiments, even though challenged by academic commentators (Magas 1993, Denitch 1994, Bennett 1995, Silber and Little 1995, Ramet 1996).

There is also a strand of sociological commentary in which the assumptions are, on the face of it, quite contrary to this. Two terms are especially important here: the notions of instrumental ethnicity and situational ethnicity (McKay 1982, Cornell 1996). In the first instance, the argument is that ethnic symbols and collective 'loyalties' are mobilised specifically for the attainment of secular ends – principally of gains in political power and economic advancement. The often unstated implication is that the material ends are the principal motive force underlying ethnic claims rather than the unquestioned or unquestioning loyalty to an ethnic collectivity (Roosens 1989).

Of course both in theory and in practice one does not exclude the other; it is possible to act instrumentally and with commitment. Where material ends are contested – and not just the symbolic status of the collectivity – the commitment may be all the more deeply felt. Indeed this provides a clue to the problem of intensity – the clue being in the answer to the question 'how much is at stake?'. If groups, or individuals identifying with groups, are fighting for everything, or believe that they are, then the pursuit of ethnic ends entails a fateful loss or gain. In Milosevic's Serbian nationalism, in the Yugoslavian civil war, he set out to persuade his political constituency to place their Serbian commitment before all else by persuading them (some but not all) that they were fighting for their very existence (Bennett 1995). If the loss in an ethnicised battle – real or symbolic – is not just a matter of pride, but really or apparently a matter of survival, then everything comes together in solidifying the ethnic bond.

For the most part, however, the implication of the instrumental view of ethnicity is that there is a purposeful appeal to loyalties in pursuit of gains that are visible to some or all putative members of the group. Whether this claim 'sticks' may depend on the success of ethnic leaders in overcoming actual or potential division within the group. As Brass (1985) has especially emphasised, the battle for ethnic solidarity and for control over the symbolic markers and cultural frame of the group, is one that is played out within groups as well as between groups. Part of the whole process of defining an ethnic, ethnonational, or racialised population is the process of struggle between contesting elements within a population for the right to take the lead and set the direction of group style and purpose. Indeed this emphasis is another corrective to the over-concretised way of thinking of ethnic groups. The differences within one 'group' may be as compelling as those between different groups.

If the concept of instrumentality suggests that ethnic identity and mobilisation may be a matter of calculation rather than emotional commitment, so too does the concept of 'situational ethnicity'. This is ethnicity looked at from the individual's viewpoint, what we have referred to as the action context. Individuals move, in their daily lives, from one social setting to another, and present themselves to different sets of 'significant others' – other people whose approval matters to the individual. As Goffman and many others have argued, individuals in modern societies become skilled at judging their audiences and presenting themselves accordingly (Goffman 1969); when we misjudge, forget ourselves, or the audiences come together in the same place, we are embarrassed or worse. The children of migrants, born in the new home country, become aware of their parents' expectations and have to square these with the what may be differing expectations of their school friends and teachers. These differences are sometimes portrayed as the problems of young people 'caught between' two cultures, but in fact young people become skilled at coping with different sets of expectations, a skill that is for most people an essential, even commonplace, means of dealing with a life which crosses many institutional areas in which the audiences differ (Bradby 1999). These interstitial zones of social life are frequently the ones in which cultures change and identities are modified.

The notion of situational ethnicity certainly suggests a measure of freedom and choice in both assuming an ethnic identity and in conforming to expectations which are associated with it (Nagata 1974, Okamura 1981, Eriksen 1992, 1993b). But as we make different presentations to different audiences, so the different situations call for fine changes in our social stance and style. That is, we do not simply choose our self-presentation in different settings – rather we learn that different circumstances make different demands. This is the way in which Eriksen describes the interactions of Indo-Mauritians and black Creole Mauritians, descendants of Indian labourers and Africans respectively. There are, in Mauritius, not simply a set of expectations surrounding these two broad groupings but are subtle differences between, for example, rural and urban Indo-Mauritians and men and women. In almost all circumstances where ethnicity is important, gender and wealth are also important, and so actors learn and apply complicated guides to behaviour in different settings. This suggests that Indo-Mauritians never quite escape being Indo-Mauritian but does indicate that what it means to be Indo-Mauritian has very variable meanings (Eriksen 1992).

Part-time ethnicity

Another way of putting this is to say that no one is a full-time ethnic, at least not in the same way in all settings. This would have to include settings in which ethnicity was of virtually no account. The young student of South Asian ancestry in Britain is not a full-time South Asian, the Malay businessman in Kuala Lumpur is not a full-time Malay, the Finnish social worker in Gothenburg is not a full-time Finn. In all these instances, the salience of ethnicity varies both in its meaning and its importance and partly because of this 'situational' character of ethnicity, the actors retain a measure of control over their self-presentation. By contrast, the measure of control permitted to black – and white – actors in the Mississippi town of the 1930s was very small. Of course the rules governing behaviour for black and white citizens of Indianola, Mississippi (Dollard 1937) varied according to who was present and according to differences of class and status within both communities. But black–white relationships of equality, or of marriage, or where black was superordinate to white, were practically excluded.

We can thus imagine that any visitor to Indianola, Mississippi, at that period could scarcely fail to observe the hardness of the ethnic boundary (Barth 1969). Any visitor to present day Kuala Lumpur would take some time in learning the subtleties of context and meaning governing relationships between Malay and Chinese in the micro-contexts of action.

Ethnicity is a dimension of social action and structure in three distinct ways: as a command principle, as a flexible principle, and theoretically as a nil principle. In Indianola, Mississippi, it was a command principle, in Kuala Lumpur it is a flexible principle, and in some contexts in some societies it is a nil principle. It is a nil principle wherever ethnicity is ruled out, by law or by broad customary consensus, that is where merit and equal treatment in principle govern admission to jobs, benefits and services even if these principles are breached and circumvented (Jenkins 1986, Mason and Jewson 1992). If ethnicity is rarely a nil principle, it may sometimes be no more than what Gans has called 'symbolic ethnicity' (Gans 1979, 1994).

Theories of decline and persistence

We have discussed ways of understanding the origin of ethnic systems both in the macro-structural and the micro-social face-to-face sense, in structure contexts and action contexts. This entailed discussion of what kind of social fact ethnicity represents. This question – the nature of ethnicity – is raised again in different ways in theories of decline and persistence of ethnicity and national sentiments in the modern world. Sociological theorising in the last 150 years has, in many cases, either assumed or argued the decline of ethnicity although not always of nationalism. The last two decades have pronounced this expectation to have been mistaken. At least at the outset then, theories of decline and persistence require a brief discursus of some of the principal themes of sociological theory.

Modernist theorising – the evolutionary schema of Marx, Durkheim and Weber

Marx's writings derive from Britain, continental Europe and the USA of the mid-19th century, Durkheim's from France and Europe of the late 19th and early 20th centuries and Weber's from much the same period. Common to all is a theorising of the trajectory of industrial capitalism, a social and economic system that transplanted and uprooted its predecessor agrarian, feudal and conservatively ordered societies. Marx sardonically regrets the passing of an age of chivalrous enthusiasm, replaced by the callous cash nexus and egotistical calculation. Much of what Durkheim wrote was evidence of the tension he saw between optimism for a new moral order of individualism and pessimism about the absence of constraint and solidarity in the advanced division of labour (Fenton 1984). And Weber combined his admiration for the principle of rationality – the dominant cultural mark of modernity – with his mournful portrayal of the disenchantment of the modern world. Sociological theory has been either broadly 'progressive' in its stance, where it embraced the individualising rationality of modernity; or 'conservative' and reactionary where it regrets the passing of traditional moralities, known hierarchies, and the certainties of predictable social obligations within family and wider communities (Nisbet 1967).

In most non-Marxist sociology, a dominating question has been that of the strength and nature of social relationships, obligations, and moral cultures. This diffuse anxiety about modernity focuses on the declining force of religious faith, belief and ritual, the weakening of family ties, the removal of medieval restraints on economic activity, the undermining of locale as a source of personal belonging and social integration. These are viewed as consequences of the greater mobility, flux, and complexity of modern societies. A backward looking version of this model of social change posits either the hopelessly disintegrative nature of modern life, or the need for restoration of social control, religious certainties and moral discipline. A progressive model suggests that collective life has changed irrevocably and that the social and cultural movement in the direction of individualism is irreversible. It remains nonetheless possible, it is argued, to discover or introduce new forms of social regulation and values, central among them being the value placed on individual merit, dignity and worth.

In Durkheim's work in particular it is argued that while economic life and exchanges dominate the modern social order, the economic transaction is not itself a basis for social solidarity. There is therefore a modern problem or crisis of social integration. The increased scale of social exchanges and the ever-widening scope of economic activity means that those dealing with each other are less and less likely to be part of a known and tangible community. As cities grow and receive immigrants from the countryside and small towns, there is an attendant decline of the small-scale solidarities of kinship, community and church. In the work of Tönnies this process of change is characterised as a shift from *Gemeinschaft* to *Gesellschaft*, from relationships typified by obligation, trust and permanence, of which the family is the model type, to relationships based on the calculation of interest and shared secular objectives (Tönnies 1963). The relevance of these arguments to theories of ethnicity is the association of ethnicity with kinship, with those particularistic ties and sentiments of solidarity, whose survival is called into question by modernisation.

Marxist thought

In Marxist thought the centrepiece is not the social bond, but class relations, transformed by the revolutionary forces of capitalism. These class relations are founded upon the exploitation of labour by capital and the inevitability of the search for profit. The economic tendencies or laws of capitalism provoke recurring crises in the sustainability of capitalism as an economic system; the growth of class consciousness and organisation provoke political challenges to the capitalist state. All these challenges will, in the last analysis, prove decisive, replacing capitalism with socialism. A new economic organisation will be dedicated to social production for use rather than profit. With the abolition of property and therefore of classes, it is a vision of the modern world which has no place for ethnicity and in which nationalism is viewed largely as a reactionary force, an ideological accompaniment to social, political and economic domination by the capitalist class (Tishkov 1997). The interests of the exploited labouring classes lie in transcending local particularisms and nationalisms by uniting as an international class of workers.

In this view of the trajectory of the modern world there are two points of entry for an interest in ethnicity. The first is that nationalism and ethnonational sentiments are viewed as distractions from the development of a rational class consciousness, the political forming of which hastens the demise of capitalism. The second is that racism is seen as having an ideological and political function within capitalism, specifically as a form of consciousness which divides and therefore weakens working-class consciousness and organisation (Balibar and Wallerstein 1991).

A consistent theme of contemporary Marxist or neo-Marxist commentary on racism has been to posit the recurrent search for cheap and exploitable labour, the use of migrant labour and female labour to meet this need, and to 'explain' the rise of racist politics and popular consciousness as responses to or functions of these divisions within the working class. The politically and economic dominant classes benefit from a divided working class; racism and nostalgic nationalism serve both as explanations of and distractions from the recurrent crises of capitalism. We discussed some of these arguments in Chapter 2.

The Marxist expectation of the direction of class and political organisation in modern capitalism has been subverted, disappointed or misconceived. Capitalism has proved to be resilient as an economic system and as a political system and, in the wake of the collapse of the Soviet Union, its satellites and empire, capitalism has achieved a worldwide dominance as practice and as ideology. The end of the Soviet empire specifically gave rise to and was succeeded by a whole series of regional and ethnic nationalisms riding high on a tide of national 'liberation' or fighting for the spoils in contested areas of new states (Kupchan 1995, Tishkov 1997).

One sociological reaction to this has been not only to pronounce Marxism dead but to pronounce all grand theory (or narratives) dead. The thing about which we can be most certain is the failure of theories which purport to offer the key to the system direction, in all respects, of modern nation-states – the implicit or explicit conception of a linear directionality of modern social systems. At the same time there are elements of Marxist thought which remain both important and persuasive. Sociology simply cannot ignore the disposition of wealth and power on the national and international stage; the sociology of identity and culture with no regard for the 'material order' is an Alice in Wonderland sociology. The drive to reduce the cost of labour in the production of commodities and services either by searching for sources of cheap labour or by intensifying exploitation in the labour process remains a central imperative of capitalist social relations and the pursuit of profit. These are reflected globally in the use of migrant labour, the move of capital installations to labour-cheap locations, and the discouraging or banning of labour union organisation in these sites.

What is currently called globalisation has important cultural dimensions, but it is also an element of something that has long been a feature of the modern (capitalist) world – the internationalisation of capital. The growing importance of transnational corporations has economic and political implications when local economic and political strategies are pre-empted by the power of the multinationals. Their importance is also cultural – many of the most prominent global companies in soft drinks, clothes, cars and electronic goods are purveyors of global cultural messages as well as of commodities (Featherstone 1990, Robertson 1992). These messages transcend national boundaries; the political and economic tendencies of globalisation undermine the nation-state while prompting some of the nationalist nostalgia and xenophobia in response to diminished local power. Capitalism is revolutionary in its social impact. Unexplained and disaffecting social change gives rise to both nostalgia and bitterness of which racialised memory forms a key part of the wistful backward glances at the cohesive and 'homogeneous' society of the past.

Contemporary sociology is sceptical of the grand schema of 19th-century and early 20th-century social theory but there is some measure of agreement about some of the principle sociological features of modern societies. Among these must be counted a steady decline in the social centrality of kinship relations, the 'thinning out' of family relations to relatively small circles of partnership and family units, and their definition as belonging largely to a private sphere, the sphere of consumption rather than production. We would also include the scale and pace of social change dictated by a series of leaps in the application of new technologies; the omnipresence, range and speed of communications, both mass and individual; and the global scale of social change in its economic, political, military and cultural aspects (Featherstone 1990).

The liberal expectancy

Although Marxist accounts regard ethnic and national formations as obstacles to class identity and organisation, the most unmistakable argument for the decline of ethnicity is to be found in the liberal–universalist sociology of Emile Durkheim. His argument centres upon what he calls the decline of the natal milieu – the locale and social obligations, especially of family, into which an individual is born. The belief that particularistic ties should decline is an element of liberal democratic ideology; the belief that they will decline is part of the sociology of modernisation. Durkheim viewed the French Revolution as the beginning of the redefinition of people as citizens, setting in train the development of laws and social institutions which recognised the freedom and dignity of the individual (Tiryakian 1971). Not surprisingly he viewed 'race' and ethnic origin as declining facts of the modern social order, precisely because both were rooted in birth.

With respect to ethnicity his most telling remarks were with respect to Jewishness in France. An atheistic Jew himself he thought that the kind of ties represented by an ethnic community such as Jews would decline in significance in the modern state of citizens. Significantly he stressed that his defence of Dreyfus and his critique of the persecutors of Dreyfus, a Jewish military captain falsely convicted of treason in a wave of anti-Semitic politics, was above all a defence of the rights of man, of the liberties and dignity of the individual (Fenton 1980, Durkheim notes on anti-Semitism 1899). This was Durkheim embracing the liberal values of the Third Republic (Fenton 1984), the same values which Balibar and other French writers have described as Universalism (Balibar and Wallerstein 1991).

This liberal view of history is precisely the view contested by Marxist thought which portrays the view as an ideological ally of capitalist development (Zeitlin 1968). In this critique, individualism is bourgeois individualism, freedoms are market freedoms, and rights are property rights. Furthermore, as we have seen, the idea of to whom full rights belonged was limited by ideas of race and by actual systems of colonial rule which reinstalled grades of participation in civil society. The French were astonished, taken aback, when slaves in Haiti took the French revolutionary message as applying equally to them (James 1938).

But the Marxist expectancy matched the liberal expectancy in foreseeing the decline of attachments of birth, whether racially, ethnically or nationally expressed. As capitalism developed, so too would class consciousness, allying men and women on a 'rational' basis, to those whose material circumstances they shared. When capitalism had been transcended by socialism, then would begin the building of a rational civil society in which men and women could relate to each other free of the encumbrances of class and birth. For these reasons those who saw themselves as building socialist states (in the Soviet Union and eastern Europe) found it hard to cope with 'nationalist' loyalties, sentiments and collectivities (Diamond and Plattner 1994, Kupchan 1995, Tishkov 1997). Political ideology indicated that nationalist forms ought to diminish; political realities indicated that national identities remained. The results were both ambivalence and genocide. By the mid-20th century this 'liberal' (and Marxist) expectancy survived if not flourished, despite and to some extent because of the massive denial of citizenship – and life itself, specifically in the Holocaust – to millions of people, on grounds of 'birth' and ethnic memberships (Bauman 1989).

In (at least) two arenas, however, sociological observers began to suggest that this expectation of the decline of ethnicity, broadly defined, was mistaken, undermined by events or informed by inadequate sociological theory. In the USA, the work of Glazer and Moynihan began to argue that, contrary to all expectation, ethnic loyalties remained important, even more important, they hinted, than class-based attachments (Glazer and Moynihan 1975). In Africa and Asia, as colonialism drew to a close, sociological, but more often anthropological, commentators began to indicate that loyalties broadly describable as 'ethnic' either remained important or had become important in new ways (Horowitz 1985). The question of the relationship of primordial ties to modernising states was raised in a seminal essay by Clifford Geertz, 'The Integrative Revolution' (1973).

New states and the integrative revolution

The problem of the integrative revolution was defined by Geertz in terms not far removed from the questions we discussed in connection with Emile Durkheim. That is, a central question in modern societies was, 'if old moralities and solidarities have diminished, how can we create a new morality based upon the mutual respect, obligations and values of the modern citizen whose main allegiance is to a set of principles rather than a set of persons?'. Edward Shils had previously discussed this problem in a frequently cited article whose main point was to make the distinction between 'primordial' and 'civil' ties, the former the kind of ties associated with birth and kinship, the latter associated with citizenship of a modern state (1957). While the main question in Durkheim was how the modern (liberal, citizen-based, individualist) state could develop the institutions, laws and civic ethics appropriate to an 'advanced, complex' society, the main problem addressed by Geertz and Shils was how 'civil' ties could contend with the persistence of 'primordial' ties of the kind which Durkheim assumed were in decline.

These writings introduced the term primordialism, denoting a fundamental attachment grounded in early socialisation This term has persisted as a focal point of a debate about the very nature of ethnicity as a social bond and identity (Eller and Coughlan 1993, Hutchinson and Smith 1996). The early writers were arguing that the persistence of primordialism was a specific problem of new states, particularly those developing in Africa and Asia in the wake of the formal 'winding up' of colonial regimes. And they were concerned with the general problem of primordialism and not, as later misdirected critiques appear to believe (Eller and Coughlan 1993; see also Grosby 1994), with defining ethnicity as quintessentially a primordial type of attachment. The functioning of liberal democracy, the structures of citizenship and the social and cultural integration of new states were all threatened by primordial attachments and loyalties.

One representative case is drawn from the views expressed by members of the Linguistic Committee which met on Indian independence to implement the proposal that internal boundaries be redrawn to correspond to linguistic areas of India. Nehru was appalled by their petty jealousies, which were standing in the way of his vision of a secular Indian citizenship. He regretted that 'some of the ablest men in the country came before us and confidently and emphatically stated that language in the country stood for and represented culture, race, history, individuality and finally a sub-nation' (Geertz 1973).

The attachment to an 'impersonal' sense of citizenship in new states could not be guaranteed as long as there was tension between the desire for modern efficiency and the wish for social recognition and dignity, which the state could not always provide. People were not always ready 'to subordinate familiar identifications in favour of a generalised commitment to a civil order [if this was to] risk a loss of definition, or worse, domination by some other rival ethnic, racial or linguistic community' (Geertz 1973). It is at this point that the most cited definition of primordiality is made:

> One that stems from the 'givens' – or more precisely, as culture is inevitably involved in such matters, the assumed givens – of social existence: immediate contiguity and kin connection mainly, but beyond them the givenness that stems from being born into a particular religious community, speaking a particular language, or even a dialect of a language, and following particular social practices. These congruities of blood, speech, custom and so on, are seen to have an ineffable, and at times overpowering, coerciveness in and of themselves. (Geertz 1973)

These primordial ties threaten national unity which is 'maintained not by calls to blood and land but by a vague, intermittent, and routine allegiance to a civil state, supplemented to a greater or lesser extent by governmental use of police powers and ideological exhortation'. We may think that sub-group attachments are consistent with nation-state membership, even essential to them. Durkheim certainly argued that this was the case, as do contemporary advocates of pluralist democracy. But, Geertz argues, by contrast with occupational, professional and party loyalties, primordial loyalties may compete with the state because they command the whole person in preference to, or at least 'before' the state. The types of primordial ties which are seen as working in this way are those based on kinship or quasi-kinship, race, language, region, religion or custom.

The 'givenness' referred to does not mean some sort of biological essence conveyed in the blood stream through inheritance. Rather it means that identities are internalised as people learn to whom they are obligated and how they should behave; and that under some circumstances those identities take root deep in the person and in collective expressions. They are learnt in such a way not quite that people can never imagine anything else but that letting go would be difficult and risky; a certain strength of sentiment would be invested through socialisation in a group such that any individual would find it difficult ever to forget that he or she were a Sikh, Hausa, Malay, a Telugu speaker, or a Karen. If he or she did begin to forget, there are many circumstances in which there would be others ready to remind him.

Primordial ties

The use of the term primordial by Geertz and others does not exclude the recognition of an opportunistic and socially constructed view of ethnicity and culture. The fact that language differences can give rise to conflict in some circumstances but not others is itself an illustration of the idea that cultural diacritica may or may not be 'seized upon' to become the defining boundaries of group relations. Similarly, the claims for dominance by the Javanese in Indonesia is an example of a group mobilising cultural difference to mark the group and advance its pretensions to elite status and superiority (Geertz 1973). Geertz certainly recognises that sentiments of the kind he calls primordial may be manipulated by politicians who can, in a new democratic system, appeal to 'people like us' defined along lines of cultural, religious and other cleavages.

He suggests that in Sri Lanka:

> The rise to power of Bandaranaike in 1956 on a wave of cultural reli-
> gious and linguistic revivalism undermined the authority of the English
> speaking and biethnic Colombo patriciate by appealing openly to the
> primordial sentiments of the Sinhalese, promising a Sinhala only
> linguistic policy, a place of pride for Buddhism and the Buddhist clergy,
> and a radical reversal of the supposed policy of 'pampering' the Tamils,
> as well as rejecting Western dress for the traditional cloth and banian of
> the Sinhalese countryman... the institution of universal suffrage made
> the temptation to court the masses by appealing to traditional loyalties
> virtually irresistible and led Bandaranaike and his followers to gamble
> on being able to tune primordial sentiments up before an election and
> down after it. (Geertz 1973)

This is not a view of primordiality, let alone ethnicity, as simply a 'given' whose force cannot be escaped. Geertz does, after all speak of assumed culturally defined givens. But it does entail the specula-tion, if not the assumption, that such attachments have enough strength and persistence to be capable of being the object of a successful appeal – and this at least appears often enough to be the case. What is wrong is any assumption that culture and religion are always the source of conflict and are always 'primordial', deeply felt and socially ingrained.

To take the argument further we may consider Geertz's reference to 'the sorts of primordial ties that tend in one place or another, to become politicised'. It is possible to put it rather differently. Those groups who identify as ethnic (or linguistic and regional) groups may not in all circumstances have a primary loyalty to the group – the very thing which Geertz sees as threatening liberal democratic institutions. Their real grievance may be that to the extent that they see their fate bound up with a group, they suspect or fear that this group is less than fully incorporated or less than fully rewarded – on a categorical basis. So that a person in a group identified as A, within nation-state B may not be saying 'I am A first and foremost' as a potential threat to B; rather the person or collectivity may be saying, 'if you want us to become good Bs make room for us As'. This is exactly the structure of argument used by non-Malays at the time of independence (Ratnam 1965). In this sense, the members of a group may, at least up to a point, accept civic values (democratic process and citizenship) and with rather lukewarm affection accept that they belong to political state B, but protest that they are excluded or less than fully included in it. To the extent that this is the case, the irreconcilable conflict becomes less stark than Geertz supposes.

People like us

Identifying 'people like us' is the bread and butter of the politician's appeal to sections of the public – or even in forms which suggest an appeal to the whole, or nearly whole public. The politician who makes a successful identification is the one who diagnoses a sentiment shared by a big enough segment of the voting public (however diffusely) so that we speak of the appeal as catching a mood, touching a nerve or riding a wave. This diffuse public may be conformed by class, gender or ethnicity, or other identities such that the message catches the individual who thinks 'she is talking about me – and people like us'. In the example of Sri Lanka, Bandaranaike knew how to identify 'people like us' and we may suppose that Milosevic had similar success, at least for a time, with

Serbians (Bennett 1995). The essence of Geertz's argument is that in new states, where citizen identifications are uncertain and 'people like us' are not sure that the state is including or benefiting or honouring them, primordial attachments of many kinds compete often successfully with appeals to throw in one's lot with the state. It should be clear that this failure to throw in one's lot with the state, in states where citizen loyalty is fragile, is not simply because there is a countervailing primordial tie. Of course the concept of primordial tie includes the idea that it is deeply felt; but it is not simply because it is deeply felt that it poses a threat to the state or intervenes between the individual and loyalty to the state. The source of the disaffection may be in part instrumental based on a view that by claiming and emphasising their identity as As they stand to gain, or that as As they are currently being treated rather poorly. This accords with the sense in which ethnic identifications have been described as instrumental, opportunistic, situational, constructed or even invented (Hobsbawm and Ranger 1983, Roosens 1989).

The question of choice is crucial. It points again to the idea of societies differing in the degree to which identities and roles are ascribed, as against 'open' and rewarding 'achievement' rather than any characteristic socially endowed by birth or socially fixed memberships. Certainly the phrasing of ethnicity as situational and instrumental and opportunistic is compatible with an action framework. The individual actor is viewed as making a calculation 'will it reward me to identify as an A in this situation?' Similarly, the idea that people identify in different ways in different contexts implies a measure of choice and openness in social life quite contrary to the idea of ethnic and racial categories as being ascriptive.

This equation of a 'situational' view of ethnicity with 'choice' need not be complete. In Malaysia three pan-Malaysian categories – Malay, Chinese and Indian, or an even simpler categorisation of Malay and non-Malay – are quite coercive categories in many respects. But different ethnic identities may be relevant in for example, all-Indian social circles where distinctions between Muslim, Hindu, Christian and Sikh or Tamil and Punjabi become in context more significant than the Malay/non-Malay distinction (Nagata 1974). It is possible, in other words, for ethnic identities to be both coercive and situational.

An expression of the same theme, of strategically selected collective identities, can be found in the idea of construction and invention. The idea of invention derives principally from theories of nationalism and the work of Hobsbawm and Ranger (1983) in which they and others argued that nationalisms rely on selective 'reading' of history, even a rewriting of history, in order to construct traditions, images, heroes and myths which then become the basis of the claim that there is a nation with a common folk and way of life, and that its history is glorious, or tragic or both, and its future bright and uplifting. The inventionist argument has equally been applied to ethnicity claims so that not only are individuals seen as choosing between ethnic identities, or choosing none at all, but that equally there may be a collective mobilisation of an ethnic category in which the category itself is invented or reinvented by a careful and conscious compilation of cultural history (Roosens 1989).

Affect and kinship

The association of ethnicity with 'high affect', a deeply felt and enduring identity and allegiance, is expressed through reference to the bonds of kinship. Certainly the notion of primordialism, in its guise as denoting deeply felt attachments, associates affect with kinship. Part of the task of sociological exploration is then the nature of the relationship between ethnicity and kinship. There are two main ways in which this has been discussed: one has been to see ethnic attachments as an extension of kin and extended kin ties, the second has been to refer to quasi-kinship where ethnic bonds are presented as if they were kin bonds.

As is the case with nationalism, the rhetoric of ethnicity is replete with the language of kinship. The curiosity is this: where kinship ties may be the most stable is in the relatively 'closed' community, prior to migrations, urbanisation and social mobility and it is in these instances, especially if contact with 'others' is slight, that the elaboration of kinship ties into ethnic ties may be least developed (Linnekin and Poyer 1990). As Eriksen has so cogently argued, ethnicity should be seen as a dimension of a relationship, and it is in relationship with others that ethnicities thrive. It is in the context of new states and modernising societies that ethnicity has been seen primarily as an extension of extended kinship when members of families have become mobile and moved into new sets of relationships outside the restricted locales of birthplace. Some of the best known research and interpretation of ethnicity in Africa relates to social processes of mobility and urbanisation (Cohen 1974).

Three features of these studies are of immediate relevance to our discussion. One is that ties described by these researchers as ethnic are in part a function of real (not fictive) kinship. The second is that these ties are not 'simple' kinship ties but take on new meanings in urban settings, including the redefining of the boundaries of the groups – typically by broader amalgamations of groups which may have been seen in a smaller setting as different. And the third is that these new ethnic ties, more or less linked to real kinship, are not necessarily intensely felt and all-encompassing in the demands they make on the individual.

There are good sociological reasons for this last point. The person who moves out of his or her home community into the growing urban centre and encounters familiar and unfamiliar others, becomes newly aware of his/her ethnic identity. This is precisely the story told by the Copperbelt studies which described African villagers moving into cities and relying on extended kin connections to survive in the new arena (Cohen 1974). The fact that few of one's closest group may be available is a cogent reason why wider circles become the defined group boundary, the amalgamations where kinship stretches into quasi-kinship. But it is in these urban circum-stances where a new set of lessons is also learned – or may be. That is the necessity of getting along with 'others'. The very circum-stances which make the person acutely aware of their ethnicity are the same ones which may demand interethnic co-operation, or at least 'getting along'. Thus one report indicates (Lloyd 1974) that people did feel their ethnic attachments but did not describe them as all-encompassing; the structures of everyday life (the workplace, the marketplace, the labour union) were such that interethnic co-operation was frequently called upon. In similar vein, if not for all the same reasons, new urban Africans speak against 'tribalism'. The connection of ethnicity with kinship is not in this instance a recipe for its being all-embracing; nor is it so intensely felt that all action is predicated upon it – quite the contrary (Grillo 1974).

If this is the case it suggests that something else has to explain the intensity of feeling apparently associated with ethnicity, at least and especially where this 'intensity' is linked to seemingly intractable conflict and violence. For this reason it seems that Horowitz (1985) has misplaced his emphasis on kinship as the 'cause' of the intensity with which ethnic sentiments are felt and thus the root of the intractability of violent conflict – the implication being that ethnic 'warriors' are quite literally fighting for their brothers and sisters. No doubt where conflicts do arise and are ethnically structured the affect associated with kinship plays its part. But on its own it can hardly be seen either as the source itself of the intensity of affect and certainly not as the source of the 'inescapable' conflict. To this extent the critics of a vulgar primordialism are certainly right. The horror in these ethnic conflicts is not the simple equation:

kinship and extended kinship = ethnic loyalty = unalterable boundaries of difference = antagonism, violence and conflict

This equation does not work. The horror is that in ethnic conflicts of the kind exemplified by Rwanda/Burundi (Evans 1997) and Bosnia, people who have learned to live alongside each other, notwithstanding ethnic difference, find themselves in circumstances where survival has become wholly ethnically defined. In these circumstances people do murder their neighbours – despite the lessons they have learnt.

'It is true I killed your parents. It is true. I had orders.'
'Who ordered you?'
'The school headmaster C.M. I killed with a lot of other people. There were 42 in the group.'
Mr K. stared at him.
'My father was your god-father. You were his neighbour. I don't understand how you could do that. You were my friend. You were like a brother.' (*Guardian* report on massacre of Tutsis in Rwanda, 1 May 1995)

Furthermore the 'Family – ethnicity – intensity of feeling – protect your own – inescapable conflict' set of linkages does not always work, because several other links in the chain do not always work. The first link – family–ethnicity – does not always operate because people do not always translate their family ties into wider ethnic ties. Where family life is important – and it is certainly more important in some societies than in others – then if family ties are translated into ethnic sentiments the ethnic sentiments derive some of their intensity from the fact they are grounded in socialisation and identity formation. We may find many instances – in the biographies of ethnic warriors, those who take up an ethnic cause, of the ethnic identity being learnt at the knee of the father and mother and brothers, sisters, uncle and cousins. But it need not and does not always happen in this way. We also know that there are at least three other possibilities – other than the family–ethnicity–intensity equation. One is that socialisation in the family may not stress ethnicity. It may stress, for example, the learning of a broad set of values among which ethnic identity comes low down the list, or even take the form of a counter-ethnic message. The second is that a loose ethnic identity may derive from family but without the intensity of feeling – a socialisation which foregoes any moral imperative to 'die for your people'. And the third is that whatever lessons the person learns in socialisation may be drastically modified as young people re-form their identities in young adulthood.

If some of the family–ethnicity linkage has worked we certainly cannot always expect the 'protect your own–inescapable conflict' sequence to follow. For this to follow there must be – at the point of socialisation and/or through the experiences of adult life – a set of circumstances which makes the message 'protect your own–fight for your people' the only one which makes sense. In other words, there must be a problem of desperation and survival. It seems that in many circumstances – certainly in the many instances where armed conflict is at a local level, where violence comes close to home – precisely this kind of desperation and struggle for survival is entailed. But it is certainly arguable that the reason the ethnic sentiments are strongly felt is because survival is or appears to be at stake and not the other way round. (To clarify, the 'other way round' would be that people fight for survival in a desperate unremitting way because all-powerful ethnic sentiments are involved.)

The problem then becomes one of explaining how this 'set of circumstances' occurs. We may speculate that it occurs when:

1. Cross-cutting ties lose their influence.
2. When there is a general breakdown of civic ties such that either state-derived forms of non-ethnic adjudication cannot be relied upon. This would argue against Geertz by suggesting that ethnic ties are strong because civic ties are weak and not that civic ties are weak because ethnic ties are strong.
3. When the state itself acts in an ethnically informed way; when state power is wholly or almost wholly identified with an ethnic group.

These 'types' may well fit the case of examples both from African states and from Yugoslavia. In the case of some African states, state power may be weakened for both economic and constitutional reasons. The problem of integration may be encountered – the inability of states to 'tie in' and win the support of (some) ethnic groups – because the persistent problems of economic development in a world economy which favours the rich and powerful gives new states little to offer. If for these and other reasons, such as the relative weakness of the state's own ability to offer promotion and mobility as state functionaries, the state fails to tie in its would-be citizens, then family/extended family/ethnic loyalties may be a matter of survival. And, to repeat, this will be especially the case where the state itself talks of an exclusive ethnic language which systematically excludes sizeable segments of the population.

In fact this latter problem occurs both in poor 'modernising' states and, in some cases, in rich developed states, racialised unreconstructed America being an example of the latter, apartheid South Africa being another with an ethnically defined barrier between the rich and poor sectors. All African states with dominant ethnic groups, not always numerical majorities, such as Sudan, Rwanda, Ghana, Nigeria and Kenya (see Horowitz 1985), may be prone to the same kind of problems. Malaysia may prove to be an intermediate case which avoids the problems of the thoroughgoing identification of state power with one ethnic group, the Malays, because countervailing interests prevent this, making ethnic compromise and a modest, if not wholehearted, 'non-ethnic' democracy the basis on which non-Malay ethnic groups are 'tied in' via both economic and political means (Horowitz 1989).

Summary

This discussion has proceeded from a theoretical examination of the quality of ethnicity as a dimension of relationships as primordial, situational, contextual and instrumental to a discussion of the kinds of circumstances in which ethnicity takes on both a prominent place in action and structure and may be imbued with intense sentiments. The link with kinship is clearly an important one, partly because, the arguments of the anti-primordialists notwithstanding, there are circumstances in which the kin–extended kin–ethnicity linkages may be made, and this will be all the more compelling when people reside in states and societies where dependence on kin, not just for private personal supports, is woven into economic and political life. But the kin–ethnicity linkage is not a necessary one; it may or may not be intensely felt; and where it is intensely felt, its roots in kin or quasi-kin may not explain this intensity. These are important conclusions for the judgement of the power of persistence of ethnicity in the modern world, for the understanding of the apparent drama and acuteness of ethnic conflict, and for the understanding of the problems which Geertz (1973) denoted by the phrase 'integrative revolution'.

One key to the understanding of the intensity of ethnic sentiments is exploring the associations with kinship and face-to-face interactions. The micro- and meso- or 'institutional' spheres represent the areas of everyday life in which individual actors work out their ethnic identities. These frequently constitute, we suggested, areas of indeterminacy within which new identities are formed and acted out within differing situations. Kinship is an important element of these micro-spheres but neither ethnic identity nor the intensity with which it is felt can be read off from the fact that some of its roots are in kinship relationships. Just as a wider set of macro-contexts give a frame to ethnicity which no individual actor can remake or escape in a moment, so do wider circumstances influence whether kinship and other regional, language and communal attachments are translated into unremitting ethnic oppositions. In particular we suggested that the weakness – particularly the economic and political weakness of some new states may mean that ethnic ties are strong because civic ties are weak. This is the reverse of the assumption or argument that civic ties are weak because ethnic sentiments are strong.

The answer to the question of whether ethnic ties should or should not be regarded as primordial is therefore that they may be or they may not be. In any case, as we saw, primordiality does not itself exclude a certain situational, instrumental or 'invented' character pertaining to ethnicity – another reason why, in the study of contextualised ethnicity, our focus should be on the context as much as on the ethnicity. The same is true if we look at another type of post-colonial society – the societies which were colonial rulers, rather than colonised, such as Britain, France and Holland.

This chapter also opened up the question of ethnicity as a set of problematics: theories of origin, theories of intensity, and theories of decline and persistence. In theories of origin we examined both macro-contexts within which ethnic identities and allegiances have emerged. In theories of intensity we looked especially at the nature of the links between kinship and ethnicity, and the debate about primordiality. The theories of decline and persistence, perhaps more than other questions, connect us directly to the general terrains of sociological theory both about the very nature of ethnicity and its sources in modernity.

Much of this debate has surrounded the question of the 'liberal expectancy' – the sociological and moral tendencies which underscore 'Universalism' both as principle and as fact. We shall return to this question in Chapter 8. We should be clear about the constituent elements of the liberal expectancy. It is simultaneously economic, social, political and cultural. The (liberal) economic expectation is that modern rational economic calculation drives out particularism; the social expectation is that the milieu of birth recedes in its salience; the political expectation is that forms of universal franchise and citizenship supplant ascriptive ties and identities; and the cultural expectation is an expression of all those tendencies which lead towards homogenisation both national and global. None of these expectations is fully met in the modern or the post-modern world but not simply because ethnicity has survived to confound them.

Chapter 4

Racialisation and Ethnicity in the Economic Context

In this chapter we discuss the relationship of ethnicity to class structure and the division of labour. The latter part of the chapter is an account of America as a slavery and post-slavery society.

The interdefinition of ethnicity and class

The class situation of any ethnic group is commonly a primary influence in giving the group its character and shaping the group's relations with others. We do not often find a complete correspondence of ethnicity with class position although the association of an ethnic group with a class, or more narrowly an occupation, is found in many societies: the Chinese with trading and commerce in South East Asia, Indians as cane producers in Fiji, African Americans as an urban working class, as service workers, and as greatly over-represented among the urban poor. But ethnic groups are also typically class stratified and the class identities of a group's members cut across their ethnic identity. An educated middle class or elite within an ethnic population will often provide political leadership, but also stand to be accused of being remote from their poorer brothers and sisters, of betraying them or of not understanding their lives. Where migrants become urban minorities, middle-class community leaders and professionals may act and be called on to act as intermediaries and brokers between an ethnic community and the state or receiving country.

The class and occupational concentrations of ethnic populations are typically based in fact and reproduced in myth. In Malaysia (Malaysia: Seventh Malaysia Plan 1996–2000) 28 per cent of Chinese were engaged in wholesale and retail trade compared with

12 per cent of Bumiputera (Malays and others) – a significant occupational concentration. Less commonly observed is that almost half
of all Chinese in Malaysia are production workers and agricultural
workers. Despite class differentiation within a group, an ethnic
group's class or occupational concentration means that class experience is mediated by ethnicity. Ethnic or racial ideologies always
threaten to cut across the shared class experience of say, the black
poor and the white poor in the USA; in business and commerce,
ethnic networks directly influence the way in which business is
carried out.

This 'interdefinition' of class–ethnicity and ethnicity–class, is
both cultural and material. Ethnic groups have determinate class
positions and it is not simply a matter of 'ethnic meanings' being
'superadded' to class structures as if the latter had a reality base
which the former lacked. Ethnicity is sociologically grounded in
the lives of families, neighbourhoods and schools, and in the class
structure of a society; ethnicity may be, and frequently is, a
primary basis of mobilisation in political action and voluntary
associations. With regard to class and economic position, as we
argued in Chapter 1, ethnic groups are encompassed within specific
locations in the division of labour and the class structure, and these
positions are often unequal. The ethnically defined system of
inequality, the class-situated ethnic groups and the ethnically
ordered division of labour are the classic loci of what are simultaneously economically ordered ethnicities and ethnically framed
economic structures.

The external definitions of ethnic groups are compelling and
constraining where they form part of laws regulating housing,
labour, migration, citizenship and political participation. In the case
of the USA, ethnicity has been highly racialised and collective identities have been described and understood in a language of race. In
much of the present chapter our discussion of the USA will be set
within a model of class and racialisation.

The actors' frame of reference

In the study of ethnicity actors' definitions can scarcely be ignored,
and in practice rarely are. But classes may form part of an analytic
system which does not depend in the first instance on an account of
the actors' point of view. We can define social classes by reference
to property, capital and wage labour or by reference to occupational

categories, in ways which do not depend on the actors' view of their own class position or their class attitudes. In practice, however, social, cultural and ideological constructions invariably enter into class relationships and the understanding of them.

In racialised societies both political power and economic dominance are simultaneously class structured and ethnically or racially structured, the USA and South Africa being the prominent cases of racialised societies. In these countries a 'race–class' debate – a debate about the 'primacy' of one or the other – has been central to political action and academic commentary (Wilson 1980, 1987, Lipton 1985, Marks and Trapido 1987, Wolpe 1988). In apartheid South Africa (1948–94) black South Africans formed the greatest part of the working class, the service workers and the rural poor. But the idea of an interethnic class alliance with white workers was almost unthinkable, given the ethnically privileged position of the latter.

Class structures

Class structures, classes and class relations express sociologically the social form which economic relations take. In a feudal or tribute-bearing society, a class of commoners or producers tied to the land yield part of the product of their labours to an overlord or a dominant institution. This was the kind of society to be found in the Hawaiian islands at the time (1778) that Captain Cook came across the islands by chance on his voyage across the Pacific. Contact with British, American and other foreigners and the introduction of trans-Pacific commerce destroyed and transformed that economy and that culture within the space of 70 years (Kame'eleihiwa 1992). In a capitalist society, economic relationships are built upon the private ownership of land and the means of production (capital) and wage-paid labour; the latter constitutes a class which reproduces itself by selling its labour power. In the classic conception of capitalist societies a bourgeois class or capitalist class – which owns and controls the means of production and 'purchases' labour power – is matched by a wage-labouring class, the working class. The interests of these two classes are seen as inherently opposed. The wage-labouring class has historically been viewed as having its characteristic form in factory-based commodity production with routine or skilled manual work; this remains the case in many countries and industries. In most older capitalist industrial societies the proportion of workers engaged in manual and factory-based work has declined steeply with a growth in the service sector and in professional and administrative employment.

Transcending capitalism

In no advanced capitalist society, characterised by manufacturing and commodity production, has the potential for class conflict led to the kind of class revolution which socialists expected. What the world has seen of socialist revolutions have occurred in Russia, one of the least advanced of the European countries, and in China, a predominantly agrarian society; as well as in Cuba and, under different circumstances, in eastern Europe. In Russia, and more properly the Soviet Union, a socialist state took on the role of forcing, with much brutality, a collectivisation of land and 'modernisation' of agriculture while introducing primary industries and state-directed manufacturing on a grand scale (Hosking, 1985). In the former Soviet Union, it is certain that this socialist experiment in industrialisation and the planned control of an industrial economy has been abandoned; in China, socialism/communism appears to have been abandoned in all but the outer forms. In the Soviet Union and in the 'satellite' countries of eastern Europe, the communist period up to 1989 was characterised by a high degree of centralisation of power in a state apparatus dominated by the party.

These structures collapsed throughout the Soviet Union and most eastern European countries in a very condensed period between 1989 and the early 1990s. Capitalism and the social and political doctrines which typically accompany it – an individualist social ethic, market economics and the argument that political freedoms depend on market freedoms – have gained the upper hand. This is true not only in the USA, Germany, France and Britain – the 'older' capitalist economies, but also in the expanding economies of the Pacific Rim countries. These last include above all Japan but also Australia, New Zealand, Malaysia, South Korea, Indonesia and Taiwan. Most of the eastern European countries, including what was East Germany, now consolidated in a unified Germany, and Poland, Hungary, the Czech Republic and others, are now enthusiastically embracing both a capitalist ethos and capitalist practice.

The persistence of class inequalities

Since social and political science failed to predict this dramatic turn of events it would be most imprudent of late 20th-century social scientists to pretend to be able to predict where these old and new capitalist regimes will lead us in the new century. We can, however, observe some facts which constitute an economic 'field' in which ethnic identities act. Among these facts are the continued importance of classes and class inequalities, the dogged persistence of poverty in advanced economies, in most countries a growing divide between possessed and dispossessed, the recurrent crises of capitalist economies, and the world movement of labour in which people from poorer countries seek entrée to the expanding and rich zones of the world. Each of these features of modern economies has the potential for being converted into the politics of ethnicity: urban concentrations of disadvantaged minorities and the politics of welfare, security and class protection; the identification of an ethnic group with poverty and exclusion; the ethnic ramifications of economic collapse as in the attacks on Chinese merchants in Indonesia; and the politics of immigration and refugee status.

Migrant labour is engaged typically on greatly unequal terms, both economically and politically, that is, in poor work accompanied by no rights or limited rights. And with the increased movement of both capital and labour, and the reducing of trade barriers, the capitalist economies are increasingly a world economy, accelerating the competition between countries and zones. In its political and cultural as well as economic forms, this process is the one we know as globalisation (Robertson 1992). Given the great disparity between rich and poor zones of the global economy, opportunities to work in the rich sector are eagerly sought. There is now scarcely an area of the world where there cannot be found a bitter politics of immigration and refugee control. In contemporary China, the modern sector's attitudes towards internal in-migrants is familiar to observers of migration in post-war Europe: 'Country cousins take rap for rising crime in Shanghai', *Financial Times* 8/9 August 1998. With economic development there are three million in-migrants in Shanghai who have built the highways and skyscrapers. But with workers laid off from state-run enterprises, local resentment grows, and the in-migrants are widely seen as associated with crime. 'The quality of these people, the "waididren", people from out of town, is not the same as locals'(*Financial Times* 8/9 August 1998).

Global competition

The countries of the European Union fear competition from South East Asian producers, notwithstanding the 1997–98 crisis in the Asian region. International capitalists struggle to secure a foothold both as investors and as sellers in the great population centres, especially India and China, which represent such a huge percentage of the world's population, and will dramatically increase that share in the coming decades. The struggles for control of Central Asian oil illustrate China's increasing power and influence (*Guardian* 1997d). At the same time those 'developing' countries themselves seek to establish their place in the world economy by a mixture of attracting external capital and endogenous growth. Many of these newly expanding economies face the problem of attracting international capital while meeting stringent requirements of the World Bank or the International Monetary Fund. Countries seeking to attract inward investment attempt to guarantee to those who would invest in them a measure of internal social and political stability, balancing this against the revolutionary implications of capitalist development. In the aftermath of the 1997–98 crisis, Asian states had to balance the wish for economic recovery against the demands made by creditor institutions; economic liberalism threatens social control. These facts of contemporary economic relationships influence ethnicity in both its global and local contexts.

Racialisation, ethnicisation and classes

We have argued that ethnic identities and racialization developed within three key contexts of the modern world, especially the modern world of the last three centuries in which colonial and imperial powers of Europe, and latterly the USA, imposed their will on countries of Africa, Asia and the New World. Those three key contexts are slavery; colonial settlement and rule; and the internal dynamics of capitalist democracies of the West. Within these historical trajectories we have spoken of post-slavery minorities, indigenous peoples, urban minorities, ethnic groups in plural societies and the proto-nations. These types of ethnic groups are illustrated through the case studies presented in Chapters 4–7: African Americans as a post-slavery minority, Hawaiians as an indigenous people, Malaysia as an example of the post-colonial plural society, and British and other European examples of urban minorities; with, in some parts of this book, examples of 'proto-nations' or ethnonationalism.

The class-economic contexts of these types of ethnicity are different in form and emphasis. In post-slavery societies the key economic issue has always been 'what was to be the post-emancipation economic destiny of former slaves and their descendants?' They might remain as formally free labour on plantations, or become smallholders or sharecroppers; in several cases their place as fiercely disciplined plantation labour was taken by new importations of labour. Where, as in the USA, there is a large white population as actual or potential competitors, the class interests of whites have been critical in shaping the class fates of Africans.

In post-colonial societies a matching of ethnicity with class position has been an inheritance of the colonial order where labour was imported for specific purposes and domestic ethnic difference was significant in, for example, recruitment into the army and state bureaucracies. The key questions for the post-colonial social order are then: Will the class and division of labour specialisations of the colonial period persist? Will any ethnic group achieve a position of dominance in the post-colonial state? Will elites be multi-ethnic?

In societies where indigenous peoples have been dispossessed of their land we will find not only the survivors of the indigenous population and the colonial settlers but also a 'third force' of migrants who are neither indigenes nor representatives of the colonial ethnicity. In New Zealand there are European or Pakeha New Zealanders, Maori, and new in-migrants from, for example, other Pacific islands and Asia. But whereas the collective interest of in-migrants is the removal of obstacles to mobility, the economic interest and cultural imagination of indigenes is bound to the land. By the 1990s the characteristic politics of indigenous peoples are land claims, reparations and cultural dignity. The case study of the class context of ethnicity and racialisation in the remainder of this chapter is the USA as a post-slavery society and the position within it of African Americans.

The USA: slavery, racialisation and class

Even in 1991 the US population is described unequivocally as belonging to different 'races'. People of Hispanic origin are listed separately but with the note 'persons of Hispanic origin may be of any race' which presumably means that persons who are 'ethnically' Hispanic by country of origin and language may be white, black or 'other racial' origin. 'Other races' are cited as including Native Americans, Asians and Pacific islanders (Table 4.1).

Table 4.1   US population by racial and ethnic group, 1990

	1000s	%
All races	248,710	
Black	29,986	12
White	199,686	80
Other races	19,038	8
Hispanic origin	22,354	9

Source: Adapted from US Bureau of the Census (O'Hare *et al.* 1991)

African Americans, slavery and post-slavery

The great moments of America's ethnic history were, following Wilson's 1980 periodisation, racialised slavery from the mid-17th century to 1863; post-Civil War reconstruction and subsequently the making of segregated America up until 1954; the post-1954 de-desegregation and civil rights period (Wilson 1980).

The period of slavery, early 17th century to 1863

The enslavement of Africans in the New World is an instance where class position and racial or ethnic definition virtually coincided. In the American south in the period immediately prior to the Civil War almost all Americans of African descent were slaves and there were no slaves who were not African Americans. In the early years of colonial incursions into America the settlers had enslaved some Native Americans; the imported European workers were indentured labourers whose conditions were not – in the earliest period – readily distinguishable from that of Africans (Jordan 1968). But the relative failure of the attempts to enslave American Indians and the eventual sharp distinction between European and African servants/slaves (Klein 1967) led to a situation in which only Africans were unequivocally regarded and treated as slaves.

Although white men from Europe were affected by ideas associating Africans with low rank or slavery itself, prejudice alone cannot account for their enslavement. Superior armed force, a ready supply, and the inability of African states to protect themselves or their people – as well as traders and others who collaborated in the slave traffic – all played important parts. But once slavery was established and racialised – that is unequivocally linked to Africans and blackness – white men and women had powerful reasons to distinguish themselves both from Africans and from the unfree condition.

Slavery flourished in the upper south – Virginia, North Carolina and neighbouring states – where tobacco was the principal crop. Competition with other tobacco-producing areas almost led to some of these states abandoning slavery. The demand on the world market for cotton and the success of cotton growing in the American deep south – Mississippi, Alabama, Louisiana – revived slavery and led to upper south slave owners selling their slaves into the deep south.

There were of course African Americans who were not slaves. Indeed a very small number owned (African) slaves themselves. (Franklin 1943). Plantation slavery had only taken root in the southern states. In the north, black Americans were typically in service and labouring occupations and there experienced fierce racial discrimination (Litwack 1961). In the south about one sixteenth of African Americans were free men and women – but their social political and economic position was marked by discrimination and sharply confined by *de facto* and *de jure* restrictions. Only a few succeeded in establishing themselves in rewarding and reasonably secure trades and occupations (Franklin 1943, Hermann 1981). With these important exceptions we can be confident in saying that the fit of ethnicity and class position was almost perfect – all slaves were black/African and the great majority of African Americans were slaves.

Slaves as a politically conscious class

This may appear as a sound recipe for a collective consciousness in which slaves recognised their shared class position and their shared ancestry in a powerful combination of shared memories. Several things conspired to ensure that although this always remained a possibility, and one which occasionally flickered into life, for the most part collective consciousness faced formidable obstacles and collective action even more so. Plantation life was confining; slaves were rarely permitted freely to leave the environs of the estate and usually when they did, they were carefully watched. Although some observers have suggested that uprisings and revolts were numerous (Aptheker 1987), significant rebellions were few.

This was not because slaves were docile – as their masters sometimes wanted to believe – but because the material circumstances were stacked against them. White masters and those who did their bidding – the slave drivers and patrols – had the overwhelming command of superior force. Slavery was a system sustained above all by coercion, by sheer monopoly of the means of enforcement.

Slaves passed word from one to another as they moved – at their masters' wish – around the south – but the movement of slaves was also a method of breaking up solidarities. The break-up of family liaisons (Genovese 1976, Gutman 1977, Litwack 1980) was used as a method of control and slaves who were viewed as likely organisers of 'trouble' were moved on and brutally treated. Frederick Douglass, who later became famous as a campaigner against slavery and a post-Civil War politician, describes in his autobiography how he was detected as being too clever and thoughtful (Douglass 1962). His master hired him out to a small farmer who was tacitly deputed to break Douglass's spirit by force.

Some of the earlier commentators on slave plantation life emphasised the degree to which slaves 'accepted' their position (Elkins 1976), especially if they had been born into slavery. Other commentators have shown that slaves adopted ways of coping and resisting (Huggins *et al.* 1971, Rawick 1972, Genovese 1976). But even the boldest among them were for the most part only able to express their defiance as individuals.

Although slavery was, in America, a common condition of Africans and their descendants, their experience varied, as did the detail of their material position. The condition of unfreedom was fundamental but the particular combination of circumstances could vary significantly. There was a social distinction between house slaves and field slaves. The great houses of the master and his family commanded a retinue of servants, nannies, and trusted managers, whose daily life was different in several respects from the labouring slaves in the tobacco, sugar and cotton fields. Those slaves who came into closest contact with their masters in these ways sometimes were viewed as having gained a step in status. The manager of a Mississippi plantation was recognised by his masters as a skilful and resourceful worker of more than usual benefit to the slave owner. When lands of the ex-slave owners were threatened with confiscation in the brief period of 'radical reconstruction' in the south, his former owner preferred to bestow his land on his ex-slave than see it fall into the hands of the 'carpetbaggers' – northern fortune seekers who came to the south after the Civil War (Hermann 1981).

Slavery was racialised domination; it was also expressed as sexual domination. Slave masters ruthlessly exploited their female slaves who were forced into giving sexual favours to their owners. From these relationships stemmed mixed parentage children who were, at best, regarded with some affection by their father – as well as by their mother.

Mixed descent

No one can be sure to what extent these and similar liaisons produced a population of mixed descent in the American south. For a long time it was argued that a singular characteristic of the American 'race system' was that it defined people as black or white with no intermediate categories. Stephen Small questions this (Small 1994). It is certainly true that some records and indications of public recognition show that 'coloured' became a significant social category in parts of the south as it certainly did in other 'bi-racial societies' – such as Jamaica and South Africa.

To be sure in a society which placed such social significance on skin colour there were situations in which 'lightness' of skin among people of colour was regarded favourably by black and white alike. In North America and South Africa (Watson 1970) passing for white took place, but passing for white – by light-skinned people with some African ancestry – was more a mark of the hardness of the boundary between black and white. It showed that social recognition was what mattered – 'racial' categories are always a matter of social recognition and social definition – but it also showed that they mattered by way of defining people unequivocally as 'one or the other'. So, in the slave system and in the social and economic world which developed out of it or after it, there were social distinctions among African Americans which rested both upon the social status system of colour as well as the slow growth of class differentiation among African Americans.

After the American Civil War

The ending of slavery was the result of the victory of the free-labour capitalist north over the agrarian, slave labour and conservative south. Neither in the north nor in the south was there any clear picture of what a post-slavery society would be like. Many white people in the northern states, in which slavery had been abolished in the early part of the 19th century, believed that they stood to lose by slave emancipation. Northern Federal soldiers were persuaded to fight the Confederacy, the traitorous secession, but there were bloody riots in New York and other cities against conscription. Most white southerners believed they were fighting for survival in defence of a way of life. Greatly underrecognised in history, almost 200,000 former slaves fought in the Union colours. It was not until 1998, 133 years after the end of the Civil War that the contribution of black soldiers was formally and publicly recognised.

Post-slavery America: racialised competition

Black Americans recently out of slavery became politicians (none so spectacularly successful as Frederick Douglass), became tradesmen and service workers (tailors, barbers, gardeners, carpenters), some formed a small *petite bourgeoisie* of shopkeepers, ministers of religion, funeral directors and others, and a small number became professional men – educators, lawyers and doctors, almost all trained in racially segregated institutions (Frazier 1957). Some of these classes served both of the racialised populations – the gardeners would certainly tend white men's gardens and the tailors mend white folks' clothes. Many – the funeral directors and ministers of religion – had an ethnically exclusive clientele.

But the great majority of black men and women in the period after slavery continued to labour on the plantations, became sharecroppers and small farmers – a social class position which they shared with thousands of white southerners who were equally poor or at best made a meagre or modest living (Gutman 1977, Litwack 1980). Others who were unable to survive in the harsh environment of agricultural wage labouring and sharecropping became victims of the southern penal codes in its legitimate and illegitimate forms and spent much of their lives in penal servitude working in pointless labour or in public works contracted to the prisons by public authorities (Wilson 1980).

There can be few better illustrations than the American south of the way in which public authorities turned poverty and abject economic distress into crime by making 'criminals' of debtors and vagrants. Once in prison they were 'legitimately' required to work for nothing and southern states got roads built, trenches dug and swamps cleared by coerced labour of black men under the surveillance of armed white guards. If in many societies physical coercion usually lies below the surface, in the American south it was unmistakably on the surface so that all could see what it meant. And it was racially defined.

These are some of the 'hard' facts of economic life in the south – which maintained this profile for much of the period from 1865 to 1918 and even longer for those who remained in the south after the great exodus. The destinies of the poor – a majority of all southerners – were largely in the hands of large landowners, the bigger farmers, the banks, the railroad companies and the textile mill owners, the company stores and the judicial system. This was true for black and white alike. What happened to them, how they lived and died was a direct consequence of the political and economic system of the old south in which small farmers, sharecroppers, and landless labourers found mere survival all they could hope for or expect. Eventually, the plantation owners themselves – who above all depended on labour, however poorly remunerated – increasingly looked for and found ways of mechanising crop control and harvesting so as to reduce the need for labour to a minimum. To take no account of these facts of life is to imagine that the history of the American south – in slavery and post-slavery – is a history of 'race relations', which it is not.

The transition from racialised slavery to a white supremacist regime has appeared to many as inevitable. But as Vann Woodward has famously argued, the period of reconstruction in the south after the Civil War held out the possibility that a non-racial social order could be constructed (Vann Woodward 1964). For a decade or so the ex-slave population participated in politics, held public offices and made small gains over and above the gain of freedom, at least as long as the north retained a military presence in the southern states and was disposed to punish the secessionists. By the end of the century the defeat of the south was utterly secure and the failure of reconstruction to provide a basis for real social and economic enfranchisement of the black population was abundantly evident. Political manoeuvre, popular prejudice and class interests combined to make this so.

First of all, as Camejo (1976) has shown, the old ruling class – the white plantocracy – merged with or was replaced by new financial interests in the south and neither they nor their capitalist counterparts in the north had any interest in achieving a social and economic revolution for the sake of human equality (Camejo 1976). In particular, men who were persuaded that property was a sacred right were ill-disposed to take land redistribution further than was necessary to disable the social and political class that had fought to defend slavery. The combination of respect for property by those who had most, and the fear of economic competition by those whites who had least, subverted any real prospect of creating an economic base from which the ex-slave population could find a place of dignity in the post-war south.

By the 1880s and 90s one of the real threats to the position of the new southern elite came from the possibility that the propertyless agricultural labourers and sharecroppers, and small farmers, black and white alike, might set aside their suspicions of each other in a recognition that 'they were in the ditch together' (Vann Woodward 1963). White populists led by Tom Watson recognised that they could gain by solidarity with black farmers and farm workers in their united struggle against the banks and large landowners (Vann Woodward 1951). They never presented their alliance as a crusade for interracial harmony but as a practical and unsentimental collaboration grounded in their shared class interests. Proponents of white supremacy and Democrat opponents of the populists provoked violence to undermine the efforts of the black–white alliance in populism and Watson's protection of his black colleagues provides one of the few instances of late 19th-century American history where whites united with blacks in armed self-defence.

The role of violence

Indeed the part played by violence throughout this period, and later periods, of American history should never be underestimated, much of it violence by whites against blacks. In the period after the Civil War the Ku Klux Klan was founded and the movement and its sympathisers have now been responsible for nearly a century and a half of violence against black Americans. In answering the question of how to explain the position of black Americans in the period since the Civil War, violent coercion should never be omitted from calculations. By 1900 all the southern states had decided – at least their white voters had – to create and perfect white supremacist regimes (Silberman 1964). And these were enforced by the monopoly of violence by the institutions of the states and their functionaries. The threat of whites uniting on a class basis with blacks was averted by the simple technique of appealing to the group self-interest and racialised pride of whites, their political masters promising that however hard and meagre their own lives were, they would be guaranteed that one segment of the population would be permanently 'below' them.

Tom Watson, the white populist leader who had allied with the 'coloured' farmers, himself was persuaded that he and his followers stood to gain more from racial than from class solidarity and he spent the last part of his political career arguing for the disfranchisement of blacks in the southern states and justifying this argument by reciting the familiar repertoire of racist slurs best calculated to gain support among resentful and angry whites (Vann Woodward 1963). By the early part of the 20th century virtually all prospects of white–black alliance in class struggle had been dashed and a system of racialised domination, enforced by 'legitimate' and extralegal violence, was firmly established.

From slavery to wage labour and ethnic competition

The class context of ethnicity in the American south, and in America as a whole, was a critical fact in shaping people's lives, in how they survived or did not, in how they thought of their past, present and future, and in how they sought to resist or overcome their circumstances by individual action or by forming allegiances and alliances both within and without the socially defined racial boundaries. After emancipation, this class context changed crucially from one in which black men were almost all slaves, and white men – among whom class differentiation was critically important – were variously plantation and slave owners, small and medium farmers, agricultural labourers, tradesmen and urban workers. The class disposition of whites was of paramount importance in shaping how they saw African Americans – as enemies, as necessary labour, as competitors or as actual or potential allies. The class position of African Americans was also important in how they saw themselves; over the period of 140 years since the end of slavery black Americans have embraced a wide spectrum of social and political ideologies. They have seen themselves as Africans, as Americans, as workers and labour unionists, as Democrats and as Republicans, as Christians and as Muslims, and as black and as the prophets of a non-racial America (Draper 1970, Marable 1984).

The class and political struggles of 1880s and 90s had left America as a thoroughly racialised society. The class discontents of the white poor among small farmers and labourers were diverted by political racist appeals; movements towards class-based interethnic solidarity were squashed by inducing whites to accept the gains of a white supremacist society. In the last quarter of the 19th century the Colored Farmers Alliance had collaborated politically for a time with white farmers and the Populist Party. In the early 20th century black and white miners struck in solidarity in the Alabama coal-fields. These were to prove exceptions to the rule.

Since the turn of the century the northern migrations of black Americans and their incorporation into an American urban prole-tariat has shifted the class–ethnicity axis. For much of this period black Americans formed part of the American working class, a part which was excluded from more desired jobs, prevented from joining unions or entering skilled trades (Drake and Cayton 1962), and subject to a ceiling in promotion within industry and commerce.

The movement into urban manual labour was also a shift, for African Americans, from south to north. By the end of the 19th century northern cities like Chicago and New York were home for a small but growing number of black southerners. This movement was accelerated by the absence of workers in war time and the temporary cessation of white in-migration from Europe. As soon as the First World War ended, a struggle for jobs, housing and ameni-ties ensued and was seen in racial terms. This was the occasion for a succession of bloody riots in urban America. White workers sought to protect themselves from competition with black workers by retaining control of segregated labour unions which exercised power over entry to employment.

In this situation, some black leaders concluded that the way to persuade employers of the value of black labour was to encourage black workers to remain outside labour unions, thus promising white employers a non-unionised labour force which could be drawn upon to replace white workers. The more these strategies were followed – by white labour unions, employers and some black organisers – the more it became possible to set white against black in class conflict. Wilson has demonstrated how black workers were used to break white workers' strikes; a racialised order served the interests of employers (Wilson 1980).

Throughout the period violence was used against white as well as black workers – this was the age of the Pinkerton security agencies, the private police of American capital – and it was not until the late 1930s that labour union solidarity of white and black again became a possibility. This was especially so in new industrial sectors where CIO (Congress of Industrial Organisations) unions were predominant as against the AF of L (American Federation of Labour) craft unions which had almost always protected white workers against competition from black workers By the end of the 1930s and the introduction of New Deal policies designed to rescue American capitalism from the devastation of the 1929 collapse, the USA was moving towards the period of accommodation marked by the ending of formal segregation and the Supreme Court reversal in 1954 of the separate but equal doctrine which had provided the underpinning of a racialised system of domination. The organised struggles of black people and the effects of black participation in the Second World War effort brought down a formal system of racial oppression which had lasted for more than three quarters of a century (Buchanan 1977).

The shifting centres of gravity of American capitalism have, in the last few decades, found ever-decreasing need for the unskilled or lesser skilled urban industrial occupations which so many 20th-century African Americans filled. A combination of racial discrimination, segregation (Massey and Denton 1993), the compelling power of racist ideas, and the class trajectory of black Americans in the history of the USA has, by the end of the 20th century, consigned millions of black Americans to a life at and beyond the very margins of society (O'Hare *et al.* 1991) (Table 4.2).

Table 4.2   USA: black and white population by occupation – selected occupational groups shown

	White Male %	Black Male %
Managerial and professional	27	13
Service	9	18
Semi-skilled labour	19	33
	White Female %	Black Female %
Managerial and professional	27	19
Service	16	27
Semi-skilled labour	8	12

Source: O'Hare *et al.* 1991

William Julius Wilson: the significance of race

William Julius Wilson's periodisation of racialised America has informed the account just given: the slavery period as phase one, plantation economy and racial caste oppression, the 1880s to the 1940s as phase two, industrial expansion, class conflict and racial oppression and post-Second World War as phase three, progressive transition from racial inequalities to class inequalities (see also Boston 1988, p. 10). Wilson's analysis was a very great advance on 'race relations' theories, which concentrated on prejudice and racialist attitudes. It signally achieved a 'unification' of the analysis of racialisation with class structures in American society and history. His main argument was that formalised racial oppression had been the hallmark of the period up to the 1960s; when these formal structures were removed or at least delegitimated, the specific historical class position of black Americans became the main cause of their continued disadvantage.

His work was however not well received in some quarters for two main reasons:

1. The fact that, as the title 'the declining significance of race' implied, his work appeared to suggest that racism and discrimination were no longer 'important'.
2. His use of the term 'underclass' to describe those black Americans trapped in a multi-stranded web of disadvantage resonated with right-wing descriptions of ghettoised Americans as failing through their own 'deficiencies'.

This could have been avoided if Wilson had made it clear that he did not intend the first. The second seems to be unwarranted.

He uses the term underclass to describe the class position of that large proportion of black Americans for whom a racialised poverty reproduces itself, not by the failings of the poor but by the fact that opportunities for the urban poor, black and white, to 'escape' are rare and meagre. His argument appears to suggest that class structures reproducing black Americans in poverty had become especially significant at the moment that formalised racial oppression – legitimated segregation, disfranchisement, the formal structures of white supremacy – 'ended'. But he actually gives an account of a racialised class system in which class relations were never free of a simultaneous system of racial oppression, a point which he himself captures by his reference to the interaction of 'the economy and the polity' in all the stages he has depicted. To put it bluntly, African American slaves were simultaneously coerced by slavery and racial oppression; black sharecroppers were impoverished simultaneously by the nature of sharecropping itself, which similarly oppressed the southern white poor, and by the institutions of segregation and white supremacy.

There is little need to look far for an explanation of continued impoverishment of the mass of ex-slaves in the period 1865–1900, and beyond. Members of the white majority intended this to happen and systematically set about denying civic and economic improvement to the majority of black southerners; by and large they succeeded. The small moves which were made in the direction of land redistribution in the radical reconstruction period were annulled in the 1880s and 90s and the civic participation achieved by blacks in this period was eradicated by 1900. There was nothing mysterious about this; it was precisely what was intended by a sufficient majority of elite, middling and poor whites. As black labour moved out of the south from the 1880s onwards, new racialised class structures were constructed in the urban north where black workers became service workers and unskilled industrial workers but, in almost every conceivable sphere, faced a ceiling of 'closure' beyond which they would find it extremely hard to advance.

Wilson correctly argued that economic tendencies in modern America – the declining need for unskilled labour, deindustrialisation in the wake of competition with new low-wage economies, the growth of sectors of the economy which required high educational credentials – worked particularly hard against African Americans, given their historically inherited position. The implication – that delegitimating racism and racial discrimination held out the possibility of only limited gains for a relatively few black Americans and that any other advances could only come from restructuring the class system itself – was inescapable. And structural class 'reform' was on no one's political agenda except in the 'reverse' direction – that is, the rolling back of welfarism and indeed the programmes of affirmative action which had aided the social mobility of the new black middle class.

If the simple emphasis on class structure is flawed by the neglect of the fact that it is a racialised class structure, the flaw of the emphasis on 'race' is the failure to be explicit about economic or class processes which affect people irrespective of ethnic group. Where 'racial difference' is seen to be a crucial variable, or the one in which we are interested, then the tendency is to compare (for example) black and white populations in the USA. But it is important to remember that economic changes will typically have their effects across populations even if they affect some more than others. Boston's discussion of marginalisation illustrates this very neatly.

Marginalisation and ethnicity

In order to clarify the understanding of the position of black workers, Boston conceptualises the black working class as comprising three segments, the primary, secondary and marginalised. The primary is defined by higher paid and relatively stable employment in profitable and well-founded industries; the secondary by labour-intensive work in less stable industries; and the third is defined as those who do not 'have a full time attachment to a job', the unemployed, involuntary part time and 'welfare and poverty populations' (Boston 1988, p. 49).

The last category corresponds closely to what other commentators have referred to as the 'underclass'. In Boston's description 'marginalisation is a dynamic process related to business cycle behaviour, growing automation of industry, the export of jobs abroad, relocation of industry [and] the declining industrial base'. He then charts the fall and rise of the numbers of black and white marginalised workers as a proportion of the potential labour forces. One interesting result is that the curve of growth in the proportion of potential labour forces who are marginalised is identical for black and white workers. The economic changes – automation, relocation, export of jobs abroad – have a general impact. But at the same time it is important to note that the proportion of black workers who are marginalised is double the proportion for whites, both at the beginning and end of the 12-year period which Boston has described:

> In 1970 the percentages [of workers who are in marginalised positions] for white and black respectively were 7.7 per cent and 15.3 per cent. In 1982 these percentages were 14.6 per cent and 27 per cent respectively. (Boston 1988, p. 49)

Similarly the new black middle class has grown in a period when the proportion of all workers who are in the classes of occupation typically described as middle class, the professional, managerial and administrative, has been growing in the labour force as a whole.

This segment of the labour force had accelerated growth from the 1960s onwards, coinciding with the period which saw the successes of the civil rights movements and initiation of programmes to reverse over a century of discrimination in employment. Historically, the black middle class has been small and dominated by small business enterprises, self-employed and employed professionals, and providers of services largely oriented to black customers. Racialised markets excluded black entrepreneurs from white clientele – the successful minister had a black congregation – and so racial discrimination 'provided' a market and severely limited it. By contrast, the new professionals, among whom university academics would be a good example, are often in large institutions numerically dominated by whites, with black and white customers – students. This is a significant step beyond the pre-1960 period when all major and minor universities, black and white, were ethnically segregated.

The provision of services and running a business largely within the ethnically segregated community may mean that the business class retains its ethnic or racialised identity, promotes that identity among its clientele, and may further develop the politics of ethnic promotion, racial advancement and nationalism. Thus it has been suggested that the Nation of Islam (black Muslims) in America has, at periods of its development, pursued a petty bourgeois philosophy encouraging both black entrepreneurship and racialised market loyalty (stock black products, buy black). Boston (1988) has suggested that it is from the ranks of the new professional black elite, in particular the academics, that the black neo-conservatives have been drawn, reflecting their position as black professionals working in predominantly white institutions.

The changes in class structure affecting all populations will influence the class structure of the black population and these changes in turn affect relationships within the black population. In particular they affect dependency – for example, the dependence of ethnic entrepreneurs on ethnic clientele – and integration – the degree to which an ethnic middle class detaches itself from an ethnic working class and poor. This last argument was particularly important to Wilson, who argued that the growth of the new black middle class had produced a class detached from the largely disadvantaged mass of the black population (Wilson 1980, Small 1994).

Racialised structures, such as housing segregation and job discrimination, are an often decisive element of class structures which themselves change in ways we have already described. The continued significance of discrimination and segregation in American society is evidenced both by Massey and Denton's (1993) demonstration that segregation continues to influence black American social experience and economic fate, and by Small's (1994) and Omi and Winant's (1986) analysis of racialisation in the age of the delegitimation of formal racism.

They convincingly argue that when racism, predicated on the recapitulation of ideologies of inherent inferiority, is no longer possible, at least outside the far right, the appeal to racialised beliefs among white Americans takes on a set of coded forms. As in Britain, appeals to 'law and order' sentiments contain thinly disguised messages associating black youth with crime (Solomos 1988, Solomos and Back 1996). The same may be said about disparagement of welfare dependency, attacks on single parenthood, and of course the widespread appeal to 'rolling back the state'. The far right in America combines anti-statism and racism in close correspondence with each other and Omi and Winant were close to the mark in their prediction that extreme anti-statist movements might turn to terrorism. White anarchist anti-statism and racism appeared to combine in the 1998 murder of an African American in Texas. In Britain 'getting the state off people's backs' the Thatcherite slogan, included attacks on programmes designed to implement equal opportunities.

We should be careful not to imagine however, despite the power of racism, that white racism always got what it wanted. The history of black civic and economic participation is not only a history of closure, but also a history of resistance and organised political action, as nationalist, revolutionary, civil rightist and mainstream local and national political projects show (Marable 1983, 1984). One of the features of the American political configuration is that black voters are sufficient in number, whether as a majority – in a particular zone – or as a potentially decisive minority, that they are 'worth courting' by both black and white politicians. But where black political leaders acquire high office they may, if they wish to strengthen their power base, need to create and maintain support among white voters and institutions, limiting their ability to be exclusively ethnic 'nationalist' in ideology.

Cultural survival

The struggle for cultural survival is particularly important for the theme of ethnicity since the obliteration of ethnic solidarity was one of the first tasks undertaken by those who enslaved Africans and their purchasers who profited from their labour. Africans who spoke each other's language were separated so that solidarity was frustrated and slave owners kept a close watch on the non-work activities of their slaves, fearful of any signs that shared beliefs and practices might develop into resistance. This illustrates that racism – or racialised categorisation in social structure – is not simply a malign form of ethnic signification – although it is that. In the sense that ethnicity is often used – the attribution of social significance to descent and shared culture – slavery and forms of racial oppression were designed to erase ethnic identity. The racialised American social system has been built around a super-category, designed by a dominant class, whose sociological function was to override all other categories and self-definitions. Resistance to this took the form of cultural creativity which in part took the stigmatised category – black – and made it the symbol of claimed self-definition. black Americans took a racial category and recreated and re-presented it as African American ethnicity.

In contemporary America this struggle continues as African Americans living in the modern south look to demote all those cultural *significata* of white supremacy and equally resentful modern whites seek to reclaim them as a form of politicised cultural nostalgia. The Confederate flag and the singing of Dixie are the two most potent symbols of a social system which, whatever else it was, was a white supremacist order. Thus the 1990s' American south is punctuated by the cultural politics of historical symbols – plans to remove statues, reinstate them, play Dixie, ban Dixie, and fly the Confederate flag or tear it down:

In South Carolina Governor Beasley has crusaded to lower the Confederate battle flag from the Capitol in Columbia where it has flown beneath the American and South Carolina flags since 1962. Stiff resistance has been led by the state chapter of the Sons of the Confederate Veterans... In Virginia the Senate voted to retire the state song Carry me back to Old Virginia because of its references to 'darkies' and 'old massa'... The newest targets are the obelisks and statues that stand as monuments to the Confederate dead in almost every southern courthouse. In Franklin Tennessee a black resident filed a lawsuit in federal court seeking removal of that town's Confederate soldier statue as well as $44 million in damages... and a Confederate battle flag was spray painted on a monument in Hayneville Alabama to a civil rights worker who was shot to death there in 1965. (*Guardian* 1997b).

The American case provides us with illustrations of all the themes we introduced earlier in this volume. It illustrates racist doctrines in action in that slavery and post-slavery white supremacy was 'justified' in all the modalities which we described – theories of racial hierarchy, inherited character difference, socio-cultural incompatibility, and racial theories infused with themes of class dominance. It shows that ethnic difference was erased in face of the imposition of the category slave–black–negro. America is also one of the societies (apartheid South Africa was another) in which this system of racial categorisation succeeded in racialising virtually every conceivable facet of human existence, from the broad sweep of social, political and economic structure, to the minutiae of everyday life, interpersonal etiquette, and the outward appearance and the inner soul.

This racialised saturation runs so deep into socialisation, into memory, culture, love and hate, that it is small wonder that people may be affronted by any suggestion that 'race' can be neglected in sensible analyses of American society. This racialised saturation also illustrates that when a system is wholly predicated on categorical domination – as the USA was, certainly from 1863 to the 1954 Supreme Court decision – then any departure from this order is perceived as a threat. So ways of walking, dressing, speaking, the mere inclination of the head, are regulated in the enforcement of the racialised system. Thus Martin Luther King's refusal to answer to the call 'boy' was a revolution on its own. So was Rosa Parks' refusal to stand up – her action on a segregated bus in Montgomery, Alabama, led to the Montgomery bus boycott, a landmark in the civil rights struggle (Marable 1984).

The race and racism discourse

A discourse of race and racism predominates in this account of the American case. The discourse of ethnicity is equally applicable but has had a curious place in American commentary. It is significant that the discourse of ethnicity has been so predominantly applied to white populations in American society. All through the period that we have described, millions of (white) Europeans were arriving in the USA, fleeing religious and political persecution and economic despair in their own country (Handlin 1973, Yinger 1994) and entering the spaces opened up by the advances of capitalist industrialism in urban America. These in-migrants too faced hostility, some of it phrased in terms similar to that applied to African Americans and many Italian immigrants were initially treated as and sociologically categorised as 'black' (Gossett 1965, Handlin 1973, Yinger 1994). In the longer run they were also initiated and socialised into a social system which was already predicated on racialised categories; a significant element of learning that they were Americans was learning that they were white Americans.

Whatever hostility white European immigrants did face, they were never confronted with the utter determination of white America to exclude them civically, economically, culturally, and politically. American social observers appear to have dwelt long and hard on the question of why the racialised social inequalities of African Americans have been reproduced so persistently. But, we have argued, the answer appears to be relatively straightforward: if African Americans absolutely or proportionate to their numbers did not gain entry to favoured economic niches after emancipation - landowning small farmers at reconstruction, entrepreneurship, skilled unionised labour as America industrialised, the upper echelons of clerical administrative and professional employment – it is because this is what the more numerous and more powerful whites intended. The agents of exclusion have been many, depending on the crucial gates to be opened at different points of American history; the complicity of white elites in enforcing white supremacy in the segregation period give the lie to any simple notion that black advances have been resisted only by white workers fearing competition (Camejo 1976).

The racist notion that African Americans have prompted their own lack of advancement is belied by the overwhelming evidence of the way in which opportunities have been seized when they have been there, and of the contribution of black resistance to the eventual formal ending of the system of white supremacy. Similarly Steinberg's classic analysis of the fortunes of successive immigrant groups in America – whose children and grandchildren form the ethnicities of contemporary America – disposes of the culturalist accounts which imply different aptitudes in different groups conveyed by their cultural fit with individualistic and competitive America (Steinberg 1981, Woo 1990).

America in the 1990s presents at least three contexts of ethnicity:

1. The racialised identities of white and black America for which the pattern was set both by the system of racial slavery and the post-slavery order of white supremacy.

2. The ethnic identities of white European immigrants and Hispanic immigrants responding to specific demands for labour in industrialising urbanising America.
3. The genocidal treatment of native Americans, reduced to the margins of American society for much of recent history and now reemerging as a social and political force in their efforts to control their own destiny.

Ideologically and culturally, this has now produced a situation in which the white Anglo-European hegemony can no longer be taken for granted, challenged not only by organised African and native Americans, but also by a generalised politics of culture and ethnicity in which ethnic claims are advanced as a means of fighting for position in both collective and individual terms. There is no clearer evidence of this than in the reaction which it has produced, not only in reactionary – if coded – restatements of racialised privilege, but also in liberal anguish both over the 'threat' to individualism posed by collective claims and the challenge to 'European' culture posed by a culturally phrased ethnic politics (Schlesinger 1991).

Summary

Although ethnic groups cannot be understood wholly as classes or as fractions of classes, nonetheless the intersection of class and ethnicity is one of the keys to understanding ethnicity. The historical formation of ethnic groups is, in very many instances, class situated and this is especially true of those populations whose common heritage includes experience as migrant workers, both voluntary and coerced. Where there are concentrations of ethnic groups at specific points of the division of labour and in particular class locations then the identification of ethnic identity with occupation, work sector and class position is powerful. This is true of trader minorities such as the Chinese merchants of Jamaica, or Gujarati small businessmen in Britain, and of labouring minorities such as Africans enslaved in the Americas, or Indians as field workers in post-slavery colonies. The linking of class and occupational locations with specific ethnicities usually becomes attenuated as the successive generations of migrants' children enter diverse sectors of the economy. Class differentiation then becomes an element in the cultural differentiation within an ethnically defined population. In ethnically organized struggles, the fact of class differentiation will prompt allegations of ethnic disloyalty much in the way that social mobility among majorities prompts accusations of class disloyalty.

Class experience is crucial in shaping the experience of ethnic minorities and majorities and in forming the ethnic identity itself; shared class experience becomes part of a collective memory which contributes to the collective ethnic self-image. Similarly the class-based political concerns of both minorities and majorities influence the way in which ethnic groups view each other. This is illustrated in our account of the tension between class interests and racialised sentiments among the rural poor, black and white, in post-slavery America.

In our extended discussion of the class location of African Americans we showed that there have been critical changes at decisive historical junctures. The period of slavery, the post-slavery system of segregation and diminished citizenship, and the period of civil rights and some social mobility, showed how the USA has been a profoundly racialised social order. Wilson's thesis that 'race' has become less significant was criticised for implying that racial discrimination had diminished in its effects. But he was essentially right in showing that broad economic changes affected both white and black Americans adversely, even though, because of their historical situation, African Americans were more adversely affected than others. Where there are groups, socially defined as different within the ethnic formation of a society, who view other ethnic groups as threatening competitors, the defence of class interests becomes highly ethnicised. Ethnic closure of social mobility or labour market entry, as was the case with white exclusion of black workers from many market spheres, constitutes an ethnic tactic in a class contest. It is not so much that the defence of ethnic interests replaces the defence of class interests, rather that the defence of class interests takes an ethnic form, given the significance of the ethnic formation within society. It may equally be said that the defence of ethnic interests is class situated. This has provided a detailed case study of a post-slavery ethnicity; the next chapters will look at plural societies, at dispossessed indigenous peoples and at Western nation-states as further examples of the class structuring of ethnicity.

Chapter 5

Class Structures, Ethnic Formations: Malaysia, Hawai'i, Britain

This chapter examines the relationship of ethnicity to class structure in a colonial and post-colonial society, in a case of land dispossession and an indigenous people, and in European post-colonial coloniser societies. Malaysia, Hawai'i, and Britain are the principal case studies.

After slavery: 'coolie' labour, colonies and post-colonies

Slavery in the New World has been a principal site for the racialisation and ethnicisation of populations. In the middle and later 19th century slavery was in many instances replaced by other forms of coerced labour. Labour from India and China, brought to Fiji and Trinidad, and known as 'coolie' labour, was used in mass crop production such as sugar – in conditions similar to slavery in several respects, without the labourer being the property of the master. Indian labour was recruited into several British colonies, typically after the ending of the slave system. This was the case in Jamaica, Guyana, Trinidad and Mauritius, and in Fiji Indian workers were used in preference to indigenous Fijians whom the British administrators sought to 'conserve' outside the plantation economy (Scarr 1984).

   In Peru in 1862 there was a new interest in slave trading as Peruvian guano mining companies looked for a source of labour which they found by trawling the Pacific for Polynesian islanders who were seized and brought to work under conditions of slavery. Most died within months of arrival in Peru and the Guincha

Islands through lack of immunity to Western diseases, overwork and neglect; the dead were dug into pits in the guano mines and some of the nearly dead were thrown onto 'compost heaps' (Maude 1981).

In Hawai'i a sugar plantation economy was established after slavery had been abolished both in the British colonies and the USA. Labour was recruited from China, Japan, Korea, Portugal and the Philippines and a large number of smaller sources. In Malaysia, under the auspices of British colonial rule, Chinese workers were recruited into labouring in the tin mines and Indian workers onto the rubber estates and the railways. In the British African colonies of Uganda and Kenya and the island of Ceylon (now Sri Lanka), Indians were brought to work on plantations or on specific projects such as railway building.

These mass movements of labour were fundamental to the development of new economies in the colonised countries. Although workers sometimes moved on or returned to their former country, many of them, along with their descendants, gradually came to settle in their new country and to regard it as their home. Indigenous populations – Hawaiians in Hawai'i, Fijians in Fiji, Malays in Malaya – largely remained outside the modernising cash economies in which the imported workers laboured; for many years populations, defined by ethnic origin, lived in enclaves quite separate from each other.

The relationship with other ethnicities in the new country was crucial to the hardening of ethnic identities. This was especially so when the in-migrant workers or their children began to leave the plantations thus potentially bringing them into economic competition with the local population. Ethnic consciousness was intensified when former colonies became independent. Indigenous people were likely to regard the presence of incomers as unwonted and illegitimate. Competition for resources was marked by ethnic resentments. Similarly, competition in the political sphere acquired ethnic contours, as was evident in the early post-independence politics of Malaysia, Sri Lanka, Trinidad and Fiji (Ratnam 1965, Milne 1981, Eriksen 1992, Little 1994).

The way in which ethnic groups regarded one another was in part a consequence of the policies and practices pursued by the colonial power. The colonial rulers reinforced or even 'created' ethnic differentiation by treating populations as separate entities and selecting distinctive groups for specific occupations as in the military and the police.

Malaysia: ethnic formation, class structure

The case of Malaysia provides an excellent illustration of the intersection of class and ethnic categories and of the need to place understandings of ethnic phenomena within a context of class structure and process.

The Malaysian population in 1995 numbered 20.69 million and can be viewed as comprising three principal ethnic groups: the Malays (55 per cent), the Chinese (30 per cent) and the Indians (9 per cent). There are also non-Malay indigenous groups (6 per cent) in the sparsely populated East Malaysia or North Borneo (Malaysia: Seventh Malaysia Plan 1996–2000). The Malays' long-established settlement of the region ensures that they unequivocally regard themselves as the 'natural' indigenous people of the country although they do not deny this status also to the small number of non-Malay indigenes. There is internal differentiation within these three major groups – for example between Tamils and other Indians among the Indian population, or in religious terms between Hindu and Muslim Indians. But the compelling fact of the social and political construction of ethnic identities in Malaysia is that these three major groupings – Malay, Chinese and Indian – supersede other categorisations in importance. The Malays historically consider themselves 'the people' of the region, political parties were formed as ethnic (described as 'communal') blocs, and there are clear regional concentrations by ethnic groups.

The identification of ethnic groups with classes in Malaysian society is a long way from being 'perfect' – by comparison with our example of slavery and African origin in the United States. There is ethnic differentiation within classes and class differentiation within ethnic groups. Among Malays in the colonial period there was a fundamental class distinction between the mass of Malay peasant producers who lived in the Malay villages (*kampong*) and the Malay upper-class, the Sultans and chiefs who formed the conduit through whom the British exercised 'indirect rule'. The Sultans had no final effective political power but had control of the governance of all affairs affecting Islam and Malay custom (Husin Ali 1991).

As the British colonial system progressed, a small but growing number of Malays were recruited into lower middle-class clerical and service occupations mostly connected to colonial administration. But at the point of independence (1957) very few Malays counted among businessmen and entrepreneurs, either of the *grande bourgeoisie* (big business) type or of the *petit bourgeois*, small business and traders. Indeed very few Malays were in any kind of urban occupation and there was virtually no Malay 'industrial working class'.

By contrast, many Chinese and Indians were largely identified, in the colonial period and at the point of independence, with the two economic sectors for which they had originally been imported as labourers – tin mining and rubber production. The Chinese also formed a substantial part of the commercial and capitalist class in Malaysia and the largest part of the local bourgeoisie. Indians too had diversified into business and trading sectors and a small proportion had also moved into professional occupations such as the law and medicine. In short the Chinese, and to a lesser degree the Indians, had entered what is often referred to in Malaysia as the 'modern sector', including urban professional and business activities.

The links between migration, ethnicity and business enterprise have been reproduced in many historical cases. Jomo's account of how in-migrants became involved in business, while few indigenous Malays did, could be replicated beyond Malaysia in many other instances:

> The ethnicity of many ostensibly Malay businessmen can usually be traced to Arabs, Indians and those who are now termed 'Indonesians'. Chinese specialisation in certain economic and occupational roles often involved sub-ethnic specialisation as well, that is following dialect group or kinship lines. This suggests that the organisation of capital in the frontier economy relied greatly on kinship and other similar relationships. Having secured niches in the colonial economy, the reproduction of these class and occupational roles tended to preserve the sub-ethnic, and therefore the ethnic patterns of specialisation as well... By contrast the Malay upper class and peasantry had fewer opportunities or motives for entering entrepreneurial activities. (Jomo 1988, p. 245)

These economic and occupational concentrations are linked to the geographic concentrations of ethnic groups in Malaysia, with Chinese concentrated in west coast urban areas and Malays in rural *padi*-producing zones, especially along the east coast of the peninsula.

At the time of independence by far the great majority of Malays were agricultural peasant producers, isolated geographically in the *kampong*, the Malay villages, and with only partly developed political consciousness.

Table 5.1	Employment in Malaysia, 1995		
	Bumiputera	*Chinese*	*Indian*
Percentage of all employed	52.4	30.3	8.4
Percentage of all employed in agriculture	62.1	12.3	6.4
Percentage of all employed as doctors	33.4	32.1	32.0

Source: Seventh Malaysia Plan Table 3.2 and 3.4 (adapted)

Significant changes in the class structure, and the ethnic dimensions of the class structure, in Malaysia, have taken place over the decades since independence. The most significant of these has been the enlarging of the middle class of teachers, civil servants, administrators, university academics and related professional and semi-professional occupations, and the enlarging of the urban working class, particularly in new manufacturing industries. The ethnic dimension of this class structural change is that, in entry to both these modern occupations, Malays have been favoured as a calculated instrument of state policy (Lim 1985). At the same time Malays have begun to form a section of the capital-owning class. This was again encouraged by a state policy which viewed the concentration of Malays in the 'traditional' sector as actually and potentially a serious political problem. The class differentiation among Malays has in this period altered significantly so that it now incorporates not just a traditional elite and a peasantry – the Sultans and the villagers – but also a *grande* and *petite bourgeoisie*, an administrative and political class and an urban working class.

Some Chinese settlers in Malaya entered into agricultural and small trading economies alongside the Malays and there remains a minority of Chinese who are assimilated to Malaysian rural life. But the greater number of Chinese in Malaysia remained in or near the tin mining areas to which they were originally recruited, the business and commercial sectors which they successfully entered, and the urban production employment of which they still form the greatest part. Thus all three major ethnic groups in Malaysia can be described as class differentiated, despite a historical and in some respects continuing set of class–ethnic identifications: the Malays with the peasantry, the Chinese with tin mining, with business and commerce and with factory work, and the Indians with rubber tapping, lower grades of administration, and the professions, notably medicine (see Table 5.1).

When Malay peasants came into contact with Chinese (other than as co-agriculturalists) it was in specific economic relations, that is with Chinese as traders, as money lenders, and other commercial relations in which the poorer Malay peasant stood in a disadvantageous relationship to the Chinese. Jomo, commenting on the early attempts to foster a Malay business class, observes this commercial nexus between Malays and Chinese:

> The disappointing results of the early efforts to create a class of Malay capitalists frustrated the few existing capitalists as well as those with such class aspirations. Their frustrations were, understandably, directed primarily at their competitors among the already entrenched bourgeoisie, typically identified with the Chinese bourgeoisie. Also, since it was mainly Chinese businessmen who occupied those less-monopolised positions in the economy to which a newly emerging bourgeoisie could aspire, frustrations stemming from inter-capitalist rivalry were increasingly expressed in ethnic terms. Furthermore they were often also the capitalists who dealt directly with the Malay masses, especially in commerce and credit, that is, the sphere of circulation, and hence were a convenient target for the mobilising of popular resentment. That this Chinese bourgeoisie did not actually dominate the economy was therefore quite irrelevant to Malay bourgeois aspirations. (Jomo 1988)

Jomo goes on to say that 'given such a strong identification of ethnicity, or "race", with classes or class fractions, the most convenient ideological banner with which to mount a political and economic challenge was obviously ethnic'.

When in the 1969 elections Chinese-supported parties made electoral gains, the subsequent celebrations in the capital city ended in ethnic riots (see Chapter 6). One result of these disturbances was to strengthen the ideological case for Malay preference in Malaysian social and economic policies. This was predicated on the argument that the underlying cause of intercommunal violence and tension was the relative economic disadvantage of Malays and their non-participation in the modern and modernising sector. Translated into class terms, this meant that the great majority of Malays were poor rural peasants, and few Malays were engaged in the urban capitalist industrial and commercial sector, either as wage workers or as businessmen. The New Economic Policy therefore was enunciated with two principal aims: the elimination of poverty and the ending of the identifying of economic function with ethnicity. An ethnic problem was seen to have a class solution, especially the concerted and planned creation of a Malay middle class and business class. Without this incorporation, Malays would continue to see themselves as the losers in their own country an outcome which would be contrary to their view of the independence settlement. As one Malay writer phrased his view of the constitution:

> The entire compromise clearly indicates non-Malay acceptance of the historical fact that Malaysia was a Malay and Muslim country. (Nawawi 1990)

Despite the fact that all ethnic populations in Malaysia are class differentiated, Malays have long identified the Chinese with business and wealth. This is partly because the Chinese bourgeoisie is visible, by contrast with the low profile of foreign capital, and partly because Malay peasants and city dwellers have direct dealings with Chinese businessmen, who became 'in commerce and credit, a convenient target for the mobilising of popular resentment' (Jomo 1998).

The Malaysian state has since 1969 had a relatively clear aim – the creation of a successful capitalist economy in Malaysia and the avoidance of major ethnic (communal) violence and unrest. The two are intimately related not least because Malaysia has set its sights on attracting foreign and international capital. The appearance of severe social unrest and political instability is everywhere a deterrent to capital investment, given the risk of production breakdowns or the costs of security. At the same time the Malaysian government must make Malaysia attractive to foreign investors as a place relatively free of labour unrest, irrespective of the ethnic origins of workers. Restraints on political organisations and on freedom of debate are orientated both to the management of ethnic divisions and to control or suppression of class politics and labour union strength. Husin Ali (1991) speaks of greater control of class than of ethnic politics:

> Under the present circumstances it appears that the ethnic pull is much stronger. In Malaysian politics ethnically based political parties are relatively free and vocal in expressing racial policies or ideology, whereas the life of those espousing class ideology is made very difficult; in fact they can and have been restricted or proscribed.

Although ethnic politics may mask popular resentment about inequalities in general, the theory that ethnicity subverts class politics has to be qualified. In Malaysia ethnic divisions *per se* also pose a serious threat; the political economy of ethnicity and class in Malaysia is a balancing act. The government can afford neither a class revolt (such as South Korean workers staged against their job insecurities in 1997) nor ethnic riots. Peasant poverty may be represented as 'Malay poverty' and business wealth as 'Chinese wealth', but no one can afford an ethnic war.

More than one in five of all Bumiputera (mostly Malays) are employed in agriculture, compared to, say, Indians for whom it is less than one in sixteen. However much the government is determined to help the Malays, there is no obvious solution to peasant poverty. On the one hand, this is a result of the fact that economic policy in Malaysia is largely directed towards development of the capitalist modern sector which entails a combination of securing foreign investment with state-managed domestic capitalism. On the other hand, peasant poverty persists because state governments cannot simply manage an economy which is dependent on world commodity prices. Rice for domestic markets may be price supported or subsidised but not rice or other commodities on international markets. Much rural poverty or economic survival depends on the fluctuation of world rubber prices, themselves subject to demand in Western markets for cars and sporting goods.

The political will to eradicate rural poverty is weakened by the class configuration of the Malay ethnic population. The Malay state-promoted businessmen share political power with an older elite class of Malay landowners. Land reforms which would benefit Malay peasants will not recommend themselves to those whose land could be divided up. There have been some modest successes in tackling rural poverty by new rural land clearance schemes and assistance to Malay rural poor in starting new enterprises. But a high proportion of Malaysia's peasant class live in poverty or close to it and remain subject to external market fluctuations, as do rural producers globally. Most of Malaysia's poor are rural and up to half of the peasantry live in poverty (Jesudason 1989). In 1995 mean monthly household income for all Malaysia was 2,007 RM; for Bumiputera it was 1,600 RM, for Chinese 2,895 RM and for Indians 2,153 RM (Malaysia: Seventh Malaysia Plan, Table 3.6).

The success of the post-independence Malaysian state is not in solving the problem of rural poverty but in creating the conditions for revolutionary capitalist progress in the modern sector. Manufacture – for example of cars and electronic goods under the aegis of Japanese investment – has joined oil and primary commodities (tin, rubber, palm oil) and traditional agriculture in the widening scope of the Malaysian economy. The Prime Minister has set out his '2020 vision' of Malaysia as the site of the MSC – the Media Super Corridor – a major player in the global economy (Jeshurun 1993). In ethnic terms the success has been in avoiding major ethnic cleavage – by contrast for example with Sri Lanka – and in promoting the Malays into political and business middle- and upper-class positions. Especially at the elite level above all in Malaysia, Malays and Chinese (and others) need each other – it is a multi-ethnic elite:

> Malays and Chinese comprise a small elite circle [who] are interlinked politically [in the government and the National Front], economically in joint ventures, and socially in club memberships. (Husin Ali 1991, p. 105)

Ethnic integration is class specific. Among factory workers some attempts at cross-ethnic collective action are successful but trade unionism is restrained both by communalism and by general curbs on their powers and activities (Ackerman 1986, Khan and Loh Kok Wah 1992, Boulanger 1996).

The entry of Malays into urban and manufacturing economies as wage labour may in the longer run foster a class and labour union politics which is non-communal; in the short and medium term ethnicity or 'communalism' continue to predominate. This type of intersection of class and ethnicity is closely related to the politics of culture and ethnicity in Malaysia. The support for a more 'funda-mentalist' Islam is, for example, more evident in specific class groupings – among the rural poor and some sections of the Malay urban middle class (Khan 1998, Schmidt *et al.* 1998).

We shall return to these questions of culture and politics in Chapters 6 and 7. In the remainder of this chapter we examine examples of two other characteristic ethnic-making contexts – the dispossession of indigenous peoples and the formation of urban minorities in Europe.

Hawai'i: indigenous dispossession

The islands of Hawai'i were first populated in the period around the 3rd to the 5th centuries AD by people migrating from the South Pacific islands now known as the Marqesas Islands (Oliver 1975). These were Polynesian peoples who shared cultural similarities with other peoples of the South Pacific, people who now live in Tahiti, the Marqesas Islands, New Zealand (Maori) and other islands to which the ocean-going Polynesians travelled and settled. The population of the Hawaiian islands grew steadily through the ensuing centuries with some continuing traffic between Hawai'i and their islands of origin. The estimates of the population of Hawai'i by the end of the 18th century have varied. For some time there was general agreement around a figure of some 400,000 based partly on Captain Cook's estimates when his ships first came upon the islands. More recent commentators have suggested that these were underestimates and point to a figure of up to 1 million, part of a general reestimation of the pre-European contact populations of the Americas and the Pacific (Stannard 1989, 1992). The effect of the new estimates is twofold: it suggests a great vigour and success of the societies in the pre-European contact lands, and puts a higher estimate on the magnitude of the social and physical devastation caused by the advent of Europeans.

There was no immediate intent on the part of the English sea-captain James Cook to colonise the islands but the reasons for his and other adventures were intimately connected to European expansion and domination. The voyagers sought new sea routes which would give their sponsors an advantage in international trade and commerce, and some looked, for example, for plants which would provide cheap food for slave economies. Hawai'i was not immediately colonised partly because of its isolated position and potential colonisers did not see the advantages which might accrue from such a venture. But the advent of European-introduced firearms to the islands accelerated the process of consolidation of the islands – spread from east to west over several hundred miles – under a single rule, guided by the first King of the Hawaiian kingdom, Kamehameha the First. A formally sovereign independent Hawaiian kingdom survived until 1893 when the annexationist party overthrew the last monarch, Queen Liliuokalani, by force of arms. Although the Federal US government did not immediately agree to the proposed annexation, by the end of the century the islands had become an annexed territory of the USA which they remained until 1960 when Hawai'i became the fiftieth state of the USA.

The illegal overthrow of Queen Liliuokalani's government (Loomis 1976), and the fact that the 1959 advent of Hawai'i as an American state did not consult the native Hawaiian people to seek their consent, form the basis of present claims concerning the illegitimacy of the American regime and for claims about dispossession of lands. A large proportion of land ownership and use in the islands is now politically and legally contested, especially those lands which were ceded to the Federal government at the time of the illegal overthrow, and ceded back to the state of Hawai'i in 1960. It is also apparent that large portions of land designated under the Homelands Act passed during the territorial period have not benefited Hawaiians in the way the legislation intended (Buck 1993).

The present population of the islands is about 1.2 million, about 20 per cent of whom can claim some Hawaiian ancestry and can make a claim to all those lands appropriated from the people of the islands. Tens of thousands of others of Hawaiian descent live in other states of the USA (Barringer *et al.* 1995). The recent history of Hawai'i is part of a pattern of European and American colonialist expansion, imperial rule and economic exploitation, but it also differs from other cases in important respects. The early European disinterest in colonisation permitted a period of change which was managed and directed by the sovereign kingdom. But even then – in the first half of the 19th century – the economic impact of European contact was very considerable.

First, a trade in sandalwood denuded the islands of the tree and irretrievably disrupted the economy and ecology of the land. Then, the use of Honolulu and Lahaina as ports of call integral to the international whaling trade compounded the destruction of traditional taro growing and fishing economies and their concomitant ways of life. The destruction of a civilisation resulted from the combined effects of the introduction of diseases, of economic intrusion, political disruption, and of cultural demoralisation in the wake of Christian missionary activity. A population which may have neared a million in the latter part of the 18th century was little more than 30,000 by the end of the 19th century. This is a story of devastation that is replicated right across the Americas and the Pacific.

Throughout the 19th century, although the Hawaiian government survived, it was under ever-mounting pressure from American economic interests in the islands and the steadily growing realisation of the military strategic value of Hawai'i. Hawaiian monarchs might wish to preserve their own autonomy and the best interests of their people but American military threat, usually signalled by the stationing of military vessels just off the islands, undermined the freedom of action of the home government. By the middle of the century the government found itself compelled to permit sale and purchase of land in a system of Western property ownership and control which was alien to the people and the customary way of life.

Although early in the 1830s there had been experiments in plantation economies, by the 1860s the sale and lease of land had
prompted further land speculation and the 1871 Treaty of
Reciprocity with the USA made possible the subsequent widespread
expansion of sugar plantations. The Treaty allowed for the entry of
Hawaiian sugar tariff free into the USA and later permitted 'in
exchange' American use of Pearl Harbour whose strategic importance was now recognised.

Although in the 1870s and 80s a certain compromise between the
kingdom's interests and those of planters and other trading interests
permitted a period of relative stability – best represented in the reign
of King David Kalakaua – the last Queen's attempts to preserve
some autonomy in the Kingdom prompted the planters and their
allies to plot the overthrow (Liliuokalani 1964). By then sugar plantations were spread through the islands largely worked on by
migrant labour imported from Asia (Lind 1938).

The early 19th-century co-existence, with some intermarriage
(Adams 1937) of white European and American incomers and
Hawaiians, followed by the importation of several hundred thousand 'Asian' plantation workers (Lind 1938, Kent 1993), many of
whose descendants remained in the islands, laid the foundations of
the present ethnic demography of Hawai'i. In a 1990 population of
just over a million, whites, principally American 'mainlanders', are
a minority but at over 30 per cent form the largest single ethnic
population. Those of Japanese descent (25 per cent) form the next
largest group, among whom, until recently, out-marriage has been
relatively uncommon. Few Hawaiians of 'unmixed' descent survive
but the Hawaiian ancestry population has grown steadily in the
present century, most of this population being of mixed ancestry
following intermarriage with white Americans, Chinese, Filipino,
Portuguese, and others (Hormann and Lind 1996).

In 18th-century Hawaiian society the primary class distinction
was between *ali'i* and *kama'aina*, the nobility and the common
people who owed allegiance to them and bore tribute to them in the
form of labour, produce or service. Rules governing relations
between chiefs and commoners, and between men and women,
were guided by *kapu*, a system of prohibitions enforced by severe
punishments. Care of the land centred upon the production in irri-
gated fields of the taro plant which was the basis of *poi* making, a
staple food along with fish. The surviving signs of ancient Hawaiian
culture are to be found in (for example) what remains of *heiau*
(temples), burial sites, petroglyphs, some part-excavated village

settlements, and, in non-material culture, the chants, legends, the hula, and a vast accumulation of knowledge about the ocean, fishing, canoe construction, and health and spiritual welfare (Handy *et al*. 1981).

The effect of European diseases introduced after 1778 was, as mentioned, severe and widespread. But the effect of European trading contact was similarly damaging to the indigenous society and economy. The foreign traders dealt with *ali'i* in order to gain access to land and acquire sandalwood. The fragrant trees were collected by *kama'aina* and delivered to traders who paid the *ali'i*, but the latters' lack of knowledge of trade meant that they were prey to disadvantageous deals and tempted by payment in kind with worldly goods previously unknown to the islanders. This process, followed later by the whaling trade, undermined the island social order and the relationships between chiefs and common folk. By the time the missionaries arrived in 1820, and began to tell anyone who would listen that Hawai'i was a debauched and immoral civilisation, the processes of demoralisation, depopulation and consequent neglect of agriculture were evident.

Some individuals and families among the *ali'i* class of Hawaiians formed liaisons with and intermarried with white Europeans and Americans who came to the islands as traders, missionaries, or as naval officers and men. As some incomers provided valuable services to the Hawaiian chiefs and the kingdom – in several instances serving as ministers providing valuable knowledge about America and beyond (Daws 1968, de Varigny 1981) – there was formed an upper class composed of ruling Hawaiians, incomer Europeans and Americans, and intermarried families which created links between both groups. The incomers needed the co-operation of the Hawaiian nobility because the latter was the formal government whose actions mattered, and could provide access to land. Romanzo Adams (1934), the distinguished first professor of Sociology at the University of Hawai'i, argued that this legitimisation of 'inter-racial' marriages at the upper-class level created a different ethos and doctrine of 'race' in Hawai'i compared to otherwise similar places. The part-Hawaiian-part-*haole* fraction of Hawaiian society was both class and ethnically defined. It was prominent in the ruling elite of the kingdom, and it was a mixed ancestry group which created a new ethnicity, the *hapahaole*, in upper class Hawai'i.

In the Grand Mahele of 1848–50 (Chinen 1958, Kame'eleihiwa 1992), an act which parcelled out land among the crown, government, nobility and common people, the share allocated to *kama'aina* was tiny and the general debilitation of the population was one reason why most made little progress in registering claims for land titles. Some *ali'i* sold or leased their land and a market in property was one of the changes which facilitated the foundation of a plantation economy. Crown and government lands were, as we indicated earlier, lost in the illegal overthrow of 1893 and the subsequent annexation of Hawai'i and its admission as a state in 1959. Some of the people who were successful in holding on to their land, adding to it and becoming more wealthy than ever in this period – the latter half of the 19th century – were precisely members of the *hapahaole* ethnic class grouping which we have described.

The Hawaiian people, with some access to land and sea as a basis of subsistence, weakened by disease and falling in numbers, were not in a position to fill the need for labour in the new plantation economy. So while Hawaiians remained marginalised both socially and geographically in the islands, the plantation became the centrepiece of the Hawaiian economy. This created another system of class relations – and of ethnicity. The plantation economy grew rapidly through the 1870s, a decade after the abolition of slavery in the USA. In much the same way as Caribbean plantations imported Indian labour, and later Fiji built a sugar industry on the backs of Indian labour, so the Hawaiian sugar economy depended on imported Asian labour. The first migrant workers were from China, the second group from Japan and after both these sources ended, Filipino labour made up the largest single group.

The sugar and later pineapple planters always sought to benefit from ethnic division in the labour force. Different immigrant groups worked on specific plantations and were housed together in simple dwellings at the place of work (Takaki 1984, Beechert 1985). Lind has described how in-migrant workers became racialised by the circumstances of plantation life – the 'plantation as race-maker' in his vivid phrase:

> Beginning with Chinese in 1852 and continuing later for nearly a century, plantations brought in varying numbers of Portuguese, South Sea Islanders, Japanese, Germans, Norwegians, Koreans, Puerto Ricans, Russians, Spaniards, and Filipinos. Each was imported primarily to provide part of the essential supply of docile unskilled labour, and, under the segregative system of labour control then in force, each group came to be recognised as a separate and distinctive – but clearly subordinated – race... Part of plantation strategy in securing effective control over their

workers, was to place them in work crews and segregated communities or 'camps' of those with similar ethnic backgrounds. (Lind 1996)

Organisations of workers were largely – until the 1930s – ethnically based, thus precluding pan-labour force organisation and encouraging ethnic rivalry; different groups were paid different rates of pay depending on rates negotiated at the point of entry. As tens of thousands of workers came into Hawai'i the planters had an interest in finding diverse sources of labour – newer groups were more easily controlled and also cheaper. Thus the planters and their representatives developed successive ethnic stereotypes. As Chinese workers became settled they came to be viewed as less docile than the Japanese who came later; and so with later groups. Diversifications within groups, as well as different sources of labour, were seen as beneficial to planters. When the earliest migrants came from China the plantation managers kept a careful eye on language and district of origin differences among the workforce. Both in recruiting and in using labour, diverse distinct groupings suited the employers. Thus Lind concludes, 'the plantations, in a very real sense, created most of Hawai'i's "races" by first introducing groups of peasants from widely separated and overpopulated areas of the world and endowing them with a distinct racial identity' (Lind 1996, p. 114).

Regimentation of daily work and control over the non-working hours of workers were common features of plantation life and Lind has described the regime as similar to slavery (Lind 1938). When ethnic-based unions protested in the 1920s repression was fierce, and when interethnic unionism developed in the 1930s force was used to suppress demonstrations. The most notorious case of suppression of a peaceful demonstration was police action – tear gassing, hosing and gunfire – mobilised against multi-ethnic unions in the Hilo Massacre of 1938 (Daws 1968, Beechert 1985, Puette 1988). The stark openness of class struggle and the disciplining of workers and their families was at its greatest in the 1880–1939 period, the heyday of Hawai'i as the 'sugar-coated fortress' – an economy dependent on plantation crop production and the growing importance of Hawai'i as a base for the US military.

In this same period we find the most open indications of racism and ethnic division. Racialised categories transcended ethnic identifications and the Asian workers and their descendants were portrayed as a 'Yellow Peril', dangerous and threatening to 'American civilisation', inherently incapable of advancement, or of being assimilated in what was increasingly an American society. As were Indians and Chinese in Malaysia, the Japanese in Hawai'i were viewed as owing first allegiance to their home country, in their case to the emperor of Japan; cultural difference was construed as political threat and alien danger.

The fact that Hawaiian society was most openly racialised in the period of plantation dominance adds weight to the argument that plantation systems are 'race-makers' and provides evidence of the collusion of racialisation with class relations and the disciplining of labour. Hawaii in the 1930s was also a highly militarised society with over 10 per cent of the population military personnel. Many military men were southern Americans; and whatever region they came from, they had been raised in a pre-war USA which was a segregated society still openly predicated on ideas of racial inferiority and superiority. Some of these racist attitudes were directed towards Japanese workers and their families. This manifested itself in the disciplining of plantation labour as we suggested; but it was also seen in another typical class context of ethnicity – competition in trade and in labour markets. When Chinese and later Japanese plantation workers left the plantations, they sought work in the urban centres in trades, labouring and services. Where this brought them into competition with *haoles* and Hawaiians – for example in small building works, repair work, laundries, restaurants – the grounds were set for anti- 'Asian' sentiments.

In some instances these sentiments were specifically anti-Japanese, who as an ethnic population, and the largest group in the islands, were especially likely to be suspected of disloyalty. This was partly because of the generalised influence of 'Yellow Peril' thinking, and partly because the older generation still retained traditions and symbols of Japanese attachment – in dress, religious worship, custom, speech, and respect for their emperor – so as to give superficial plausibility to the prejudice that they were 'un-American'. Anti-Japanese feeling reached its height in 1929 when a young Japanese-ancestry boy kidnapped and later killed a young white schoolboy (Daws 1968, Lind 1996).

But in other instances the sentiments expressed by the white American elite minority in Hawai'i, in this period effectively a colonial dominant class, elided Hawaiians with Chinese and Japanese and all other so-called 'alien' groups. This was evident in the Massie Case in which the wife of an American officer in the US Navy stationed in Hawai'i claimed to have been raped by local native men. In the climate of hate and hysteria which followed the case on the mainland, white women were portrayed as constantly in danger of attack by savage native men (Daws 1968, Lind 1996). There was no foundation to her claim but her mother subsequently had a defendant shot and killed in an effort to extract a false confession from him. When the mother was charged with the unlawful killing of the Hawaiian defendant, and found guilty, she was sentenced to one hour's detention – served, with drinks, in the governor's office (Daws 1968). These events of the early 1930s show that Hawai'i, as a colonial society in which power resided in white (*haole*) business, military and political circles, constructed a racialised view of the many ethnic populations in the islands, sometimes including the native Hawaiians in a general category which covered non-white, as being alien, dangerous and culturally and constitutionally inferior.

The Hawaiians were largely – although not entirely – absent from the plantation economy. But they also – like the Malays by contrast with Chinese and Indians – did less well in the 'urban' sector trades and services to which former plantation workers and their children gravitated increasingly in the 20th century. A portion of the *hapa-haole* class retained a certain status in Hawaiian society, and other Hawaiians entered public service occupations such as the police force and fire services. Yet others left the islands for California and other states (Barringer 1995). But the majority, as a dispossessed people whose ancient culture had been mocked, devalued or trivialised (Obeyesekere 1992, Buck 1993, Trask 1993), and whose rural subsistence provided only a meagre living, remained economically and socially marginalised. As Maori in New Zealand and aboriginal peoples in Australia, the Hawaiians were expected by many to diminish to disappearing point and they were at best the object of patronising welfare. The Hawaiian Homelands Act of 1920 provided for small parcels of land to be made available to native Hawaiians but benefited very few.

In the 1990s the pattern of marked relative disadvantage persists. This does not mean that all those of Hawaiian ancestry are poor in health, welfare and income, but it does mean that native Hawaiian share of disadvantage is disproportionate. In the 1990 census, of those families classed by the census as Native Hawaiian 18 per cent had family incomes less than $15,000 compared with just over 10 per cent of the whole population. The average family income for native Hawaiians was nearly $9,000 below the average family income for the State of Hawai'i and Hawaiians were overrepresented in low-pay labouring occupations (US Bureau of the Census, 1993). Percentage enrolment in the University of Hawai'i system is below their representation in the population, but has been growing through the 1990s. On several health indicators native Hawaiian health compares unfavourably with the population as a whole. In the 36–65 age group the rate of hypertension is 197.2 per thousand population compared to 130.3 in the wider population (US Bureau of the Census 1993). These kinds of patterns of relative disadvantage, sometimes much more acute, are to be found replicated among Native American Indian peoples in Canada and the USA, among Maori in New Zealand, and dispossessed indigenous peoples in many countries. It is almost always accompanied by higher rates of imprisonment and in dramatic cases, brutal treatment and death in the prison system (Hazlehurst and Hazlehurst 1989).

The pattern of cultural demoralisation has, however, been transformed from one of near desolation to one of revival and celebration. This political and cultural effervescence is found in all the contexts of dispossession which we have mentioned and to which we shall return in the discussion of the politics of ethnicity.

Britain and Europe: post-colonial migrants to the metropolitan centres

The European societies – and we shall look primarily at Britain – became post-colonial in a rather different sense. From the end of the Second World War they largely divested themselves of their colonial possessions and by the 1950s and 60s had begun to receive growing numbers of in-migrants from the societies which were or had been their colonies. In many instances – in the case of Jamaica for example – these included the descendants of enslaved labour. Britain, France and Portugal were post-colonial and post-slavery societies but in a significantly different way from Brazil and the USA – their slave-holding possessions had all been at some considerable distance from 'home'. They therefore had some, but very few, descendants of enslaved populations within the home society. But debates about slavery and, subsequently, a social and political consciousness of empire endowed all these societies with a colonial mentality which shaped their views of later migrants from their colonies (Kiernan 1969, Rich 1986).

Although in small numbers, Africans and Indians had come to Britain long before the tens of thousands who came in the 1960s and thereafter. Probably the first Africans to come to Britain were soldiers in the Roman Imperial Army (Walvin 1973, Shyllon 1977). Later travellers to Britain were often of high social status: African princes and scholars visited Britain in the 18th and 19th centuries and the Hawaiian royal family of the later 19th century were acquainted with the British royal family. Their summer palaces in Hawai'i now display gifts sent to them by Queen Victoria or her relatives.

Others coming to Britain were in service positions and in the 18th century black African young men were fashionable as servants in the homes of the wealthy; paintings of the period often show an elaborately dressed African boy-servant in a domestic scene (Walvin 1973, Dabydeen 1985). Africans and Indians also came to Britain as sailors and traders, and port towns, such as London, Glasgow, Bristol, Cardiff and Liverpool, in the early 19th century developed small black populations some of which persisted into the 20th century. Relations between these populations and the white indigenous population were varied, historians citing instances both of hostility and solidarity (Walvin 1973, Shyllon 1977).

In the latter part of the 19th century racial attitudes became notably harsher and these attitudes were closely associated with class, status and power (Lorimer 1978). These were linked to class attitudes in that the portrayal of (particularly) black people as constitutionally weaker, as suited to menial labouring, and as potentially threatening and dangerous, were similar in tone to the views which middle and upper classes in Britain took of the urban proletarians. Irish workers in English cities were viewed in much the same way (Miles 1993). Ideologies of class and ideologies of race have frequently been either parallel or linked, portraying one class of people as suited to inferior tasks, as constitutionally inferior, and as posing a danger and threat to ordered society.

Theories of white Aryan superiority and the societies promoting ethnological or anthropological studies of racial difference flourished among the status seekers of the new middle classes (Lorimer 1978). A view of 'natives' as dangerous was stimulated by the periodic order crises of imperial rule: the Morant Bay Uprising in Jamaica and its suppression illustrated how imperial rule was ultimately sustained by superior force of arms. Imperial wars and the suppression of uprisings in the latter half of the 19th and much of the 20th centuries, provided occasions for the reiteration of the theme of 'white civilisation' as well as for popularising jingoistic patriotism and empire (Rich 1986).

Throughout this period of the last two centuries Britain had received large numbers of in-migrants from Ireland and continental Europe. In Victorian Britain and the first decade of the 20th century both Irish and Jewish in-migrants were targets of hostility to incomers (Foot 1965, Holmes 1988). Irish were treated with disdain and portrayed as 'animals' in a way that later non-white in-migrants were to experience and socialist writers Marx and Engels spoke of the Irish as part of the 'ethnic trash' of English cities. The Irish worked in service and labouring occupations, remitting money to their families and enduring the ethnic prejudice which, often as not, was anti-Catholic prejudice. The *Manchester Guardian* (4 July 1852) reported a violent attack on Irish people in Stockport in the north of England:

> We regret to have to record one of those disgraceful riots which exist only where the lower class Irish dwell in considerable numbers – arising out of the perpetual feuds between the Irish Catholics and lower class of English factory hands.

If the account is accurate the 'riot' was an assault on the Roman Catholic chapel by a gang of English workers who destroyed the iron altar rails with axes and sledgehammers, and:

> Proceeded up to the altar and tabernacle, and rapidly destroyed these; females it is said being as eager and active in the work of destruction as males.

In the subsequent fighting one died and others were seriously injured. In the campaign to enact aliens legislation, Jews were spoken of as the sewage of Europe emptying into Britain (Foot 1965) and other groups such as Lithuanian miners migrating to Scotland were described as threatening the health and good 'stock' of the native population (Holmes 1988).

In the period immediately after the Second World War the main populations entering Britain were peoples – Polish and Italian among them – displaced or made stateless and refugees by the war and they came in considerable numbers in the late 1940s and early 1950s. The Irish continued to constitute a major source of in-migration to Britain and in most years after the war they were the largest single source. All these in-migrants provided much needed labour in a labour scarcity situation which characterised the decade and a half from the end of the war. In response to the same labour shortages, by 1950 migrants from former colonies began to arrive in Britain. In the early years Jamaica was the largest single source and Jamaican men and women, and labour migrants from

Barbados and other Caribbean countries, were recruited to meet labour needs in transport and nursing (Lawrence 1974). By the later years of the 1950s workers from India and Pakistan began to arrive in larger numbers and eventually outstripped Caribbean arrivals and settlers both as new migrants and as a proportion of the total population.

Class and ethnicity: migration and urban minorities

The migration of labour on a world scale is not new – as previous examples have illustrated – but it is a growing and seemingly permanent feature of the modern global economy (Castles and Miller 1993). Those people from the Caribbean countries and from India and Pakistan who came to Britain in the 1950s, 60s and 70s were matched by people from the same countries migrating to the USA, Canada, Australia, New Zealand, Norway, and other countries; most came from countries, regions and even families with traditions of migration in search of income to remit to their home country and where they went was partly a product of the opportunities which presented themselves. People from the Caribbean had worked on the building of the Panama Canal and from India had worked on building railroads in Kenya and Uganda. Migrant labour is attractive to employers because it is commonly less expensive than indigenous labour since migrant workers are likely to be comparing their wages with meagre possibilities of income in their home country. The use of migrant labour is invariably a net saving to the immigrant-receiving country since they avoid the costs of social reproduction of workers and their families in accepting mature and sometimes skilled workers into the labour force. The less social rights incoming workers have, the more this is true.

Migrant workers may also be less likely to organise and protest about their working conditions if they are worried about their right to stay; they may be vulnerable to explicit and implicit threats from their employers and be more willing to do work which is dirty or dangerous and evades safety regulations.

Throughout Europe in the last four decades these characteristics of immigrant labour and class experience have been repeated (Castles and Cosack 1985) both with respect to workers from former colonies and to internal migrants within Europe (including Turkey), formerly from southern Europe, more recently from eastern Europe. By the 1990s all the more prosperous European countries had foreign-born populations from 3 per cent up to 8 per cent of the total (Yinger 1994) and with their children added in would roughly double those percentages.

Portugal has been for much of the post-war period (and before) one of the less economically prosperous zones of Europe and workers from Portugal migrated to other European countries, especially France and Germany. Since the revolution of 1974 and the ending of a long period of authoritarian rule, and the entry into the European Community in 1986, there has been greater social open-ness and economic progress in the country. Decolonisation was an important dimension of the creation of modern Portugal since the overthrow of Caetano's government was much spurred on by opposition to the prosecution of imperial wars in Portugal's African colonies.

Economic opportunities and the need for manual workers, especially in the building industries have meant that Portugal itself has become an immigrant-receiving society as workers from the Cap Verde islands seek work in Lisbon and its environs. In the 1990s Portugal had to face the question of racism within its own borders as two Cap Verdians were shot and killed in Lisbon (*Expresso* 1997). This was a particular shock for a country which has seen itself as part of the Brazilian (Brazil being a former Portuguese colony) pattern of acceptance of multi-ethnicity and intermarriage.

In Britain, the immediate class context of ethnicity and the new sources of migration of the 1950s, was of labour recruited into low-paid public sector work, transport and the National Health Service (Carter *et al.* 1987). The government offices which encouraged these labour flows expected them to form a pattern of 'work and return', and the great majority of men and women who came to Britain in the 1950s from the Caribbean themselves expected to return after five or so years (Lawrence 1974). In a period of labour shortage immigrant workers were largely doing work unsought by indigenous workers and so the labour market was not a primary site of conflict in the early years. Housing accommodation in a housing market where there were shortages in the post-war period, and dance halls as sites of social mixing were some of the most commonly reported areas of interethnic conflict. Visible colour difference played a key part in the perception of incomers by indigenes (see *The Times*, 'The Dark Million' 1965). Newcomers from the Caribbean and later India were defined primarily as 'coloured' and discussion of their presence in Britain was consistently phrased in colour terms, including in official documents – 'coloured immigrants', 'coloured workers', 'the colour bar', this was the phraseology by which people and relations with them were defined. The fact that immigration from Ireland remained large, and that immigration control was directed towards immigrants from the Commonwealth suggests that colour visibility and racialised categories informed post-war perceptions of the new migrations.

By the end of the 1950s the population categorised as 'coloured immigrants' was still numbered only in tens of thousands but as labour shortages gave way to some rise in unemployment a politics of immigration phrased largely in terms of colour began to play a significant part in domestic affairs. In power from 1951 to 1964, early cabinet meetings of the Conservative government began to discuss immigration control and the 'racial character of Britain' as potential election issues (Foot 1965, Sivanandan 1982, Layton Henry 1984, Miles and Phizacklea 1984, Carter *et al.* 1987).

Although the earliest discussions of multi-ethnic Britain were framed as discussions of 'integration', 'assimilation' and colour prejudice (Rose *et al.* 1969), a concern with class and class consciousness was also important. Black women from the Caribbean had been highly concentrated in hospital service and nursing occupations and men in transport services and unskilled and semi-skilled work in industry. The rather later migration of men from India and Pakistan – and from very specific locations within those two countries (Shaw 1988, Ballard 1994) – came to be concentrated in light and heavy industrial manufacture and, among Pakistanis particularly, in the declining textile industries of Lancashire and Yorkshire, in northern England.

In the late 1960s and early 1970s, they were joined by individuals and families of Indian ancestry who were expelled from East Africa, notably in the 1972 expulsion by President Idi Amin of Asians from Uganda. Many among this last migration were people who had seen relative prosperity as traders, small businessmen, shopkeepers, and professional workers, pursuits which they sought to re-establish in Britain despite barriers which they faced and despite the fact that many had lost all their assets in the process of becoming refugees. And despite racial discrimination and the widespread experience of racist abuse and violence (Virdee 1995) all of which conspired to confine 'non-white' migrants and their children in positions of social disadvantage, some of the foundations of class differentiation among the new urban minorities were being established.

The question of the intersection of class and ethnicity, especially with regard to the South Asian and Caribbean migrants and their children born in Britain, was addressed in a number of ways (Miles 1982). One possibility was to argue that the minority ethnic groups had simply joined the British working class. The great majority were in wage-paid labouring and service occupations; as bus drivers they worked with white bus drivers, as textile workers they stood alongside other textile workers, as nurses they worked alongside other nurses. Their incomes would contribute to determining where they lived and thus where their children went to school. In these ways they could be regarded as not only standing in a specific wage-labouring class position, but as sharing the class experience – and thus possibly the social and political sentiments – of the white working class.

A number of factors, however, make this understanding not so much wrong as incomplete and potentially misleading. In the transport sector for example black bus drivers and bus conductors experienced racial discrimination and hostility from white co-workers and in Bristol in the 1960s, outright opposition to their being employed as drivers (Dresser 1986). In the textile industry and other industries of a similar kind minority ethnic group workers were much more likely to work night shifts and unsocial hours and their incomes were typically lower than comparable white workers (Brown 1984). And in the hospital services, black Caribbean women were typically confined to lower grades of nursing and remained in low-paid shiftwork including hospital cleaning and as nursing auxiliaries (Carter 1997, Fenton 1988). These women commonly experienced cold unfriendliness or worse from fellow nurses and from patients, and were discriminated against in seeking promotions.

When the textile industry began to collapse in the 1970s and early 80s, as did other manufacturing industries in the Midlands, South Asian middle-aged men found themselves out of work with few prospects for new employment. When hospital and local government services – such as cleaning – were privatised in the 1980s, black Caribbean women and their white colleagues were often rehired on poorer pay and poorer conditions. As black Caribbean women who had migrated to Britain and taken up nursing jobs in the 1950s reached late middle age in the 1980s they frequently reported ill-health, disappointment with Britain, and a half-realistic dream of retiring to the Caribbean (Fenton 1988, Carter 1997). Many South Asian women worked in low-paid, arduous, insecure semi- and unskilled jobs which included airport cleaning, aircraft turnaround, motorway services, factory work, in photo processing, typewriter manufacture, hosiery, and the cloth trade generally where their employers were likely to be South Asians. In the steel industry in the Midlands, Indian men were employed in the work with the poorest conditions.

All these things taken together suggest that 'joining the British working class' hardly adequately describes the position and experience of black and Asian workers in Britain. They joined highly specific industries and services, concentrated in specific regions of the country – the South East, Midlands, Lancashire and Yorkshire, and Glasgow – and in these occupations typically held lower level positions, with poorer pay and conditions.

Gender was an important factor in influencing the work experience of people from the Caribbean and South Asia: low-paid nursing work for Caribbean women and poor-conditions service and manufacturing work for South Asian women. It was not sufficient to say that racial discrimination was simply superadded to the class experience of migrants and their families; nor to say for women that gender and racial discrimination were additional 'factors'. For many, ethnicity and gender were important constituent and defining elements of their work experience and of their broader class experience (Anthias and Yuval-Davis 1992).

The specificity as against commonalities of class experiences of whites and minorities bears upon the question of the class and political sentiments of minority populations. Minority workers in Britain showed solidarity with white workers in joining trade unions; in all sectors they are more likely than white workers to belong to trade unions and there has been no exploitation of black and Asian workers as strike breakers on the American model of the 1930s. Racialised sentiments in the labour unions have come from white trade unionists who have organised against the employment of black workers and conspired to prevent the promotion of those workers to supervisory positions On several notable occasions black and Asian workers have been forced to organise with little or no support from trade unions and at the national level the labour union movement has been slow to respond to questions of ethnic equality. One of the consequences is that although minority workers are trade unionists, they have only modest confidence in white-led unions and generally approve the idea of ethnic-specific sections within the unions (Modood *et al.* 1997). Similarly the majority of Caribbeans and South Asians have voted for the Labour Party in successive elections, but frequently with a sense that no major party responds to their concerns; many do not vote and minorities are disproportionately non-registered.

Sociologists have sought to capture this specificity of class position and class experience among minorities by referring to the special set of features of employment, working conditions, and concentrated sites and sectors of employment as constituting a subset of the working class, a 'class fraction' as Phizacklea and Miles (1980) have described the position. Throughout Europe, the correlation of migrant labour with dangerous work, shiftwork, insecure employment, and sector-specific work, combined with exploitation of their insecurities which stem from their migration/citizenship status as managed by the state in its control of immigration, confirm this portrayal of migrant workers as a specific segment within the working class. Phizacklea and Miles (1980) speak of black workers as constituting a '*racialised* class fraction' and Stuart Hall of 'race as the modality within which class is experienced' (Hall *et al.* 1978).

It is not just the external influence of racism and discrimination which influence work and class experience but 'internal' characteristics of ethnic populations. Cohesive family organisation is an asset in some forms of entrepreneurial activity – the Chinese catering business and South Asian shopkeepers are examples in Britain – and this ethnicisation of business is a worldwide phenomenon (Wallman 1979). A wider circle of ethnic allegiances may form the basis of business success in groups which have long-standing engagement in trade. Many African Asians in Britain have been able to re-establish businesses after losing all in the expulsion from Uganda. For those providing goods and services at a local level, a purchasing ethnic community with special tastes in food and dress constitutes a niche market.

Ethnic characteristics can also influence participation in the labour market and this is frequently gender specific. South Asian Muslim women in Britain have, over two decades, been recorded as low participants in employment outside the home, less than one in five being classed as employed in labour force surveys. Much domestic employment of the home-working type goes unrecorded and employment among Muslim women is gradually rising (Modood *et al.* 1997) but the generally lower participation reflects attitudes to family and the role of women (Modood *et al.* 1997).

By contrast Caribbean women in Britain have participated in the labour force more than any other ethnic population, partly reflecting their initial entry to Britain as single independent migrants, and partly reflecting established traditions of independence within the family of Caribbean women. Thus ethnicity as well as racism influences work and class experience (Anthias and

Yuval-Davis 1992). This should not be taken as a reading of fixed cultural attributes of ethnic groups. In all instances the established preferences and attitudes are significant and influential but all are equally subject to change. One important dimension of the cultures of urban minorities, especially where they have recently migrated from village societies and non-urban economies, is the set of cultural expectations surrounding the behaviour of men and women. But these can change quickly and neither in so-called 'traditional' societies, nor among minorities in modern urban societies, can these be seen as the simple reiteration of a pattern of the subordination of women.

These arguments sought to draw the theorisation of ethnicity and racism into the general orbit of a political economy of capitalism, a much wider ambition than simply accounting for the class position of minorities. Racialised class fractions were seen as performing a determinate function with capitalism, specifically in the unending search for cheap and exploitable replacement labour. Racism as a central dimension of political discourse was viewed as performing a specific ideological function, as appearing to answer the questions (for example about order, about unemployment) raised by crises in capitalist economies.

There remain difficulties in this approach which have become more evident as changes in the last decade or so have become more evident. The framework depends heavily on the notion of the vulnerability of migrant workers and particularly addresses populations in which the migrant generation preponderates. In this sense the sociology of ethnicity in this form is really a sociology of migrant labour, or of migration and racism. It reflects two common and virtually universal facts:

1. That capitalism on both a national and international scale demands fluidity of labour and finds in migrant labour an inexpensive and exploitable source.
2. That this is frequently accompanied by racist ideas, from indigenous populations and from the governments who have facilitated their entry.

But the theory says rather less about the voluntary characteristics of ethnic groups as against the involuntary dimensions of the experiences of racialised populations. It tends to assume that racism has its way in simultaneously suppressing minorities, in heartening sections of the majority, and providing the ideological solution for despairing and floundering ruling political parties. Some of these processes have not, in Britain, turned out in quite the way which prognostications of the 1980s and 90s predicted.

The class–racism argument as we have described it has always been uncomfortable with social mobility among minorities and has tended to focus on the persistence of disadvantage (Ballard 1992) and lower-class position among immigrants and their children. The existence of middle classes among racialised minorities does not invalidate theories of the persistence of disadvantage. In the USA, the emergence of a substantial and growing middle class among African Americans has to be taken side by side with the evidence of the persistence of enormously disproportionate disadvantage among America's black urban poor. But the evidence of growing class differentiation within and between ethnically defined populations in Britain runs counter to the implication of an inescapable racialised oppression.

The survey of Britain's ethnic minorities in the 1990s suggested that three broad categories could be established (Modood *et al.* 1997). The first group included Chinese and African Asians and was in several respects economically advantaged. The third group comprising largely Pakistanis and Bangladeshis had a greatly disproportionate share of economic disadvantage. The second group was intermediate, containing Caribbeans and Indians. In both of these there was evidence of middle-class status, improved income levels and higher occupational status, alongside evidence of the perpetuation of disadvantage and poverty. Similar studies confirm a pattern of social mobility among urban minorities in Britain (Iganski and Payne 1996) and these and other studies indicate a clear pattern of difference by gender and ethnicity. It is apparent, for example, that young British born women of Caribbean ancestry have experienced greater economic success and social mobility than young Caribbean men (Modood *et al.* 1997). The evidence suggests that, for future social mobility, class at entry may be decisive (Modood *et al.* 1997).

In America and Britain middle-class status grows among both ethnic minorities and majorities, at the same time that there is a hardening of social exclusion and underclass status among both majority and minorities. Changes in class and economic structure which are 'blind' to ethnicity, nonetheless affect minorities dispro-portionately (Srinivasan 1992). If supermarkets bankrupt the corner shop, they do so indiscriminately, but many minority entrepreneurs will be hit. Equally the success of young British black women depends on part on the opportunities which open up for young people generally and women in particular. It is possible that the greater economic mobility of young black women in Britain reflects the gender bonus in the feminisation of occupation structures. The conclusions about whether social exclusion is intensifying is not necessarily the same answer as that to the question of whether specific minorities are 'trapped' in disadvantage.

Summary

Just as plantation slavery created the context of racialised identities in the New World so did subsequent migrations establish ethnic groups in non-slave plantation work and in the recruitment of labour into metropolitan urban centres. Workers from India were recruited into plantation economies in the Caribbean, Malaysia and Fiji and from China to many of the same destinations. In the examples we have examined in this chapter, the Chinese and the Indians in Malaysia are descendants of workers recruited into mining and plantation economies; in Hawai'i, Chinese, Japanese and Filipinos were three of the largest recruited labour groups – the British as a colonial power refused the Hawaiian authorities permission to recruit Indians. The pattern of recruitment and the mode of employment of plantation labour in Hawai'i (that is in segregated groups) meant that the plantation was, in Lind's phrase a 'race-maker'. The colonial past, and its present effects carried forward in colonial mentalities, form the background to migrations from former colonies to former colonisers (Grosfoguel, 1997) – of, for example, Jamaicans to Britain. Migrant workers in Britain and Europe have filled typically low-paid and less-desired niches within the class and occupation structure; the futures of the daughters and sons of migrant families are shaped by their class experience and their experience of racism; they are shaped but not fixed.

Chapter 6

Politics and Ethnicity

Power is organised formally and informally and in public and private arenas. The most visible politics are found in constitutional forms, systems of governance, and public, legitimate party and pressure group mobilisation. These are the types of politics with which we are primarily concerned in this and the subsequent chapter. We will be especially concerned with the way in which states give substance to ethnic categories, to the way in which the public conduct of political affairs is expressed in a language of ethnicity, and to the way in which groups organise and advance their interests under a banner of ethnic identity. That is to say we are concerned with:

● the state and ethnic groups
● the politics of culture and ethnic ideologies
● ethnic group mobilisation.

This is not an exhaustive list of the forms which the politics of ethnicity may take. In emphasising the politics of culture we are giving less attention to the analysis of electoral politics, although studies of this kind have contributed a great deal to the understanding of contemporary ethnicities (Husbands 1991b). In democratic political systems the ethnic arithmetic of electoral politics can be crucial to the achievement of ethnic political ends and to the responsiveness of the political system. If a minority ethnic group is geographically spread and elections are constituency based the group will have great difficulty in advancing its cause. If competing parties can afford to ignore minorities without cost they may well do so. And then if the same group is both economically excluded and politically neglected, the conditions are set for the politics of frustrated ambitions and desperation. Electoral arrangements, especially proportional representation, make a real difference to the extent to which minorities can make their voices heard in elections.

Within individual state systems, economic and political power are typically interdependent. Just as economic wealth may be the basis of political power, so too political power can be the basis of wealth. This is true of corrupt regimes where individuals have made themselves and their families wealthy on the basis of political power – Mobutu in Zaire, Marcos in the Philippines, and Suharto in Indonesia. But it is also possible for whole groups to elevate their position through a position of dominance in the political system. In South Africa the Afrikaaners had been preponderantly farmers and largely excluded from the Anglo-dominated capitalist class. Their position of hegemony in the post-1948 regime enabled them both to enter the capitalist sphere and to bring large areas of the economy under state control (Adam and Giliome 1979). In Malaysia from 1970 the Malays drew on their leading position in the political system to create a Malay middle class and entrepreneurial class, partly through insisting that Malay individuals or institutions should have favoured access to loans and investment funds. Prior to this Malays had largely been excluded from the modern sector of the Malaysian economy (Jesudason 1990). In this way political power not only promotes economic power but also promotes the economic power of a distinct ethnic group.

The sphere of politics is, then, the sphere of the exercise of power and in particular of formal and organised state power. It is also constituted by the political organisation of parties, pressure groups and associations and it entails the mobilisation of political symbols and the politicisation of cultural symbols. Our interest is in the way in which these political institutions and processes have or acquire ethnic significance. The place of ethnic categories in the creation and development of modern states is central to this question.

States, nation-states and ethnic groups

The states of modern Europe for all their unique histories broadly share the concept of the *nation*-state. As Gellner (1983) has argued, they have all tended to follow the principle that nations should have state systems which give formal political expression and autonomy to their nationhood. Correspondingly, states are nations composed of people with a claim to common culture and ancestry; nationalism is the doctrine of promoting the correspondence of nation and state (Gellner 1983).

There are three questions with respect to nation-states which are of particular interest to the question of ethnicity. The first is that the concept of nation raises the same question as the concept of ethnic group: how far do we regard nations as grounded social realities and how far as the constructions or inventions of the political imagination of groups whose interests they serve? (See Chapter 7 for a suggested middle position on this question.) It is partly an empirical rather than a purely theoretical and conceptual question – some nations are more invented than others. Hobsbawm has argued that at the point of creation of the modern Italian state the 'standard' Italian language was spoken by less than 3 per cent of the population (Hobsbawm 1990). Cultural homogeneity was something to be created rather than the foundation upon which the nation-state was built. At the same time, modern peoples who call themselves, for example, Serbians, Quebecois, Hawaiian, or Albanian can claim a real commonality of language and continuity of place and shared history which is at least 'plausible' when constructed into a national claim.

The second is that the formation of states as nation-states implies the cultural definition of an ethnic majority. That is, within the concept of nation is an idea, which may be more or less explicit, of who and what comprises the nation. In a narrow ancestral or even biological idea of the nation, either multi-ethnicity within the nation is excluded, or minority ethnicities are defined as less than full members. This was true where whiteness was an essential dimension of the concept of member of the nation and full citizen of the USA, Australia and South Africa. In all three until relatively recently only 'whites' had full access to citizenship and political participation. In other circumstances, the definition of the nation or the ethnic majority may be predicated on a concept of a group bounded by language, of common religion, or a combination of cultural and 'racial' characteristics. The claims of the Kosovo Albanians to independence or greater autonomy within Serbia/ Yugoslavia are based on the fact that 90 per cent of the people of Kosovo speak Albanian, are Muslim, and dispute the language of education (Serbian or Albanian) with their Serbian masters. In Britain the ideas of who and what is truly British and English has variously been grounded on claims about culture, about religion and on racialised ideologies. Islam and Hinduism have been central to the definition of Pakistan and modern India. The concept of a nation, defined by ancestry, religion or language, will necessarily include some and exclude others; equally the concept of ethnic majority entails the concept of minority. Majority and minority self-conceptions are shaped by each other and are defined in relation to each other. If multi-lingualism is an index of multi-ethnicity, then the 'most' multi-ethnic states are, excepting Canada and the USA, also among the poorer states (Lazcko 1994).

The third point is that the construction of purportedly homogeneous nation-states has never been perfect. The project of cultural homogenisation, which Gellner (1983) regards as a necessary adjunct of modernisation, is never fully achieved, both because subsequent migrations interrupt the process, and because cultural minorities within the wider embrace of a nation-state do not, or do not wholly lose or give up their distinctiveness neither do they give up their claim to distinctiveness. An English-dominated British state has not finally driven out Welsh language and identity nor has the Castilian Spanish state driven out Basque language and identity. As we suggested earlier in this book, such populations and the claims they make are properly regarded as 'proto-nations' since they mount a political expression not only of ethnic solidarity but also of a right to self-governance whether as a new state or as an autonomous nation within a multinational state. If ethnic ideologies define nations, ethnicity may define citizenship within nation-states. Examples earlier have shown this: 'white only' access to full citizenship in the past in the USA, South Africa, and Australia; and communal electoral rolls in Fiji and New Zealand where voting has been partially defined by ethnic group membership.

We referred previously to the politics of recognition and the politics of resources and distribution (Taylor 1992). Economic marginality, blocked mobility and poverty bring their own indignities so that the search for recognition and the search for material improvement can be analytically, but not substantively, separated. If young Muslims in Bradford, England, are angry it is not so easy to disentangle three likely sources – the experience of economic disadvantage, the insults of racism and the sense of affront at the slights on Islam (Samad 1992, Lewis 1994). So the demand for cultural recognition and the pursuit of resources for a group, or for individuals as members of a group, go hand in hand. This is true of policies which are designed to reverse the effects of historical discrimination and disadvantage, that is of policies of equal opportunity, positive action and affirmative action. In this sense anti-discriminatory policies and practice are a spur to ethnic group definition and mobilisation.

Ethnic identities become the vehicles for the achievement of both collective and individual goals.

The politics of culture

In Chapter 3 we discussed the concepts of primordiality and of instrumental and situational ethnicity. The instrumental concept suggests either that groups mobilise to pursue collective interests or even that a collective identity is constructed in order to make material gains. The shared symbols of a group become the source of solidarity, the means for promoting unity, and the banners under which people march, literally or metaphorically speaking. In this sense, the concept of instrumentality represents a challenge to the idea of authenticity. There can however be no prior judgement that the shared symbols and cultures, which express the solidarity of a group, have no real grounding in the lived experience and the hearts and minds of the people. Taking the instance of shared language and the wish for a language to survive, in case after case language loyalties have been the prompt for action or have been an important motive force in mobilisation. The nationalist Albanians of Kosovo (in 1998) revolted against their children being taught in Serbian; the black African children of Soweto (in 1976) rose up against the state's insistence on teaching them in Afrikaans. These cultural attachments and loyalties depend both on the intrinsic value attached to (say) a language and to the fact that a symbol, a language, a flag, a statue or commemorative event can appear to encapsulate the fortunes of a whole nation or ethnic group. Orange Order groups in Northern Ireland speak of preserving their traditions and culture by marching through towns and cities to commemorate a military victory over Catholics.

The very words used to describe people are contested because they are rarely simply descriptive, rather they carry with them the connotations of dominance or subordination, superior and inferior status, and privilege or stigma. The insulting intent of 'nigger' in the USA and 'kaffir' in South Africa is unmistakable; in other instances the import of names for people is more subtle.

This cultural and political import of words includes objects and places as well as people. In the wake of political and cultural revivals of suppressed groups, and in the dissolution of states and empires, it is common to see the tearing down of statues, the rewriting of history books, the renaming of streets, towns and mountains.

In Russia on the collapse of the Soviet Empire, a team of historians was set the task of rewriting school history books. All the newly independent post-Soviet states face a huge task of cultural rewriting and renaming. Where Russian minorities are left behind (Kolsto 1996), as for example in Latvia, they are obliged to watch the downgrading of the symbols of Russian superiority while the Latvians rejoice (Skultans 1999). In New Zealand, the name of the country itself is contested. Those who favour the renaming as Aotearoa may cite the better known form – New Zealand – for the sake of recognition, while many use the combined form Aotearoa/New Zealand. In Australia in 1998 the New South Wales state government raised the question of the naming of Botany Bay Park 'as an act of reconciliation between black and white Australians'. Botany Bay has been viewed as the 'birthplace of white Australia' commemorating the landing of Captain Cook in 1770 and the subsequent claiming of the land for the British crown. The proposed name change coincided with the Australian 'Sorry Day' in which white Australians sought to register their regret at the past policies which had systematically divided aboriginal families. Previous name changes in Australia had been reversed after white conservative protests (*Guardian* 1998).

Almost all the African states which gained independence in the 1960s renamed the country and principal cities – Zaire for Belgian Congo, Harare for Salisbury in Zimbabwe (once Rhodesia). India has renamed states and cities whose immediately previous names – such as Campbellpur – bore the marks of imperial rule through the names of administrators, politicians and military men. New Zealand has renamed Mount Egmont as Mount Taranaki but retains Palmerston North, Hastings and Hamilton in the North Island, and Christchurch, Canterbury, Nelson and Queenstown in the South Island.

In the revived political consciousness of historically suppressed populations names associated with stigma and derision are rejected and replaced. 'Nigger' is not accepted in the USA except when it is used by African Americans; where private use by whites is made public, as occurred in the O.J. Simpson trial, the perpetrator is disgraced. The policeman who gave evidence in the trial for murder of the former footballer had his evidence discredited when tapes were played in court exposing his use of 'nigger' in conversation. In South Africa in 1997 a rugby coach lost his job when he was heard speaking of 'kaffirs'.

Language and cultural symbols

The cultural politics of ethnicity and nation come to the surface in these discussions of names for places, buildings and events. The often sharp and bitter debates punctuate longer running contests about the dominance of specific cultures and languages. One of the great difficulties in the concept of the 'multi-cultural' society is the incorporation of the idea that cultures are equal in worth as well as existing side by side in mutual tolerance. Languages are suppressed, defended or promoted, precisely because people sense that a language is an item of culture which symbolises the value accorded to a whole population who have some sense of shared fate. We cited above the case of Albanian language education in Kosovo, Yugoslavia, and the use of Afrikaans in South Africa. Other similar cases would include the suppression and revival of Welsh in Wales, the promotion of French in Quebec, of all the non-Russian languages in the former republics of the Soviet Union and of Chinese teaching in Malaysia (Lee 1986, Handler 1988, Tishkov 1997, May 1999).

The education system thus becomes the battleground of contested national and ethnic identities. In Geertz's phrasing: 'If the general strike is the classical political expression of class warfare… then the school crisis is the political expression of the clash of primordial loyalties' (Geertz 1973). In Malaysia, Raymond Lee has argued that the cultural symbolic struggle has become a leading form of politics where minor or major gains in the use of language and symbolic forms are taken as measures of an ethnic community's strength (Lee 1986, 1990). In education there was dissension about the Chinese community's wish to establish a university teaching in Chinese – permission for it was not given. In 1998 a serious public disturbance occurred when the building of an extension to a Hindu temple was met with hostility by Muslims, including Muslims associated with a mosque which stood next door to the temple in Penang. These cultural and symbolic contests are important both because the culture and symbols themselves are taken seriously and because loss or gain in a cultural skirmish marks the power of the group to hold its own in the political struggle. Of course people feel strongly about the language they use, the buildings they worship in and the flag that flies over the courthouse; they feel these things all the more powerfully if giving ground is a fateful step back in a struggle for survival.

Types of ethnicity, historical context and the politics of culture

The types of ethnicity we defined in Chapter 1 were: urban minorities, indigenous peoples, ethnonational groups, ethnic groups in plural societies and post-slavery minorities. These we have discussed within three historical contexts: slavery and post-slavery societies; colonial and post-colonial societies; and nation-states in modern capitalism. Each of these contexts poses different problems of the politics of culture and citizenship; for each type of ethnicity there is a different framing of political goals.

These may be set out schematically as follows:

Citizenship and culture: historical contexts

Slavery and post-slavery societies: the definition of slaves as rightsless, even as less than fully 'human'; abolition and emancipation as political goals; in post-slavery, the access to full civil rights, of former slaves and their descendants; economic incorporation; the rewriting of racist culture.

Colonial and post-colonial societies: in once colonised societies the post-colonial politics of culture are about cultural renewal (of formerly devalued cultures) and the problem of the colonial mentality; about language and education; and about competing group claims in multi-ethnic societies.

In former coloniser societies it is the politics of 'coming to terms with' the end of empire. Also in once colonised societies, indigenous dispossessed groups seek to restore both cultural dignity and lost land.

Modern capitalist nation-states: the definition of the nation as a hegemonic people and culture; the place of marginalised cultures; the incorporation of minority ethnicities, both long-settled such as Roma in central Europe (Barany 1995) and new migrations.

The political goals for different types of ethnicities can also be presented schematically:

Political goals and types of ethnicity

Urban minorities: successful incorporation, full citizenship rights and (especially private) recognition within a multi-cultural society.

Indigenous peoples: language and cultural renaissance, public recognition and land rights, greater autonomy within the nation-state.

Proto-nations or ethnonational groups: public cultural recognition, status as a nation, independence or autonomy within a larger state.

Ethnic groups in plural societies: for 'incomers', full citizenship and cultural freedoms; for 'indigenes', protection of 'sons of the soil' status, cultural hegemony.

Post-slavery minorities: Either ethnic-blind incorporation, through citizenship and civil rights; or recognition within a multi-cultural whole; or cultural nationalism/separatism.

The examples of the politics of ethnicity are, in the present chapter, post-slavery and post-colonial plural societies (especially the USA and Malaysia); in Chapter 7, indigenous peoples (Hawai'i) and ethnonational politics and urban minorities in Britain and Europe.

Making political ethnicities: the USA

In Chapter 4, discussing ethnicity, economy and class, we followed a scheme of key periods of the history of black men and women in America. The same periods represent landmarks in the changing status of African Americans with respect to citizenship, civil rights and social and cultural recognition. From the first importation of

Africans into the USA colonies in 1619, through the formal recognition of African slave status in 1662, to the Independence Constitution of 1787, to the amendment abolishing slavery in 1865, represents a period of nearly 250 years in which slavery was practised and sanctioned in North America. It was virtually exclusively racial slavery – black African slavery – and those few of African descent who were not slaves had their freedoms and rights curtailed or utterly disregarded in practice. In the first part of this period it was the slave system of English colonies, in the latter part the slavery of a USA whose constitution declared all men to be born equal.

The end of the Civil War in 1865 was the beginning of a brief period of reform during which the Constitution was amended to abolish slavery and to guarantee the civil rights of black Americans. After the northern armies quit the defeated south in 1876 the civil rights gains of the post-war years began to be reversed and the scene was set for the long period of post-slavery white supremacy. New Deal legislation in the late 1930s began to make some inroads into racial discrimination and the Second World War ultimately led to the integration of the armed forces. But it was the Supreme Court decision of 1954 in *Brown* v. *Kansas Board of Education* which reversed the Court's own long-standing tacit endorsement of discrimination in the 'separate but equal' decision in *Plessey* v. *Ferguson* in 1896.

In each of these periods, citizenship and European and African ancestry were intimately and critically connected. In the first period the status of Africans, or 'Negroes' as the term then often used, was utterly bound up with the slave status and free Negroes had scarcely more civil rights than the great majority who were slaves. Those who were free were always vulnerable to being forced to prove their free status. 'Any imported Negro was presumed to be a slave, no matter what his religious or national background. So logical a connection would the status of slave and the colour black or brown have in Virginia slave codes that, in later years, a Negro or mulatto was automatically presumed to be a slave and it was incumbent on him to prove otherwise' (Klein 1967).

The Independence Constitution, which declared all men to be born equal, was the first embodiment of the Universalist rights of man philosophy. But is was silent on race and slavery and clearly was designed to leave both the slave condition and the inferior position of Africans intact. This grand contradiction persevered for almost 90 years. Several of the Constitution's clauses are clearly understood to refer to slaves and it was written in a society which neither expected nor planned slavery's end. The idea of slaves – and thus Africans – as less than full persons, is found in Article 1 section 2d which apportioned representatives and taxes 'according to the numbers of... free persons, including those bound to service for a term of years, and including Indians not taxed, three fifths of all other persons' (Ollman and Birnbaum 1990). Charles Pinckney of South Carolina, who had been a delegate to the Constitutional Convention of 1787, was later to say:

> I perfectly knew then that there did not exist such a thing in the Union as a black or colored citizen, nor could I then have conceived it possible such a thing could ever have existed in it; nor do I now believe one does exist. (Litwack 1961)

At the time of the Missouri Compromise in 1820, the great struggle concerning which states were to be slave or free-labour states, the pro-slavery proponents argued that statutes passed by states had confirmed the inferior status of Negroes – they speak of 'Negroes' and not just slaves. The states, they argued, 'had demonstrated beyond doubt that neither the north nor the south had ever regarded them as suitable members of the political community. Nearly every state barred the Negro from voting, giving evidence in court, and marrying with white persons; no state admitted him into the militia or made him a citizen by legislative act...' According to Senator Smith, 'This is unanswerable proof of the degraded condition in which Congress consider free negroes and mulattoes ought to be placed' (Litwack 1961, p. 35).

If there had been any doubt, the Dred Scott case in the Supreme Court in 1857 appeared to settle it. Scott had sued for his freedom on the grounds that he had lived in a non-slave state. The Court found that he was not entitled to his freedom and that as a slave and Negro he was not a citizen of the USA. Chief Justice Taney, pro-slavery and of the planter class, held to the majority opinion:

> The inferior condition of the Negro for at least a century before 1787 indicated that this class of people was not intended to be embraced by (the phrase) 'the people of the United States'. (Litwack 1961)

Slaves declared free by Lincoln in 1863 were confirmed in their freedom by the Thirteenth amendment to the Constitution passed in 1865, which abolished slavery, and by the northern victory over the south in the Civil War. The Civil Rights Act of 1866 and the fourteenth and fifteenth amendment were further affirmations of the civil rights of black men, including the right to vote. This civic equality flourished for a brief period after the Civil War, as we described in Chapter 4; we also indicated how and why this historical opportunity to create a free and equal society was closed off by the combined power of both wealthy and poor whites. The withdrawal of federal troops from the south left the former Confederate states to their own devices and by the end of the century a system of white supremacy was fully in place.

The civil rights protections passed immediately after the Civil War were not withdrawn, so systematic racial discrimination, segregation and disfranchisement followed indirect means, although the intentions were barely concealed. These reversals were supported by state laws, by custom and practice, and by the antipathy towards racial equality of the Supreme Court for another 80 years. Disfranchisement was achieved by means of poll tax, the white primary (which defined political parties as private institutions), literacy tests, the grandfather clause, and terror. Advocates of white supremacy made their intentions clear. In Mississippi, the constitution was revised in pursuit of a policy 'of crushing out the manhood of Negro citizens' (Silberman 1964). In Virginia in 1901 a Senator declared 'Discrimination? Why that is precisely what we propose... the elimination of every Negro voter who can be gotten rid of' (Silberman 1964). In *Plessey* v. *Ferguson*, Plessey contested a Louisiana law requiring 'separate but equal accommodation' on the railroads. The Supreme Court found that this law did not violate the Fourteenth amendment: 'In the nature of things it could not have been intended to abolish distinctions based on color, or to enforce social as distinguished from political equality, or a commingling of the two races upon terms unsatisfactory to either' (Berger 1952).

Consciousness of Africa and a celebration of black African identity has persisted from the earliest period to the present. In the slave period Paul Cuffee, the son of an African slave, had organised repatriation schemes for the benefit of Africans (Pinkney 1976) and in the early 20th century Marcus Garvey became the dominant black politician advocating return to Africa. The Black Nation of Islam, founded before the Second World War and persisting into the 1990s (Essien-Udom 1962, Malcolm X 1968, Omi and Winant 1986, Small 1994) has ideologically rejected white America and sought a 'separate territory of their own – either on this continent or elsewhere' (Pinkney 1976).

In the lowest period of the black experience in America – 1880–1954 – some black political leaders and movements, in public at least, followed policies which indicated a measure of accommodation of the brute fact of white supremacy and segregation. In league with white philanthropy, Booker T. Washington's leadership led to the foundation of many black colleges as separate institutions. In this period the meso-institutional life of America – schools, colleges, churches and places of recreation for example – produced a binary system. Some of this institutional separation has persisted despite formal desegregation, and there remains among some, a continuing faith in the idea that African Americans will flourish in institutions which they own and control. Even in movements which have embraced a 'non-racial' philosophy many were persuaded that at least a temporary separateness was necessary in a phase of restating the African American place in America. Each of these tendencies represents a curb on the simple application of the Universalist idea that the real answer to racism and its effects is the perfection of the race-blind society. For many indeed the dismantling of a racialised social order and the civic de-ethnicisation of social institutions and cultural expression have not been and are not presently the dominant thought of the politics of 'race' and ethnicity. Even the most 'integrationist' of the black American movements have periodically lost confidence in the goal of integration and incorporation. Four things have militated against integrationism: the limitations to what can be gained by civil rights, the structured persistence of black poverty and massive economic disadvantage, the depth to which racialised customs of thought are embedded in white American culture and the positive valuation of ethnic and cultural difference, both for its own sake and as political strategy. All the greatest African American political leaders, including Martin Luther King, have had to struggle with the tension between 'incorporation' and survival of black pride and dignity in a hostile environment.

Cultural struggle

In the USA in particular – but also in South Africa – the problems of racialisation and ethnicisation have also been represented as cultural struggle. In racialised societies, the categorisation of a suppressed group also implicates the categorisation of the majority and/or dominant ethnicity. If being black/African in America was defined as at least partial and sometimes near-total exclusion from civic belonging then it follows that a dominant element of inclusion was being white/European. The revolution constituted by the partial dismantling of racialisation has provoked its concomitant 'crisis' in white identities. Glazer and Moynihan are the best purveyors of the view that ethnicity remained or became (in the 1960s) a leading mode of social and political mobilisation (Glazer and Moynihan 1975) and no doubt part of this is a consequence of 'authentic' attachments to the urban ethnicities generated by the long process of inclusion of migrants into American society; each successive cohort of European migrants has faced initial hostility which has gradually receded in the face of social mobility and incorporation.

But part of 'Americanisation' has, for virtually all American urban migrants, included a process of learning that being white was a significant element of inclusion. For this reason some of the signs of 'ethnic revival' among Americans of European ancestry may be 'suspected' of being variable forms of expressing the overarching power of racialisation. In America, European ethnicity – Polish, Italian, Irish and many others – has a common denominator: whiteness, in a racialised society (Waters 1990).

At the same time political mobilisation around ethnic claims has undermined the very fabric of American nationality and civic status. This view has been expressed most vividly by Arthur Schlesinger, not as a 'new racism' but as a profound anxiety that political ethnicisation threatens that minimum of valued and shared culture which provides one of the foundations of American civic and cultural life (Baron 1990, Schlesinger 1991) and thus of the minimum necessary cohesion and viability of American society itself. Some of the profoundest expressions of this problem – as Schlesinger well knows – are to be found in the politics of culture which currently characterise education debates and policies, universities and intellectual life in its broadest definition (Goldberg 1993). Schools and universities have long been key elements of a racialised system both being virtually entirely segregated until the 1960s. Their contribution, however, was not only in how they were organised (that is practising racial inclusion and exclusion) but in what they conveyed as the key cultural messages of a racialised society. White political and economic domination entailed white domination – but not monopoly – of all forms of cultural representation including art, music, history and social science. If resistance to racialised domination correctly diagnosed this near-monopoly of cultural representation it should not be surprising that part of the cure should be understood as dewhitening and de-Europeanising history, art and all manner of cultural imagery and communication.

To Schlesinger and those who think like him this political ethnicisation of culture threatens the very core of the 'best' of the European tradition, which contains within it the 'liberal' Universalist thought that culture is not ethnically but 'humanly' defined. Can non-European (or non-white) advocates avoid the conclusion that Western philosophy is suspect as a whole if some of its leading heroes – such as Hume and Kant – can be found giving expression to racist understandings of civilisation? But the ethnicisation of culture – in all its manifestations from high culture, the so-called canons of excellence debate, to culture in its reference to daily life – does represent a threat to the Universalist ideal of humanity if it suggests that cultural expression cannot escape its ethnic foundations. As Wallerstein has so eloquently argued culture has this double meaning: as Universalism whereby culture is mobilised to indicate that differences are learned and not inherent (that is anthropological Universalism) and can express the idea that difference is 'natural' with culture as the expression of this difference (Balibar and Wallerstein 1991). If people believe the latter then they can be expected to fight tooth and nail to preserve difference – because in so doing they are fighting for survival, precisely as many ethnocultural protagonists do believe.

Malaysia and the post-colonial plural societies

It has been argued that in Malaysia the conduct of politics since independence has been aimed not at reducing difference but at reducing conflict. As we showed in Chapter 5 with respect to economic inequalities, the pivotal thought in much of Malaysian politics has been that Malays, seeing themselves as the people of the land – the sons of the soil – cannot be expected to tolerate economic and social disfranchisement in 'their own place'. In economic policy, this meant directing much effort towards inserting Malays into the so-called modern sector of the economy, in the politics of culture it has meant reassuring Malays that Malay custom, Islamic faith, and the Malay language are preserved, honoured and maintained in a position of at least *primus inter pares*.

As we saw in outline in Chapter 5, the definition of the Malays as the 'true' people of Malaya/Malaysia had been encouraged by British colonial rule. Indirect rule through the Malays' sultanate was designed to preserve elements of indigenous life, in particular the Islamic code and culture over which the sultans presided. The two principal incomer populations – the Chinese and the Indians – were imported to work in highly specific sectors of the colonial economy, thus offering them few opportunities for integration with Malays or into the 'national life' of the country. These segments were never watertight and rural Chinese in some regions became closely woven into the life of the communities in which they dwelt. As Chinese and some Indians left their initial niches in the Malayan economy, they engaged with Malays at least on a commercial basis as purveyors of goods and services, shopkeepers and other small business enterprises. Despite the brake which religion placed on intermarriage (Nash 1989), interpersonal relationships developed across ethnic lines.

Nonetheless, by the time negotiations for independence were in train it seems almost certain that the majority of those who could and did identify as 'Malays' regarded themselves as the people of Malaya/Malaysia and regarded others as guests, migrant workers or as foreigners. These 'others' had, in the eyes of many Malays, a claim to 'membership' in independent Malaysia which was substantially less than that of Malays. Both Chinese and Indians were regarded as linked to their 'homelands'; Chinese sympathies – real and imagined – with mainland China were all the more suspect as Chinese in Malaysia organised into revolutionary parties identified with the communist cause in China. In putting down the communist threat in Malaysia the British declared a state of emergency and enlisted the support of Malay soldiers in the counter-revolutionary struggle, thus creating a historic 'folk-memory' of a bitter divide.

By the time, in the 1950s, that *merdeka* – independence – became a real possibility, Malays sought protection for their 'special position' in the Malayan/Malaysian polity, a position which they viewed as threatened by any conceding of full political rights of the incomers in the new Malaysia. The ultimate spur to Malay consciousness was the proposal for an independence constitution which would have created a 'non-ethnic' citizenship of Malaysia and effectively erased their special claims – to land, culture language and religion preservation. Malay national consciousness had grown slowly in the 1930s (Roff 1994) and the sultanate itself was among the most politically active Malays. But it was increasingly joined by a small but growing class of intellectuals, journalists and teachers who stimulated political awareness nationally. The fear of losing ground to ethnic competitors at the point of independence led to the sultans, upper-class Malays, and intellectual supporters springing into action. Presenting themselves as the defenders of Malay interests, they formed the United Malay National Organisation (Roff 1994).

The discussions at the time of independence illustrate how, from the outset, citizenship was debated in 'communal' terms, communal referring to the ethnic communities which were beginning to be posited as segmentary blocks in the Malaysian state. In drafting an independence constitution, a consultative committee was established. Among the memoranda submitted to the committee were:

> This is a Malay country, which has been acknowledged to belong to the Malays from time immemorial... It is necessary that the Malays be given more votes than the other races. [Malay]

> We have lived and toiled in this country... The Chinese should have the same representation as the Malays for they have contributed most and pay the greatest share of the taxes. [Chinese]

> The Eurasian is the son of the soil and we in Malaya have no other country which we can regard as our homeland. [Eurasian]

> The Sikhs are recognised as a separate entity among the peoples of India and stand as a powerful minority that steadies the extreme views of the major races in India. [Sikh]

> Most Asiatic races require to be ruled by a benign autocracy and are incapable of ruling themselves on account of suspicion or envy of others... The English made Malaya. [British] (Ratnam 1965)

The struggles over the constitution had confirmed and hardened the ethnic identities in Malaysian politics but led nonetheless to a compromise (Ratnam 1965). Non-Malays were given the guarantees of citizenship that they demanded and Malays secured a position of primacy for Malay culture and custom, and the foundation of policies of ethnic preference in economic and institutional spheres. The constitution affirmed Islam as the official religion and Malay as an official language. Its provisions also defined a 'Malay' as the basis of preferential policies in land, education and the economy. The leading ethnically based parties – the United Malay National Organisation, the Malaysian Indian Congress, and the Malaysian Chinese Association (UMNO, MIC and MCA) – formed an Alliance which was the party of government later transforming itself into the *Barisan Nasional* or National Front. By 1998 the BN party was still the party of government under the Prime Ministership of Dr Mahatir, in power since 1981.

Although these parties within the Alliance were ethnically orientated and named, they also had specific class bases within the class-differentiated ethnic populations. The Indian and Chinese parties were largely composed of business and professional classes, while UMNO had its class basis in a Malay administrative and political elite – in the virtual absence of a Malay bourgeoisie. The post-independence compromise was seemingly successful until, in the 1969 elections, the Alliance lost support across the country, much of it to the Islamic Party. After the post-election Kuala Lumpur riots parliament was suspended for two years.

As Horowitz (1989) has argued the prospects for stable integration in Malaysia may have appeared poor at independence; the prospects were better in Sri Lanka. Over three decades later the results appear to be almost the reverse, with Sri Lanka embroiled in a seemingly unsolvable civil war and Malaysia having achieved that modicum of ethnic peace which has accompanied the growing prosperity of the country and some of its people.

The two features for which some commentators have most berated Malaysia – some restraints on freedom of expression, and a system of ethnic preference for Malays – are the very ones which have made a measure of national integration possible. The distaste of some commentators for the Malaysian system suggests a view of democracy which assumes that the 'proper' form is based on universalistic citizenship and unrestrained public debate. As Horowitz and others have argued, the aim of the Malaysian state has been not to reduce difference but to reduce conflict (Horowitz 1989).

The most overt and alarming signs of the potential for ethnic conflict were witnessed in 1969 when Malays reacted violently to Chinese displays of celebration at election results which were viewed as advancing Chinese ethnic interests. The Kuala Lumpur riots were viewed then and have been portrayed ever since as a stark demonstration of what can happen if ethnic competition is so bitterly contested. All commentators appear broadly to agree that an underlying cause of Malay discontent was their belief that they were economically disadvantaged in 'their own' country and that incomers (that is, the Chinese) were rich and getting richer. For this ethnic discontent to be possible, we should be careful to note, requires the prior condition which we have already partially explained – that is, that people see their own circumstances and those of others in primarily ethnic terms.

The response of the Malaysian state – a response which required the collaboration of non-Malay representatives – was to reaffirm the Malays' special position as already established in the Independence Constitution and to attack what the political elite saw as the real cause of Malay discontent, that is, their disproportionate representation among the poor and economically worse off, and their corresponding underrepresentation in the business class and among educated professionals. Affirmative action to improve the economic position of the Malays was the aim of the New Economic Policy (NEP) which has remained a cornerstone of Malaysia's political compromise since 1970 (Jesudason 1990).

The chief areas of privilege for Malays have been four: protection of Malay land ownership, access to scholarships and thus to higher education and professional social mobility, favourable terms in access to home ownership, and favourable treatment in business loans and other measures designed to increase Malay participation in the 'modern sector' – capitalist business enterprise. While there is disagreement about how successful these have been, there is general agreement that they have been successful enough to allay Malay fears of being 'losers in their own country' and enough to create – almost as a direct intent of public policy – a substantial Malay middle class grounded in professional, civil service and administrative occupations and a growing rate of business participation. All of this has been underlined by a Malay political dominance such that it is difficult to conceive anyone other than a Malay and Muslim as Prime Minister with Malays occupying most of the 'commanding heights' of the Malaysian polity. The instrument for this achievement has been the Alliance Party and its successor the National Front, a political party which incorporates all ethnic groups but in which the Malay partner – the United Malay National Organisation – has unquestioned pre-eminence. When the NEP was reviewed it was clear that any conclusions that the achievements (in promoting Malays) were 'unfinished' and partial were simultaneously arguments for the perpetuation of the policy ; to conclude that the policy had achieved its aims was to argue for phasing it out (Malaysia: Seventh Malaysia Plan 1996–2000).

At the same time the government has continually stressed the need for national unity and implements this by discouraging or debarring open and potentially sharp debate of Malay 'privileges' of all kinds. In these circumstances, many if not all political questions – whether about higher education, languages of instruction in schools, and about manifestations of Islamic practice – are effectively ethnicised

(Lee 1990). That is, it is hard to conceive of policies without seeing them simultaneously in their ethnic significance.

Two macro-level problems face the Malaysian state: maintaining the confidence of investors who are willing to underwrite the continued growth of Malaysia's capitalist economy, and ensuring ethnic peace. In order to achieve the first the government has to try to guarantee political stability and to oversee stable industrial relations; to achieve the second the government has seen its task mainly as dealing with potential Malay 'ethnic' discontent – of the kind we described above. Therefore both a sharp and well-developed class politics and a fierce and intense ethnic politics are seen as posing a threat to the Malaysian compromise.

Some labour questions are likely to become more acute. As home-based workers see their incomes rise their competitive differential with workers elsewhere (for example the USA, Japan) diminishes and governments can either try to forestall domestic income gains or look to migrant workers for lower wage costs – for example the employment of large numbers of Indonesian and Bangladeshi workers in construction – both of which paths contain political dangers. At the same time the embroilment of the Malaysian (and other South East Asian) economies in a global capitalism means that the domestic government is not always able to dictate the terms of development within its own state boundaries. In order to win international investors, Malaysia and similar economies may have to concede to the 'liberalising' demands of either international capital or governments (for example the USA) who seek to collaborate. The relative weakness of South East Asian economies in 1997–98 has shown how countries like Indonesia become highly susceptible to pressures from the International Monetary Fund. To a lesser degree, Malaysia (being in less of a plight than Indonesia) also had to consider the choices between local political control and Monetary Fund assistance. To date it has resisted becoming a client of the IMF.

Meanwhile the success of the NEP in creating a Malay middle class has created a social and cultural distance between prosperous urban Malay and poor rural Malays. In Malaysia, as elsewhere, one of the responses to economic and social disadvantage has been an intensification of attachment to the symbols and rules of Islam. Overwhelmingly, support for PAS, Malaysia's Islamic party, is greatest in rural areas occupied chiefly by relatively poor Malays. (By contrast support for parties of the left with an ideological class basis has been largely identified with Chinese ethnicity). These are the agrarian Malays, outside the so-called modern sector, whom the NEP has barely touched, land reform having been consistently overlooked in programmes to assist Malays. If their discontents are channelled into an Islamic party then they pose a real threat to the National Front which depends on securing majority Malay support for UMNO. So the government, in which UMNO has the leading part, must strive to appear faithful to an Islamic Malaysia while constantly falling short of the kind of Islamification which discourages international investors and destabilises ethnic relations at home – since Islam is so closely bound up with Malay ethnicity. This kind of balancing act is reflected in the statements of leading figures in the Malaysian government.

The ethnic categorical definition of social, political and economic transactions and dispositions constitutes a macro-social constraint in Malaysia – what Boulanger has termed the 'ethnic triad hegemony' (Boulanger 1996). Malaysians of all ethnic identities cannot escape the effect and meaning of this macro-social and macro-cultural fact, whether they wish to or not. They cannot escape ethnicity because it is written into the Constitution, into the names of the political parties, into choice of schooling, applications for higher education scholarships and business loans, home purchases and driving licences.This grounding of ethnicity in the macro- and meso-institutions of Malaysia indicates the limitations of approaches which view ethnicity through the choices made by individuals in micro-social interactions (Banton and Mansor 1992).

This becomes especially important in trying to reach a judgement on one of the most long-standing contentions of a standard liberal view of modernity – that processes of modernisation dissolve ethnic allegiances. The abundant evidence notwithstanding, that modernity may create ethnicity, the liberal view must be seen as depending on the argument that the growth of cities and of industrial commercial and service employment draws people into contact which they cannot avoid. The implication then is that 'blind' ethnic allegiances cannot survive these interactions (see Banton and Mansor 1992). Such a view is simplistic. To be sure the opening up of channels of interaction (same school, same neighbourhood, same factory) between people identified as ethnically different may and some-times does lead to new forms of perception of ethnic difference and to changes in the manner of what Eriksen (1993b) calls the communication of ethnicity.

But this should not lead us to conclude that the ethnic categories dissolve or that allegiance along ethnic lines is weakened; where the macro-social definition reinforces ethnicity this is most unlikely. People simply treat micro-social interactions and macro-social loyalties as different games which are played by different rules even while each 'level' significantly informs the other. Thus it is not surprising that Mariappan found that respondents indicated a willingness to envisage flexibility in some types of micro-social interethnic transactions while remaining powerfully informed in their (especially political) attitudes by macro-political structures (Mariappan 1996). In other words, people can manage their behaviour in face-to-face exchange in flexible ways which are not wholly 'commanded' by the hegemonic system of ethnic categorisation, while at the same time recognising that this category system remains powerful and all- or nearly all-embracing. To conclude from the evidence of flexibility in the micro-social spheres that 'ethnic loyalties' are breaking down fails to deal with half the evidence – specifically the evidence that ethnic categories are in some respects hardening in Malaysia as both Boulanger and Khan demonstrate (Boulanger 1996, Khan and Loh Kok Wah 1992).

Summary

In this chapter we have defined the sphere of politics and examined illustrations of the politics of ethnicity. As in the case of class and ethnicity in the two preceding chapters, we considered the historical contexts which have been classic ethnic-making and race-making situations. The contexts of slavery and post-slavery, colonial and post-colonial societies, especially with regard to labour migrations which created new ethnicities in a new setting, and the forming of urban minorities in societies of the new world and the European societies which had been prime movers in the formation of a world system. The illustrations centred upon the USA as a post-slavery society and Malaysia as a post-colonial society. In Chapter 7 we shall examine a case of land dispossession – Hawai'i – in which the politics of ethnicity are the politics of sovereignty, cultural dignity and land claims; and we shall examine the case of Britain and other European societies, post-colonial as colonising countries which have received, among other minorities, migrants and refugees from their former colonies.

Chapter 7

The Politics of Ethnicity: Hawai'i, Britain, Continental Europe

In this chapter we examine the politics of ethnicity in two contexts: land-dispossession societies and the case of Hawai'i, and post-colonial urban minorities in the coloniser societies – principally Britain; we also examine some wider aspects of ethnicity in the European context.

The politics of ethnicity in land-dispossession societies

In Chapter 2 we saw that the period of European expansion, adventure, colonisation and acquisition was accompanied by a grand cultural confidence expressed through the world views of both science and Christian religion. The peoples whom Europeans met were viewed, not in a simple or in a uniform way, but in ways which nonetheless conveyed persistent themes, of the civilised and blessed and of the savage and forlorn, themes which have been remarkably durable. The material and symbolic effects of this encounter can be explored in the history of the islands of Hawai'i in little more than the last 200 years. (Some of the main features of the modern history of Hawai'i have been set out in Chapter 5.) In the following passages we shall look at the specifically political and cultural dimensions especially with regard to the present-day Hawaiian renaissance.

Romanzo Adams has argued that some peculiar features of Hawaiian history – compared to other colonised countries – bestowed upon it an ethos of 'race relations' which marked it off from others (Adams 1934, 1937). The main reasons he advances are the broad 'equality' implied by early trading relationships, the existence of a sovereign native regime with which incomers had to deal, and the circumstances which led to legitimated and high-status intermarriages between white foreigners and Hawaiians. This meant, the argument runs, that there was no basis for the establishment of a doctrine of white supremacy: if white men married high-status Hawaiian women, they had to respect all Hawaiians; to trade meant to accept a rough and ready equality; and the authority of the home government required the respect of those who needed their approval. The earliest missionaries had to ask the permission of the Queen Regent (Daws 1968) to build homes in Honolulu; they could only do so on her authority and by abiding by the constraints that she deemed necessary and prudent. Her subsequent conversion to Christianity was invaluable to the missionaries.

There are objections to this model of foreigner–Hawaiian relations. There can be a 'rough and ready' equality in trading relationships, but in Hawai'i the greater knowledge of the outer world commanded by merchants and sailors – to say nothing of their greater firepower – was a real qualification of this equality. Hawaiians were duped, induced to enter arrangements which were much to their disfavour, and threatened with force when they failed to pay debts or meet with the conditions of deals (Daws 1968, Kent 1983). Intermarriages were respected but the effect of this was as much to create a new ethnic identity and a new part-Hawaiian upper class, rather than induce widespread respect among white incomers for Hawaiians. The most public spirited and Hawaiian regarding among this part-Hawaiian class were concerned about the destiny of the Hawaiian people; others were more concerned about their own fortunes. As we saw in Chapter 5, by the mid-19th century the sheer superior force of those who represented outside interests in Hawai'i were able to coerce or cajole the Hawaiian rulers into making the concessions necessary to pave the way for the Americanisation of Hawai'i. The autonomy and freedom of action of the Hawaiian government became more and more a fiction until it was lost altogether. The peculiar circumstances of Hawaiian history – peculiar by contrast with outright colonialism – which Adams refers to, did have the effect of curbing the development of an unqualified ethnic supremacy doctrine. But the factors which are cited as reasons, equality of trading relationships, autonomy of the Hawaiian government, and respect for Hawaiians, were progressively weakened.

Adams in fact referred to the peculiarities of Hawai'i as the 'unorthodox doctrine of race relations' – at the time of his writing in the 1930s, white supremacist views and social and institutional separation were 'orthodox' in the USA. The loss of Hawaiian sovereignty (1893) and the institution of territorial status (1900) had in fact turned Hawai'i into a society much more resembling a colonial regime than previously and Hawai'i's departure from racist orthodoxies was a matter of degree. In the territorial period real political power rested with the United States governor's office, the military authorities, and the sugar producers, their agencies, and transport companies, a group of business concerns known locally as the Big Five. This territorial regime was hostile to labour unions, antagonistic to Japanese labour in the islands, and indifferent to native Hawaiians. The survival of a number of families of part-Hawaiian and *haole* (white) ancestry constituted little or no curb on the power of a white-dominated territorial power structure.

When the transition to statehood came in 1959 the newspaper placards read 'We are all haoles now!' *Haole* was and is the term meaning foreigner but whose primary connotation has been white and American. In the territorial period and the plantation economy period the term conveyed the meaning 'boss'. The placard could be taken to read 'We are all bosses now' – meaning that democracy had come to Hawai'i. This had most meaning for Japanese, Chinese and Filipino-ancestry populations many of whom had been excluded from political participation under the territorial regime.

Hawaiians had not been excluded by birthplace requirements, but territorial status itself marked their loss of sovereignty. Statehood was seen as presenting the greatest opportunities to Japanese-ancestry Hawaiians who had begun to overcome the social after-effects of Japan's attack on Pearl Harbour. Hawai'i's Japanese had been regarded as sympathetic to Japan's imperial war aims and were accused, with no foundation, of guiding the Japanese fighter planes into Pearl Harbour. Young people born in Hawai'i of Japanese ancestry were frustrated by their parents' sentimental attachment to Japan and some tore down symbols of Japanese attachment in their own homes. The subsequent formation, after opposition from the government, of a Japanese squadron in the American army, and its outstanding war record, set the path for the 'Americanisation' of Hawai'i's Japanese. The Japanese, Filipino and other plantation workers had begun to be recruited into American-based labour unions in the 1930s and, after statehood, Hawaiians of Japanese ancestry secured important footholds in the Democratic Party.

This was eventually to provide them with a basis for electoral power in the state and for access to some leading political positions and administrative posts in the state machinery. The combined electoral and political power of the two largest groups in the islands, the whites (35 per cent) and Japanese ancestry (25 per cent), has led to the governance of Hawai'i being described as a 'haole-Japanese condominium'. In the same period the central focus of the economy has shifted dramatically from plantations (sugar and pineapple) to tourism. In the 1990s the islands' economy and much of their destiny lie in the hands of a small number of multinational corporations, Japanese and American, who control the hotel industry and the major air carriers (Kent 1983). This Japanese multinational involvement should be clearly distinguished from the Hawai'i-born population of Japanese descent. The latter have formed a substantial part of Hawai'i's working and middle classes; they do not own the leisure tourist industry.

These political and economic changes, especially statehood and the shift from plantation to tourist economy, interacted with shifts in ethnic identities and the politics of culture (Fenton 1979, Buck 1993). Improvements in general standards of living and education, the revitalisation of the Hawaiian-ancestry population, and the greater political openness of the statehood regime from the 1960s, contributed to a renewed interest in indigenous Hawaiian history and culture which has been referred to as the Hawaiian Renaissance. The advent of mass tourism interest provoked anger at the preemption of land by hotels and simultaneously made it possible for local Hawaiian musicians to earn a living from music and entertainment. Local musicians were able to thrive both at local events – social gatherings of families, church meetings, weddings, local musical competitions and festivals – and in the hotel and nightclub trade. Community events and the music recording studios, television and radio made several of these musicians very well known, and much loved, in the islands. They developed a distinctive set of styles of music which reflected old Hawaiian musical forms, 19th-century melodies, poems and ballads, and the Spanish/Portuguese influences brought by in-migrants. The popularity of Hawaiian music has played a major part in the renaissance of Hawaiian culture in the modern period (Buck 1984–5, 1993).

Three of the most popular musicians became especially important both because of their acknowledged exceptional talents and their early deaths. George Helm was a student and musician who had been a key figure in the movement to stop the American Navy using one of the islands, the island of Kaho'olawe, for bombing target practice. The movement committed to defence of the island and its historical sites, the Protect Kaho'olawe Ohana, was a model of political organisation and of the mobilisation of culture in the politics of Hawai'i. George Helm's disappearance at sea led to his coming to be regarded as a martyr to the Hawaiian cause. By the mid-1970s Helm's concern for protection of the land and the revival of respect for Hawaiian culture old and new was shared by many Hawaiians. Gabby Pahinui was probably the best-known 'slack-key' guitarist and singer and held a position as a kind of father of Hawaiian music; when he died of a heart attack at the age of 59 his passing was a public event marked by mourning, tributes from all quarters and day-long dedication of radio programmes to his music and recollections by friends. In 1997 Israel Kamakawiwo'ole also died young and his fame, and the affection for him, was marked by the decision to have a lying in state at the Capitol building. He was described, and described himself as *kama'aina*, a common man of the people. Helm was the most explicitly political of the three but Israel Kamakawiwo'ole belonged to a generation of singers who combined sometimes singing to tourists – and telling stories at their expense too – with singing at local events and evoking pride in all things Hawaiian and reminding everyone of the importance of *aloha 'aina* – the love of the land.

This was part of the cultural revolution. By the 1980s and 90s it had become or had transformed itself into a political revolution dominated by the concept of sovereignty and a material-legal as well as cultural-symbolic concern about land. The movement for sovereignty (Dudley and Keoni 1990) had as its central aim the recognition of the Hawai'ian nation as a distinct entity and the creation of a constitutional form through which this nation could govern itself. This sovereignty aim is coupled with land claims by which restoration is claimed for all lands taken illegally from the Hawaiian government and transferred to the state in 1959.

Hawaiians have been seen as a minority and an ethnic group in Hawai'i – since white arrivals and Asian labour rendered them a numerical minority. It is now becoming clear that their indigenous status, despite widespread intermarriage, was the central feature of their ethnic identity – as among Maori of New Zealand. This marked them off from other ethnic groups in the islands. Ethnicity in the case of indigenous peoples like Hawaiians is different in formation from the ethnic identities of immigrant groups and the descendants. We now outline some of the reasons for this.

Hawaiians were not immigrants to Hawai'i and by and large did not participate in the colonial economy which demanded immigrant labour, that is the plantation economy. On the contrary, whereas the plantation economy made a niche for incomers (however oppressive in the first instance) for Hawaiians it was a source and cause of further displacement in their 'own land'. That is, the plantation economy in the first instance made further inroads into native lands and in the second instance brought to Hawaii groups which would directly compete with Hawaiians once the plantation economy withered and its labourers sought places in the developing non-plantation economy, in artisanship, small entrepreneurship, professional occupations and state-sponsored forms of employment as teachers and public servants.

By contrast with the grievances of immigrants and their descendants, the material disadvantages and the cultural claims of Hawaiian communal politics were to a considerable and ever-growing extent based on land dispossession and the overthrow of sovereignty. These grievances were simply not shared with other 'minorities' in territorial and state politics. The core of the Hawaiian 'case' always had a content and a series of specific historical determinations which were entirely absent in all other contestants on the Hawaiian scene. This different core meant that the trajectory of Hawaiian claims was different from that of in-migrant ethnic groups; Hawaiians contained the potential – frequently realised in land struggles (Uyehara 1977, Hawai'i Advisory Committee 1991) – of being oppositional in a way which other minority interests were not. Other minority interests lay primarily in opening up avenues of social mobility, maintaining dignity and pride in group identity and opposing ethnic or racial discrimination. At various times, especially in the colonial period, all three of these minority group aims were opposed or deemed suspect by the economic and political elites of Hawaiian society (Daws 1968). Social mobility was blocked by discrimination and collective dignity and pride in heritage was cast as 'un-American' – as was the case during the most intense period of anti-Japanese sentiment (Lind 1996).

But in the longer run there was no central logic in the social and economic life of Hawai'i as a state of the USA which ran counter to the mobility of in-migrants, their incorporation, and the delegitimation of ethnic discrimination. The quest for reparations, the restoring of lost lands, and native Hawaiian sovereignty, all of which could be seen as 'logical' components of a developed Hawaiian politics, are all political items which are potentially oppositional. The opposition to tourism directly threatens the main economic interests in the islands, the claims of sovereignty in principle reject the legitimacy of the American government (Trask 1993), and the demand for land restoration has potential for disruption of the economy ('Land claim could reach $1.2 billion', *Honolulu Advertiser* 1996), in a way that has already occurred in Australia and New Zealand.

This is the sense in which Hawaiian ethnicity is different from that of migrant groups settled in the islands. A sociological awareness of this has been forced upon observers by the sheer persistence of indigenous peoples' movements. In the last three decades these politics have increasingly taken the direction of the politics of dispossessed indigenous peoples, following lines comparable to American Indians, Maori in New Zealand and a host of similarly placed peoples – for example, the people of Irian Jaya currently under Indonesian rule – in the Americas and the Pacific in particular. These movements identify with each other and collaborate internationally (Prejean 1994).

Although in-migrant ethnicities and indigenous movements have different aims, both are expressed through a reflexive concern for cultural recognition. The primary signs of political renewal among native Hawaiians (among all who could claim to be 'Hawaiian') were first conveyed via a *cultural* renaissance, although closely linked to community organisations. These community and political organisations resisted tourist and military land encroachment (Aluli and McGregor 1994). The revival of interest in *hula* (Buck, 1993), in Hawaiian song (Buck 1984–5) and artistic expression (Fenton 1997), in Hawaiian historical identity and in language came to fruition in the late 1960s and throughout the 1970s. These revivals were not immediately or invariably linked to the later theme of sovereignty although the potential was, in land disputes, clearly there and later realised. Cultural 'demoralisation' was frequently posed as a cause of social disadvantage. This was a Hawaiian version of the argument that people who have been induced to lose pride in their origins, in their 'culture' in all its aspects, are poorly placed to succeed at school or to compete in the market place – or to be inoculated against criminalisation. It is argued that if a people can be reeducated into ancestral cultural pride, as individuals they will succeed where once they failed.

But the politics of culture in land-disposession situations does not confine itself to culture and dignity. The cultural renaissance, once in full flow, had a momentum of its own which could not be satisfied by 'tokenist' recognitions of its importance by dominant groups within the society. Furthermore the logic of the culture argument (that is, the logic of what is entailed in the restoration of a Hawaiian cultural dignity) is quite discontinuous with apparently parallel arguments among once immigrant populations. For the latter, a modicum of recognition can be the gateway to a gradual process of social incorporation during which successive generations move, in any case, inexorably away from the cultural marks which link them to their ancestors' homelands, in Japan, the Philippines or China. For Hawaiians the homeland remains under their feet. The link between earlier ('purely' culturalist) and present sovereignty forms of cultural politics can be found in the thread which is common to both – the emphasis placed in the discourse of cultural revival on the love of the land, *aloha 'aina* or *malama 'aina*. In its 'purely' cultural form this takes the form of the reiteration of an ancient theme in Hawaiian cultural memory of the importance attached to caring for the land: the land as the source of growth, of provision of food which is materially and symbolically valued, in for example the renaissance of the historic and present value and importance of growing taro, a basis of staple food in ancient Hawai'i. Reference to the material and symbolic valuation of taro as a life-giving plant and as the basis of a past civilisation has formed a signal element of the Hawaiian renaissance over both periods – the 1970s' 'spontaneous' revitalisation of Hawaiian culture and the 1990s' politicisation of Hawaiian culture. Love of the land, caring for the land is a central element of both phases of this renaissance. A politico-cultural phrasing of this kind was never open to once immigrant populations in Hawaii.

This revitalisation or reconstruction of native Hawaiian culture has been seen as form of re-presentation of culture or of the reconstruction of 'ancient' culture whose impetus is to be found not in a naive desire to preserve or restore lost value but in its coherence with contemporary political concerns (Linnekin 1983, Keesing 1989). It has thus been argued as an instance of the 'invention of tradition' or as a case of instrumental ethnicity where constructions of the past are put to service in current political strategies. Evidently the cultural past takes on a new meaning in an utterly different context of the present (Linnekin 1983, Keesing 1989). But the argument has certain weaknesses (Trask 1993).

The first is that if politico-cultural movements of the kind represented by modern Hawaiians look to the past for their inspiration and in so doing 'reconstruct' it, emphasising some elements and neglecting others, then they are doing something which is a consistent and seemingly ever-present feature of collective memory. As those who write of cultural reconstruction would, of course, readily concede, there is no immaculate history, no unvarnished social memory of which the current forms constitute distortions or devious re-presentations. The term 'invention' is tendentious; as a term it makes its point but as a concept with a popular sense of fabrication and *de novo* creation it can scarcely escape a sense of invalidating that to which it refers.

As Eriksen has pointed out with reference to Sami politics in Norway, (Paine 1992, Eriksen 1993b) those engaged in the politics of culture are understandably enraged by an analysis which appears to portray them as mere opportunists whose real interest in their 'cultural roots' is a screen for their jostling for position. Further, in casting a kind of doubt over the authenticity of cultural concern it downplays the extent to which the cultures at issue have themselves been constructed and reconstructed a thousand times over by people and forces much more powerful than the past of present bearers of that culture. There is no better exemplification of this than Obeyesekere's (1992) account of the history of the death of Captain Cook. The captain and his men met Hawaiians when they stayed in Kealakekua Bay in 1778. Cook died after an altercation by the shore. Obeyesekere's account shows how both Cook himself, and the people of Hawai'i whom he met, have been portrayed within the Western presumptions typical of a rational and just sea-captain and 'irrational natives'.

In valuing the past, contemporary political activists in indigenous affairs will often (although not always) have come to political consciousness sharing certain democratic, egalitarian and gender-relevant values which are inconsistent with 'traditional society'. The traditional societies which lie 200 years behind contemporary indigenist politics are likely to have been hierarchical, undemocratic, unequal and patriarchal. Some versions of the politics of cultural restoration may be frankly 'conservative' as some Fijianist politics are (Lawson 1992). Many other forms are led by contemporary political and community leaders who are committed to democratic egalitarian values. We should not be surprised if there are elements of the past about which they are less enthusiastic than others and this can be shown to be precisely the case in the modern cultural politics of Hawai'i – and in many other instances too.

The social construction of the boundaries of ethnic groups can be illustrated in the Hawaiian case, again without invalidating the contemporary Hawaiian cause. The boundaries of the term Hawaiian have shifted many times over the course of the last 220 years of history, both by way of internal defining and external constraints. The possible meanings of the term include resident of the islands, born in the islands, born in the islands of some Polynesian ancestry, descendants of any Hawaiian ancestry whether or not born or resident in the islands, and of 50 per cent or more Hawaiian ancestry. In contemporary Hawaiian political struggles the question of who is a Hawaiian remains a fiercely disputed item. As a political rallying call it competes with 'local', an ethnic-like designation which simply distinguishes island born from incomers and means in effect, non-*haole* (Fenton 1979, Kanahele 1996), it is an expression of resentment towards all 'invading forces' from newly arrived mainland *haoles* to the vast billions of Japanese capital (Kent 1983). But at the same time the present-day (native) Hawaiians are the clear incumbents of a social and political inheritance stemming back to before 1778.

The politics of culture in Europe: proto-nations or ethnonationalism

The ethnic and ethnonational cultures and identities which have resurfaced, with fluctuating intensity in recent decades reflect the process of nation-state formation in Europe. Germany and Italy were unified as nation-states in the second half of the 19th century, France began to take on its modern form from the period of the French Revolution and Britain incorporated Wales (1536), Scotland (1708) and Ireland (1800) to form modern Britain long after England had taken shape in the wake of the Roman departure, and later of the Norman invasion. Since then Ireland minus Ulster has achieved its independence, Northern Ireland with its Roman Catholic minority remains the key problem of constitutional incorporation. Wales and Scotland countenanced, in 1998, different forms of constitutional devolution of power.

One of the distinctive features of this type of ethnicity is that they are represented politically by territories which have, within a wider state system, a territorial integrity and an administrative form. The question of home rule, devolution and independence, has therefore a real territory on which to found a political project. In this respect they are like Quebec in Canada, and Czech and Slovak identities in former Czechoslovakia which had already bifurcated as separate countries soon after the collapse of the Soviet Union. So too did most of the countries which reemerged as new nation-states within the territory of the former Soviet Union, the demise of which has to date given rise to 20 'new' nation-states.

Similarly, the collapse of the Federal Republic of Yugoslavia gave birth to the new states of Croatia, Bosnia (including Serbian Bosnia), remainder Yugoslavia (principally Serbia and Montenegro and including Kosovo), and Slovenia. Not only was the demise of the Soviet Union succeeded by 'reawakened' nationalisms in such countries as Latvia, Lithuania, Estonia and Georgia, it has been followed by nationalistic ideologies in Russia itself and by the resurfacing of ethnonational claims within remainder states and regions (Tishkov 1997).

In what has been termed the 'perennialist' view of nations and nationalism, it has been convincingly shown that a sense of people-hood, grounded in shared culture and historical experience, can be found among populations with a common history and persisting in culture regions, in both the ancient and modern world. Smith (1986) has referred to this conception of peoples as 'ethnie' (see under Ancestry in the Introduction to this volume) marking them off from the term nation which has been closely connected with state, in the modern form nation-state, and from the term ethnic group as a term typically applied to sub-national minorities. The term ethnie draws attention to the real basis of historical and cultural continuity of populations who have some shared sense of peoplehood.

Contrasted with this view is the modernist concept of nations and nationalism, where the emphasis is on the way in which modern states have 'created' the nations which are viewed as comprising the natural community of people within the state's boundaries. Nations on this argument do not give rise to states – or nation-states; rather states give rise to nations in the sense that as modern states take shape they actively foster the sense of national community and promote the common culture which is seen to be a requisite of nationhood. In this way Gellner sees modern states as requiring common culture such as the common language which is necessary for centralised administrations, military organisation, efficient commerce and public registrations of citizens for taxation and other purposes (Gellner 1983). The logic of a modernising economy and a state bureaucracy exerts pressure towards the elimination of particularistic cultures and languages – an efficient army and an efficient stock exchange requires that everyone understand each other. Many modern or modernising states have pushed for the creation of a common language and the perfection of standard forms of an existing language. Eugen Weber's account of peasant cultures and the project of national uniformity in 19th-century France shows how France developed a common French-speaking population – to the extent that it succeeded – through an intentional policy of cultural standardisation (Weber 1976). By being conscripted into the army or by being drawn into relations with agents of the state and by being introduced to 'standard' French usage, many and probably most peasants in France were being inducted into a sense of being French for the first time.

The perennialist and the modernist view – the view of peoplehood and enduring cultural continuity as against the 'fabrication' of cultural commonality and thus nationhood by modern and modernising states – are often seen as opposing and irreconcilable. But as Smith (1991) himself has shown it is possible to incorporate both elements in a cogent account of nation and nationalism. Some of the elements of cultural continuity and peoplehood can be seen to have long historical roots even if they have been constantly changing. Such is the case with the long development of England, the language and sense of peoplehood. This is not to say that the English are a natural community, a real family of people, or that there is a cultural heritage which marks this people off from others. It is simply to say that what is now politically represented as England has traceable origins in continuity of place, language and collective identity.

Post-war politics of immigration, ethnicity, nation and racism – Britain and Europe

Gellner has suggested that the central proposition of nationalism is that nation should correspond with state (Gellner 1983). The idea of a nation is that of a people with a shared destiny, a common past and future, and a store of customs, collective memory, and familiar symbols held in common; the term state refers to the form of organisation of citizenship, government and geographical boundaries. In Gellner's argument 'nation' may correspond with state when all those who belong to the nation are within it and there are none within it who should not be. The first means that those who are outside the state but belong to the nation should be welcomed 'back home' – an example of this is the return to Germany of 'ethnic Germans' after the collapse of communism; or it could mean that the state should be extended to bring all members of the nation under one political roof. In the Yugoslavian civil war the Serbian nationalists were defining peoples in several regions of the former federal Yugoslavia as members of the Serbian nation and therefore arguing that the boundaries of a Greater Serbia should be extended to include them.

The idea of a nation, a people conceived as sharing ancestry and culture, is expressed through empires as well as through states. Where reference is made to a family of peoples the appeal is made to shared ancestry; where reference is made to shared sentiments and ways of life, the appeal is to shared culture. In this sense Winston Churchill's use of the phrase English-speaking peoples was a cultural definition of a nation or related group of nations. So, too, the French emphasis on spreading French culture, above all the French language, throughout its empire was a cultural definition of a nation and family of nations. French cultural policy both without and within its mainland territory has been vigorously assimilationist, establishing a set of ideals of civilisation, learning, and good government which are seen as simultaneously French and universal. References to 'kith and kin' and to our cousins in the white former Empire – New Zealand, Australia, Canada and even 'our American cousins' – are a racial/ancestral definition of the nation and its extensions. The Portuguese express a concept of a shared transnational cultural domain through the organisation of countries whose official language is Portuguese and of African countries whose official language is Portuguese (Fafe 1990, Rosas and Rollo 1998).

The identification of civilisation with a national culture and language contains a contradiction. If the English-speaking peoples are viewed – as undoubtedly Churchill did view them – as the bearers of civilisation, this thought contains within it the second thought, that those who are not English/British are less civilised. The nation-centred framing of civilised values fails the test of Universalism, that is, a critical test of those very civilised values is that they include equal respect for all people. In Churchill's case we may be permitted to doubt whether his admiration for the English-speaking peoples was an inclusive one or a racialised one. He was Prime Minister during much of the period when the government began to contemplate exclusion of non-white immigrants, even in the early 1950s, when the numbers of immigrants from, for example, Jamaica, Barbados and India was still very small. The Conservative government contemplated the idea that a 'Keep Britain White' policy would be electorally successful. In every election since the 1950s, when racist arguments of this kind were being pressed on the government by constituency lobbies, references to immigration control have evoked a view of Britain as properly white – and the more so the better. If speaking English was the criterion then migrants from the Caribbean should have met the criterion ahead of anyone.

The hostility to black people was expressed in both crude and 'polite' forms; ideas of inherent racial difference were sometimes tacit, sometimes overt. The nationalist anti-immigrant lobbies spoke the language of 'race'; lower peoples were seen as threatening a 'mongrelisation' of the British (Foot 1965, Miles and Phizacklea 1984). The slogan on the poster 'If you want a nigger for a neighbour, vote Labour' was the crude message; the public face of anti-immigration politics was more 'polite' and was cast in a language of culture rather than 'race'.

This was the case long before sociological commentary began referring to 'cultural racism' as the 'new racism'. Enoch Powell, regarded in the 1960s as the arch-apostle of racism, had a view of England (not Britain) as a culture–community endangered by dilution with other cultures as the most recurring theme of his rhetoric. On the other hand his remark that even being born in England did not make you English could be taken to mean that English is in the blood rather than in the mentality. But most often he claimed that England was in danger of losing its character as a country and a culture – and appealed to all those believed the same.

This is an illustration of one of the reasons why it is possible to relate the reproduction of racism to the nature of capitalist systems, as Miles and others have so well demonstrated (Miles 1993). One of the features of capitalism is the relentlessly 'revolutionary' propulsion of social change. New modes of production, constantly changing conditions of world markets, the speed of decline of non-profitable industries and the equal speed of emergence of new ones, these are all constant and necessary features of capitalism. They are also accompanied by social changes such as the building of motorway networks, the transformation of the countryside, the destabilisation of working communities, grand irregular movements in house prices, and the emergence of new forms of leisure and popular culture, all of which are linked directly and indirectly to the dynamic and unplanned nature of capitalism. One recurrent reactive political theme in the midst of these changes is the belief that all is changing – for the worse – and is hopelessly out of control. This is why the politics of nostalgia can take the form of racism – 'the country isn't what it used to be' – as well as bitter attacks on single-parent mothers or on the moral failures of young people, these all being marks of disorienting social change which is resented or feared.

This is similar to the appeal made by Margaret Thatcher in the run-up to the 1979 general election when she said that people 'were rather afraid of being swamped' by the introduction of 'non-English' cultural strains which threatened the integrity of the familiar and cohesive culture–community. This again is a primarily 'cultural' theme citing the danger to national identity rather than to the national 'bloodstock'. This was tempered by another reference in the same speech to the 'genius of the English' for democratic government which was their gift to the world. This came rather closer to a claim that English culture (democracy) was in the national bloodstream. Like any other similar claim it poses the same contradiction – if the people have a genius for democracy then they should be able to impart it to one and all. Whether the message was cultural or narrowly 'racial', the reading was the same. The implication from the very outset of racialised immigration in politics in the post-war period was that the fewer 'non-whites' the better.

These types of anti-immigrant racism were characteristic of almost all western European societies in the post-war period. As Miles has argued, the arrangements for citizenship and the specific national cultures and circumstances in each European state made for differences in the local manifestation of racism. In Germany (Miles 1994b) 'citizenship has become based exclusively upon biological descent, reflecting the dominance of an essentialist, ethnocultural conception of the nation, and the marginalisation of immigrant populations.' By comparison, in France, the values of Universalism and rationalism have become allied with that of assimilation, with citizenship allocated by the state primarily on the basis of the principle of *jus soli*.

Jus soli refers to right according to the 'soil', that is, a person acquires citizenship principally in accordance with where a person is born, by contrast with *jus sanguinis* ('right according to blood') whereby a person acquires citizenship principally by way of descent. The implications of *jus sanguinis* are racist in a way that those of *jus soli* are not. For the implication of *jus soli* is that birth in a country and familiarisation with its customs and ideals make a good citizen of anyone fortunate enough to have the opportunity. In this sense the USA prided itself in taking in all comers and making 'good Americans' of them, corresponding to the French confidence in being able to create good Frenchmen and women wherever French language and culture were permitted to exercise their natural elegance. Thus the most celebrated case in the immigration and culture politics of contemporary France surrounded the dismissal from school of two female Muslim pupils who had come to school wearing traditional headdress. Those who argued the pupils' case did so in the name of anti-racism and respect for all cultures, including Islam. Those who argued in support of dismissal did so in the name of Universalism, the idea that religious particularism in schools threatened the secular rationality of education, a battle which modernising France had previously fought with the Catholic Church.

Although the differences between the nation-states of Europe in these respects are significant (Miles 1994b), so too are the similarities. Most western European states within the European Union have parties of the extreme right whose typical platforms include opposition to new immigration, punitive policies towards those already arrived, and opposition to closer integration within 'Europe' or favouring withdrawal from the Union altogether. Le Pen's National Front in France is the 'ideal type' of these parties. In Britain, parties of the extreme right have had virtually no national electoral success but have been influential in local elections and in specific locales, such as the north west of England and east London (Miles and Phizacklea 1979, 1984, Husbands 1991b, 1997). Their comparatively slight electoral influence may be attributed to the anti-immigration postures adopted by both major parties.

In Britain in the later 1990s this nationalist rhetoric began to turn decisively towards the question of European integration, absorption in the European Union being portrayed as a loss of sovereignty and loss of national identity, coupled with the danger of allowing both 'socialists' and immigrants in by a back door. Despite the transparent commitment of the European Union to capitalist economies, Brussels was portrayed as somehow socialistic, and the agreements on border controls as dangerous both to national sovereignty and the restriction of 'unwanted' immigrants. In the British anti-European demonology 'non-white' immigration is by no means the exclusive target. German and French enthusiasm for Europe at the level of political leadership, has meant that anti-French and anti-German themes stood to be revived by the anti-European right in Britain. Marking off Britishness by contradistinction to the continental French has been a principal way in which the shaping of British identity was achieved. France as the 'continent' and as Catholic was the mark of all that was not British (Colley 1992).

Anti-German themes were a continuation of Second World War enmities, the economic decline of Britain being a bitter pill to swallow for those who saw Britain as having won the war and lost the peace. Thus the Thatcherite ideology combined all these themes into one: the revival of British greatness, the restimulation of British entrepreneurial capitalism, hostility to Germany capped by the celebrated Ridley affair (in which a cabinet minister wrote an article about the 'German character' for which he was subsequently dismissed), the celebration of Englishness and Britishness and ultimately outright opposition to European integration. This nationalistic mix did not secure the Conservative Party a further term of office in 1997 nor did the threat that a parliament for Scotland and an Assembly for Wales foreshadowed the 'break-up of Britain' (Crick 1995, Marquand 1995, Miller 1995, Parekh 1995, Husbands 1997).

Ethnic identities and British sociology

In the 1970s and 80s the *angst* surrounding British political identities (Marquand 1995, Miller 1995, Parekh 1995) the local and national responses to so-called 'coloured immigration' was largely understood by British sociology in terms of two central constructs: class and racism. As we suggested in Chapter 5, one of the first instincts of British sociology, Marxist and Weberian, was to ask how migrant labour 'fitted' in terms of class alignment. Were immigrant workers and their families the new British working class, or a specific segment of it, and thus destined for a role in British society structured by class experience and the simultaneous experience of racism? Racism was viewed both on a historical trajectory: a postcolonial Britain reproduced the categories of colonial superordination and subordination in the institutions of a 'multi-racial' Britain; and in a class frame: racism sustained the suppression of black minorities and played to the frustrations of white British workers.

One of the consequences of a colonial-imperial past which informed the mentality of British workers and British people as a whole, was a sometimes crude, racialised notion, and sometimes a diffuse subtler one that 'coloured people' did not belong in Britain. In the minds of many whites there was almost certainly no systematic and cohesive system of racial thought, rather 'bits and pieces' of ideas, commonplace attitudes and phrases similar in their function to what Billig has described as 'banal nationalism' (Billig 1995). But the simple thought that the new migrants did not properly 'belong here' was much more widely diffused and would explain the widespread negative response to opinion questions about immigration. Even without any racialised ideology in the sense of a systematic theory of racial inequalities, this thought is powerful enough to underpin a myriad hostile attitudes. If people do not properly belong here, why do they have this job, this house, this place in the waiting room of the health centre or any other resource?

This would certainly fit with the argument that resentments about the distribution of resources in an unequal class society feed racial attitudes. This is all the more so if some of those getting rewards and resources, however meagre, are seen as having no real entitlement to them at all. In the founding of nation-states on concepts of universal citizenship capitalist democracies promise formal equality to all while the necessary functioning of a capitalist economy produces persistent and widening inequalities. And if in building the 'nation' side of the equation 'nation-state' there are ideas of who belongs (to the nation), then perceived inequalities can prompt a racist response.

At the same time the constant social revolutions of capitalism, both nationally and globally, are fertile ground for a kind of bitter nostalgia which in Britain can take the form of a perpetual sigh over lost greatness, and the disappearance of the 'red from the world map', the end of empire. An important part of this bitter nostalgia is a perception of the loss of social peace at home associated in the prejudiced mind with black youth and social unrest in the inner cities. These are the constituent parts – anti-immigration sentiments, diffuse colonial ideas, bitter nostalgia, racialised law and order themes, racialised competition for resources – which go to make up the whole.

To argue that racism ought not to be seen as a unitary whole nor as the singular cause of the fate of minorities is not to 'dismiss racism'. To do so would run against experience, in societies, including Britain, where abuse and violence is routinely experienced by minorities (Virdee 1995). It is, however, to argue both that racism is multi-dimensional with different 'prompts' as we discussed earlier, and that racism is not the sole cause of the destinies of those subject to it. Not least it would be to understate the ability of people to cope with and oppose racism and discrimination in the daily routines of their lives, both collectively and individually.

This view of racism is reflected in the fact that the identities of young Caribbean and Asian-descent people in Britain are informed but not 'determined' by racism (Modood *et al.* 1994). The political mobilisation of the collective identity 'black' was only partially successful in the British context. Modood in particular has argued that the 'political black' project foundered on the multiple source of identities open to young Caribbean and Asian-descent people in Britain. The Rushdie affair was, he argues, more important in mobilising religious identity as a form of collective identity than the experience of material and racialised inequalities. Those born in Britain of migrant families have sought ways of reconciling their ethnic identity with their sense of being in Britain or of being British (Back 1993). For young women (Bhachu 1991, Bradby 1999) this has been a delicate operation especially where they seek to reconcile concepts of gender equality with customs of a patriarchal nature in their families. For some this is an outright opposition to patriarchy including its 'ethnic' form, for others it is a creative making of new gender and ethnic identities in a way which can only be partly understood by reference to racism (Bhachu 1991, Anthias and Yuval-Davis 1992, Bradby 1999).

We shall return to some of these themes of the general theorisation of class, ethnicity and racism in Chapter 8.

Summary

The politics of culture in land-dispossession societies are guided by the twin historical facts – land loss and cultural devaluing. Where indigenous peoples have seen their land fall into the hands of settlers and invaders they have also had to withstand and recover from the insistent message that theirs was an inferior language and a primitive culture. The politics of cultural recognition have surfaced in most of these contexts especially in the last three decades, in Australia, New Zealand, Hawai'i, Indonesia and many other cases. In the search for recognition the indigenous cultural renaissance movements share sentiments and aims with other minorities; but the land basis of the politics of indigenous peoples marks them off from, say, urban minorities as the descendants of in-migrants.

Urban minorities are characteristic of European societies which have absorbed migrant workers from many parts of the world including their own former colonies. All immigrant workers face the possibility of being viewed as 'alien' strangers; those from former colonies experience the latter-day effects of the persistence of colonial mentalities. In most societies within the European Union there are political parties of the right which combine anti-immigrant sentiments with anti-European sentiments and distaste for multiculturalism (Modood and Werbner 1997). In Chapter 8 we discuss how respect for ethnic particularisms may be reconciled with an ethos of Universalism.

Chapter 8

Ethnicity, Racism and Social Theory

Announcements of the revival, resilience and renaissance of ethnicity, ethnonationalism and racism have become a commonplace of contemporary essays on modernity, postmodernity and the structure and culture of the modern world. Two quotations, only superficially similar, will provide illustration:

> For at least 150 years liberals and socialists confidently expected the demise of ethnic, racial, and national ties and the unification of the world through international trade and mass communications. These expectations have not been realised. Instead we are witnessing a series of explosive ethnic revivals across the globe. In Europe and the Americas ethnic movements unexpectedly surfaced from the 1960s and 70s, in Africa and Asia they have been gaining force since the 1950s and the demise of the former Soviet Union has encouraged ethnic conflicts and national movements to flourish throughout its territory. Since 1990 twenty new nations based largely upon dominant ethnic communities have been recognised. Clearly ethnicity, far from fading away, has now become a central issue in the social and political life of every continent. The 'end of history', it seems, turns out to have ushered in the era of ethnicity. (Hutchinson and Smith 1996, preface)

> The spectre that haunts the societies 'of the West' is no longer communism, but, both within and outside their frontiers, a series of racisms and ethnonationalisms. (Rattansi 1994, p. 1)

Revival resilience and renaissance are not quite the same phenomenon. Revival suggests the reemergence of something we have known before, resilience suggests something that never quite went away despite expectations to the contrary, and renaissance suggests something the likes of which we may have known before but has arisen with new vigour and in new forms. The term 'revival' is the least apt implying that something old has reappeared. All the examples at which we have looked – Malaysia, Britain, the USA, Hawai'i – suggest that what we now observe as 'ethnicity', is formed and takes its modern shape impelled by modern conditions. This may be a tautology – modern ethnicity must be a product of the modern world – but it is a necessary one, in order to escape the implication that all we are witnessing is the survival of group identities and cultures, something the world has always known. Anthony Smith (1981), is right in showing that modern nations and ethnonations have some of their roots in historical lines of peoplehood formation, but this does not prevent us insisting on the modernity of ethnicity. Some African countries and Malaysia, and countries like them, provide the best evidence for this. The emergence of ethnicity is correlated with the destructuring of traditional kin and tribal loyalties, is reshaped in urban settings and, while resting on real differences of language and culture, is clearly formed in the colonial and post-colonial contexts (Werbner and Ranger 1996) which gave force to collective identities which do not simply correspond to ancient cultures and ethnie.

Resilience has some of the same set of implications as 'revival' – loyalties, social ties which stood the test of time despite the effects of modernity and the competing strength of alternative identities and allegiances. Like revival it suggests that ethnicity is a definable and discrete social collective form found now, as before, and falsely expected to recede and diminish in force. The emphasis in this book on the 'types' of ethnicity and the contexts in which they are manifested suggests that we cannot routinely accept that we are everywhere dealing with the same kind of thing which merits the same name, even if there is enough similarity to group them broadly together. The expression of sentimental attachment to European origins by Irish and Italian and Polish and Scottish Americans is not really 'the same thing' as the murderous mobilisation of Serbian ethnonationalism in the former Yugoslavia, and neither are 'the same thing' as the institutional, constitutional and cultural mobilisation of communal identities in Malaysia.

Renaissance comes closest to matching the case. A set of social phenomena with at least superficial similarities has appeared in many contexts, phenomena which have important continuities with older cultures and social boundaries, but which have a specific form, shape and meaning in the contemporary world. In the cases where ethnicity is linked to the cultural effervescence of suppressed populations, renaissance as a term is particularly apt. This applies too where political vigour and new-found confidence in opposing racism and dispossession form a central element of collective ethnic identities. Renaissance seems intuitively less appropriate when the 'effervescence' is associated with seemingly arbitrary violence, glorifications of ethnonation at the expense of rivals and demonised opponents. It may be that some groups get a bad press, but Serbian nationalism appears resoundingly less appealing and sociologically healthy than, for example, the revival of Maori national consciousness in New Zealand.

In this chapter we address an interrelated set of questions. Are ethnicity, ethnonationalism, nationalism, religious identity, and racism the problem of the modern world? What do we conclude from reflecting on the 'liberal expectancy' that collective identities, which are all seen in some sense as 'non-rational', would disappear in the rational age? What sociological approach offers most insight? How does the study of ethnicity influence the discipline of sociology itself?

Ethnicity, ethnonationalism, nationalism, religious identity, racism

Although appearing superficially similar the quotations from Hutchinson and Rattansi that opened this chapter are notably different, that from Rattansi being evidently more 'critical' and sceptical than the former. Rattansi is alerting us to multiple racisms and ethnonationalisms – Serbian nationalism would fit his case – which he sees as spectres haunting the world. It would be hard to disagree with the assessment that former mono-theoretic accounts of racism should be superseded by an awareness of racisms – modes of thinking and ideological forms which bear resemblance to racist categorisation of inherence but de-emphasise biologically determinist ideas in favour of new forms of essentialising peoples. In truth the extent to which the 'old' racism was dominated by biology is grossly overstated. In any case, as Rattansi shows, and as our Chapter 2 emphasises, there has long been a grand melange of religious, cultural and bio-scientific ideas contained within the overriding faith that one civilisation, and the people who were its bearers, were superior to all others. If we broaden our understanding of racism and racisms in this way then it is clear that the cultural and political contests about language, cultural practice, collective dignity and the distribution of reward and resource, will persist. This will be so both within nation-states and across and between them. If Rattansi is also 'worried' about ethnonationalisms then it is not difficult to see what he means – the new states of the former Soviet Union and Yugoslavia present illustrative cases, and presumably he is more 'worried' about them than, say, the possibility of a devolved parliament for Scotland.

In Hutchinson's case it is much more difficult to be sure what is intended. What, for example, are the 'the ethnic movements which in Europe and the Americas unexpectedly surfaced from the 1960s and 70s'? Does he mean, in America, Black Pride and Black Nationalist movements, and if so how are these to be seen as unexpected new directions of the 1960s? The history of black American political consciousness is a long catalogue of nationalisms, Africanisms, and of recurring tension both between material and cultural aims, and between integrationist and separatist politics. The most dramatic series of breaks with America's immediate past came considerably earlier, in the wake of the Second World War which saw the integration of the armed forces and before long the decisive revoking of 75 years of white supremacist laws and segregationist practices. The kinds of ethnic identifications which others have referred to, among Americans of 19th- and 20th-century European national origins, may properly be assigned to the category 'symbolic ethnicity' (Gans 1979, 1994, Waters 1990), a far cry from battles to the death for people and culture. In the former Soviet Union people are fighting to the death – as in Chechenya – and ethnonationalisms have, as so often before in world history, emerged in the wake of collapse of empires. How long the politics of the new countries will persist in being, superficially or really, decisively ethnicised remains to be seen.

The real difficulty with Hutchinson's formulation (see earlier in this chapter), which could be found replicated in many similar books, lies in the phrase 'explosive ethnic revivals across the globe'. This groups together so many phenomena so different from each other that it loses all precision or persuasion; the phrase 'explosive' is exactly the kind of journalistic term which implies that ethnicity is a simmering brew of deep-seated sentiments, the collective human consciousness of kind which lies on or just below the surface of all social conflict. If earlier European sociology was transfixed by class, contemporary sociology sometimes appears mesmerised by ethnicity. The imprecisions are threefold: of grouping together things which are or may be very different, of failing to specify the contexts of ethnicity, and in leaving unanswered, except by innuendo (that is, 'explosive'), the question of the nature of the ethnic attachments being described.

Groupings and contexts

As we have tried to show in this volume, there is not one 'ethnicity' appearing and reappearing across the globe. We have described aspects of the colonial and post-colonial worlds, the importance of labour migration, coerced and voluntary, the renaissance of peoples who have been the historical victims of dispossession, and the unfinished work of modern capitalist and non-capitalist states in creating national cultures. These historical settings have provided the background to post-slavery racisms and anti-racisms, the communalism of 'plural' societies, the political movements of indigenous peoples, the ethnonationalism of would-be nation-states and the nationalism/racisms of established states, and finally the individual and collective identities of urban minorities in rich and poor countries. Whatever similarities and common themes they may exhibit, not least because they are in several cases juxtaposed in the same social order, it is not helpful to treat them as uniform examples of an ethnic revival.

Each of these different modes of ethnicity is defined by its historical context. In their contemporary presentations, they are situated within contexts of economic and political structure. Thus the understanding of each and any case has to be addressed within the context that in part defines it. In the case of African Americans it is impossible (or unwise) to neglect the compelling power of their vastly disproportionate representation among America's poor and economically disfranchised. Much of the post-slavery history of black people in America has been the history of the organised resistance of white Americans to the incorporation of African Americans into the mainstream of American society. As we commented earlier, the differences in success conventionally defined between African Americans and other groups, needs no further explanation beyond the fact that no other group in American history has faced the concerted national and local, official and unofficial, federal and local, and violent and subtle organised resistance to their incorporation. The slavery and post-slavery mould of racialised difference has a pivotal place in American social and intellectual consciousness. It underpins not only African American identity but also the general frame of ethnicity in American society (Kymlicka 1989).

The presence of large numbers of, or a majority white population alongside slaves and their descendants is a critical influence on the ethnic formation within a given society. Where most or all slaves were Africans, whites were keen to distinguish themselves as free and in post-slavery were determined to effect a social closure protecting themselves and excluding the black or African population. In countries where there have been substantial white populations as non-slaves, most of former slave populations have remained economically disadvantaged, usually severely so. In some Caribbean countries this is muted by the absence of large numbers of whites and by the relative poverty among Indian-origin rural labour.

The political context: ethnonationalisms and the state

The political context too is subject to great variation; contextual differences which impart a difference to the nature, form and mobilisation of ethnicity. The political context of the former Soviet Union and of Yugoslavia is one where, over the last decade, there has been a working-out of constitutional, military-guerrilla, and state conflicts. The *modus operandi* has been post-empire constitutional manoeuvring, state-minority warfare and civil war. In each of these cases, ethnic populations are represented by elites or segments which may or may not authentically represent the wills and sentiments of the people whose cause they claim to be fighting. Throughout the Western media in the early to mid 1990s, Milosevic was presented as the triumphal representation of Serbian ethnonationalism; by late 1996 his government was brought almost to its knees by one of the most vigorous and protracted public protests in recent history. Radovan Karadic was the exemplar of Serbian ethnic loyalty in the Serbian Republic enclave within Bosnia; by mid-1997 the Serbian police force was dangerously divided between his supporters and those of the new president. The importance of elites in the shaping of political struggles, including of a nationalist and ethnonationalist type, cannot be overemphasised (Brass 1991, Tishkov 1997), and this means that the nature of collective sentiment and mobilisation is always problematic. This is not to say that elite leaderships always bypass, hoodwink or beguile vulnerable or susceptible populaces. Clearly the populace will support or privately oppose the actions of elites or segments in varying degrees, but frequently it is not easy to determine how much. In Northern Ireland, how extensive was popular support for terrorist methods or armed struggle? It is almost impossible to say – and the political mood can change quickly – but willingness to use arbitrary violence has an influence disproportionate to its support; the same may be said of ETA and the Basque political movement in Northern Spain. These ethnonationalisms are distinctive by virtue of the central significance of armed violence, by contrast with cases where armed violence has been relatively rare or absent, as in Quebec, among Catalans, in Scotland and Wales. After watching the film *Braveheart* in Glasgow on Thursday you may go to your job as a trainee accountant on a Friday; in Bana Luka you may come home to find your home razed to the ground. (*Braveheart* was a popular Mel Gibson film with a Scottish nationalist theme; Bana Luka is a small town in Bosnia.)

Urban minorities

These preceding forms of ethnonationalism are different again from the political uses of ethnicity in the urban politics of advanced, rich economies. Ethnic identity is a useful symbolic weapon in American national and local politics and ethnic lobbies have influence on deci- sion making especially in foreign policy where Americans express their sentiments about their 'homeland' – the Irish about Ireland, Jewish Americans about the Middle East, and African Americans about South Africa and the African continent in general. But this is more a matter of the play of ethnic sensibilities within a welter of influences of American internal and external policies, rather than a *tout court* mobilisation of ethnic allegiances in an overtly ethnicised politics. The politics of ethnicity in America are about discrimina- tion, lobbying, the scramble for resources, and education – in short about social mobility, exclusion and inclusion. In contrast, the poli- tics of indigenous peoples are about land, historical subjugation and devaluing of a civilisation. Although cultural contest is common ground to all cases, the central impelling forces of modes of political ethnicity are significantly different in each case.

Nationalism and racism

Although they are frequently discussed as if they were simply part of the same phenomenon – the survival of collective identities – the manifest importance of nationalism and racisms can be looked at in a rather different light. Ethnonationalisms are the political expres- sion of would-be 'nations' and the wish for a state that corresponds to it, or for greater autonomy within an existing state – secession and devolution are two of the key possibilities. But nationalisms are the expression of established nation-states where the doctrine of peoplehood is mobilised for internal purposes, or where an 'our country first' politics are proclaimed in external relations – and for internal consumption. The two most notable examples of this 'little England' nationalism in recent years in Britain have been the Falklands War and the attempt to develop 'Euro-scepticism' as a rallying cry of Conservative politics in the mid-1990s (Marquand 1995, Miller 1995, Husbands 1997).

'Our country first' politics have emerged in all states of the European Union where significant minorities have opposed European integration. Despite the European Union being a capitalist project before all else, the conservative and reactionary right of Europe has taken up the cause of 'Britain/France/Denmark/Sweden first' and in many cases has combined this with internal racism and anti-immigration rhetoric. The European Union appears as a project of the *grande bourgeoisie* opposed by a combination of petty bourgeois and workers in member countries; the enemies are Brussels and foreigners. Greater freedom of movement within the Union is matched by heightened vigilance at the borders of all.

The question of where racism fits in this catalogue of ethnic particularisms, ethnonationalisms, and nationalisms, is bedevilled by the multiple uses of the term. As we argued in Chapter 2, there is a discourse of ethnicity and a discourse of racism, and considerable overlap between the two. In truth there are multiple discourses of racism ranging from explicit justifications of segregation as in the USA and apartheid South Africa; the racist anti-immigrant rhetoric in post-colonial immigrant-receiving Europe such as Britain, Holland and France; and racism seen as any politico-cultural construction which falls short of 'Universalism', as is the tendency in Balibar's work (Balibar and Wallerstein 1991). The core of racism is a system of social classification designating peoples as being of inherently unequal worth; this doctrine is allied to the systematic suppression and oppression of a people category both within the framework of a nation-state and in systems of imperial domination. Racism as such has a time and place specificity while at the same time, given the scope and duration of 'Western' domination of the modern world, it can be ascribed as a diffuse generality which portrays racism as omnipresent in 'Westernism'.

As Rattansi succinctly puts it:

> Most forms of Western racism are inconceivable and incomprehensible without an understanding of how 'Western' identities – and those of its Others – have continually been formed and created by actual and imagined encounters with the non-western Others of modernity. Identities such as 'the West' and 'European', even 'white', their conflation with conceptions of rationality, 'civilisation' and Christianity, and the superimposition upon these of images of paganism and savagery as constituted by binaries such as naked/clothed, oral/literate, technologically backward/advanced, were not already 'in place' – they came into being in processes of imperial exploitation and colonial domination. (Rattansi 1994, p. 36)

It may be argued that seeing racism in this 'imperial-colonial' context creates difficulty for an understanding of anti-Semitism; but racisms have been directed inwards, in systems of internal oppression, as well as concomitants of systems of external domination, as Miles and others have eloquently argued (Miles 1994b). Miles has repeatedly shown how forms of racism can be traced as part of the internal dynamic of (European) nation-states both in the political formation of states and the economic logic of capitalism (Miles 1993). Of course the anti-Semitism of the Third Reich was linked to the imperialism of the Third Reich; the purification of the nation within was part of the project of establishing a totalising domination in the creation of a German empire. Anti-Semitism represents the ultimate form of racism, racism as genocide, which does not posit peoples of unequal worth but posits one people of supreme worth and others, in the German case principally Jews and Romanies, as not meriting life itself.

An important question then becomes whether anti-Semitism was continuous with the project of Western rationality or the supreme perversion and departure from Universalism. There is no doubt that it can be portrayed as both (Bauman 1989). The death machines of the Third Reich were bureaucratically ordered and administered in pursuit of a science of hygienic cleansing. The eugenic theories which circulated in inter-war Germany were continuous with forms of eugenicist racism embraced in 'allied countries' and not only in minority Hitler-sympathising parties of the right. At the same time the communitarian idealisation of the people incorporated romantic 'irrationalities', as did the denial of advances in mathematics and physics as 'Jew science'. Part of the understanding of anti-Semitism in Germany must also be linked to the 'crises of capitalism' thesis. Two of the principal conditions for the emergence of Hitler and his party were German bitterness in respect of the First World War and the collapse of the Germany economy. Despite the latter part of its name, the National Socialist project was also a class project, designed to suppress working-class discontent and all the organs of their defence.

By this stage we have said enough to make the claim that 'ethnicity' is not a unitary global phenomenon, everywhere reflecting the same cultural and social impulses and everywhere fundamentally the same in its constitution. For all the superficial similarities, the underlying 'social forces' differ from context to context. We will, it seems to me, gain very little from imagining that civil conflicts in South Central Africa are the same thing as land claims and cultural renaissance among Maori in New Zealand, or that the creation of new states in former Soviet Central Asia are all of a piece with the celebration of St Patrick's day in the USA, or that the Islamic party in Malaysia can be coupled with the establishment of a parliament in Edinburgh, or that genocide in former Yugoslavia has an affinity with the survival of Welsh speaking in Wales. With regard to ethnicity we have sought to establish that it acquires its shape from its contexts, political, economic and historical. Some of these contexts are tantalisingly overlapping and Rattansi is right, in the passage just quoted, to see a common thread, through much of what we observe, of the consequences of a past and present 'Western' domination. The question of the survival of 'Western' constructions of the human project, the concern with modernity and its nature, and the post-modern frame as a mode of reflection in the sociology of civilisation is a grand enterprise and as Rattansi correctly diagnoses, a project of enormous vitality and renewed imagination in contemporary sociology. These are questions which this volume has touched upon but in the main must be seen as beyond its scope. Rattansi rightly argues that questions of identity, ethnicity and racism are central to the renewal of the sociological imagination, but in observing contemporary social changes the suggestion that the central feature of the modern world is a 'revival of ethnicity' either has little meaning or is not true.

Primordialism and ethnicity

We can, on this question of ethnicity as 'a central issue in the social and political life of every continent' (Hutchinson, opening this chapter), make one last set of observations. This requires revisiting the question of primordialism. We may recall that those who have dismissed the concept of primordial ties have largely missed the point of Geertz's (1973) argument. His is not a claim that ethnic ties are primordial but that primordial ties and sentiments run counter to civic and secular allegiances and to the status of the citizen as comprising a primary set of obligations and norms. The question of whether what is called ethnicity has a primordial character and contradicts the civic order then becomes one which can be asked in each and any observable case.

As we argued, there are clearly instances where ethnic allegiances and identities are continuous with kinship sentiments and with forms of identification which are securely embedded within the person. There are clearly instances, too, where what we recognise as ethnicity cannot claim continuity with the grounded experiences of cultural learning and all-embracing social ties. The optional identities described by Waters (1990) in her incisive account of (white) American ethnicities are different in nature from the more compelling ethnic divisions of contemporary Malaysia. The latter are not, to be sure, simply to be understood as 'primordial' but neither are they to be understood as a matter of choice in the radical individualist sense described for white Americans.

In the same vein and at the same time we cannot, from the outer appearance of ethnic conflict, conclude that the depth or intensity implied by the term primordial is necessarily present. The organisation of new states within the boundaries of the former Soviet Union in Central Asia has raised the question of religious identification and of culture and language. For this reason conflicts may be readily perceived as 'ethnic'. But the mass of evidence drawn together by Tishkov (1997) shows that we cannot assume that underlying these nation-state formations are culture communities of ancestry, religion and language which are 'simply' reemerging after 70 years of imperial Russian suppression. Enthusiasm for Islamic observance may be slight and languages may have declined; these changes are not the result of cultural imperialism alone. Local cultures have been drawn into the orbit of a wider culture and the direction in which they will now develop is an open question. It is at least a question which cannot be answered by assuming that culturally cohesive communities are reemerging from under the Russian heel.

The questions of Islam and Christianity – both as world systems of faith and ideology and as local cultures – cannot be properly addressed here but are close enough to our topic that they cannot escape mention (Said 1985, Gellner 1992, Sayyid 1997). For there seems little doubt that Islamic identification has, in many parts of the world, played the same role as ethnic and nationalist identifications in other parts – or has formed a significant element of those identifications that are also seen as 'ethnic' and 'nationalist'. The difference, of course, is that, as a component of local ethnic identities, Islam also connects peoples to a global identification. This is not without its complexities because the divisions within Islam can appear as significant as the division between Islam and Christianity, and other faiths. But even if Islam cannot be taken to be a unitary undivided whole, nonetheless in many instances it appears to represent a countercultural claim to the waning dominance of 'Westernism' and Christianity. This can be understood in part as a response to the Western dominance which Rattansi summarises and is grounded in the indignation of peoples who are responding to Western hierarchies of culture, nicely illustrated by our quotation from Trollope's portrayal of his characters' visit to the Middle East (Chapter 2).

This global influence of Islam as a world response to 'the West' is one signal component of contemporary cultural contest, both between and within discrete state systems. A second related impulse can be found in the combination of cultural indignation and sense of economic disfranchisement to be found among the poor or poorer of the world. This is exemplified by attachment to Islam among the rural poor of Malaysia whose sense of not being incorporated in the modern wealthy Malaysia is expressed more by Islamic enthusiasm than by Malay ethnicity, although both are involved (Khan and Loh Kok Wah 1992). A third source of Islamic enthusiasm is to be found in the dismay felt by more prosperous and middle-class Muslims, in societies – such as Malaysia, who have acquired increasing wealth in their modern sector and have thus brought those societies into direct contact with the materialism of a consumer culture and the delights of individualistic advancement. And fourth, we find the loosely articulated identification of nation-states with fellow Islamic countries, which poses a series of alternative international alliances to those offered by the West, or in the case of new states of Central Asia, to the receding cohesion of the former Soviet states. Insofar as these impulses towards heightened identification with Islam differ significantly in their local and global manifestations, this mirrors our caution about treating ethnicities as a unitary phenomenon.

The liberal expectancy

We have referred several times to the phrase 'liberal expectancy' in this book, evidence of the fact that it is – in one or another form – cited frequently in the context of the claimed 'ethnic revival'. Our conclusions about this argument are therefore shaped by our conclusions about ethnicity in the contemporary world. We have suggested that the argument can, for the sake of intelligibility, be reformulated as four propositions, following a broad distinction between the economic, political, social and cultural spheres. These are distinctions of convenience not to be understood as discrete spheres, but the distinction allows a closer scrutiny of the argument. As an economic proposition the expectancy is of meritocracy; as a political proposition the expectancy is of civic norms; as a social proposition the expectancy is of the decline of ethnic solidarities; and as a cultural proposition the expectancy is of a certain homogenisation within and across nation-states.

The economic proposition

An ethnicised division of labour and the practice of discrimination in the allocation of economic goods – welfare, jobs, and housing – run counter to meritocracy. It is important to remember that meritocracy is not the same project as the reduction or eradication of structured inequalities; in liberal theory meritocracy is consistent with the perpetuation of inequalities of class, since mobility and not social equality is the measure of a system of merit.

The fact that meritocracy may be purely 'formal' rather than substantial may well be perceived by those who 'know' that real opportunities are structured by inequalities as well as by honest striving. By the same token, small increments of mobility may be experienced as general evidence of social openness, sufficient at least to keep alive the ideal of the American dream or equivalent ideologies of opportunity. The question then becomes not so much is there real equality of opportunity but is there such hardening of boundaries permitting advancement to some and barring it to others that the excluded know it and cannot be persuaded otherwise. In ethnically defined economies and in an ethnicised division of labour there may indeed be no pretence that ethnic origin is irrelevant to economic participation – such was unmistakably the case in segregated America and apartheid South Africa. Both these countries now face the problem of the perpetuation of radical inequalities of wealth, opportunity and social welfare which continue to follow lines of ethnic difference in an era when explicit racist ideologies have been abandoned (Adam and Moodley 1993).

The notion of the possibility of 'betterment' for oneself and one's children is important for all ethnic groups in formally meritocratic societies; it is especially critical when there is a clear match between class position and ethnicity, as there is between African Americans and urban poverty in the USA. There is then the signal possibility that large numbers of people can scarcely avoid the conclusion that possibilities of betterment are hopelessly remote. This perpetuation of an ethnically structured class position may not – and almost certainly is not, as Wilson (1980) has argued for the USA – solely a function of the overt or covert continuation of discrimination, or more broadly racism. The fact that that country is seemingly unable to solve the problem of African American poverty has to be understood as one dimension of the fact that it cannot solve the problem of poverty.

The political proposition

The expectancy, in the political sphere, is that ethnicity will no longer be relevant to civic status. As long as African Americans were *de facto* or *de jure* excluded from voting – from the turn of the century almost all black people, who had exercised the vote after the Civil War, were disfranchised – there could be no pretence that ethnicity was irrelevant to political participation. Throughout the same period African Americans were effectively denied recourse to the courts for redress of wrongs and were treated systematically differently from whites in the judicial process. Again these formal civic inequalities have been removed, but in the USA and in Britain all the evidence shows that black people experience systematically different outcomes when they enter the judicial system, and are underrepresented as powerful functionaries – police, lawyers, judges – who operate the system. Even if all members of all ethnic origins are formally free to participate in the political system, the inequalities of wealth, of numerical minority status, and the force of racism in political ideologies may combine to result in the relative powerlessness of ethnic groups. Formal civic equality is counter-manded by *de facto* civic inequality. This constitutes a problem in any state where the formal ideology stresses the ideal of open democracy in access to power and influence. In all societies, particularly democratic ones, the practical identification of power and powerlessness with ethnic boundaries, poses real difficulties for the credibility of the civic code of equal citizenship.

The other principal context for the exercise of Universalism is in access to citizenship rather than its operation. While the Universal Declaration of Human Rights and international or multinational (for example European) courts contain principles which signatory countries subscribe to there is not an effective 'world citizenship'; to have effective citizenship is to be or become a citizen of a nation-state. This necessarily entails a contradiction. The principles of 'Universalism' affirm the rights of all men and women to justice, freedom of conscience, and dignity; they are seen as the political and intellectual inheritance of the Enlightenment. The right to justice includes equality before the law and protection from arbitrary treatment, the right to freedom of conscience enshrines the idea of moral choice and freedom from blind faith and prejudice, and the ideal of human dignity endows the human individual with a certain sacredness which would be violated by cruel punishment and affronts to the person.

The system of governance which parallels these principles is democracy, precisely because, formally or as an ideal, it confers participation in decision making on the 'choosing' individual. The contradiction lies in the fact that the linking of these rights to nation-states elevates national membership to primary importance in access to these in-principle benefits. As we have seen, the development of nation-states incorporates the creation of an image of the nation, the 'natural' members of a state system. This not only means that individuals may not gain access to any nation-state (that is the millions of refugees and stateless people), or may have imperfect access (immigrants and migrant workers), but that the nation itself is glorified and by implication other nations less valued. Ideas of race so commonly intrude upon control of immigration and access as refugees and to membership of the nation. Racist and nationalist discourses mutually inform each other and impede nation-state citizenship as the guarantor of Universalism.

The social proposition

In a sociological typification of social change from 'traditional' to 'modern' societies, formal associations supplant allegiances founded on kinship and communal memberships ascribed at birth. In Durkheim's language the natal milieu, the sphere of social ties associated with our birth, progressively diminishes in importance. This suggests that in modern and modernising societies, kinship is both narrower in its hold as extended family relationships are weakened, and looser in its grip as fewer and fewer transactions – education, welfare, economic function – are conducted through kinship. Where ethnicity is seen as an extension of kinship then the implication is that ethnicity declines with the decline of the natal milieu, and that kinship relations are properly situated in the private domain. Indeed the progress of modernity is indexed by a marked differentiation of the public and private sphere, as Weber originally argued (Gerth and Wright Mills 1961).

The social proposition of the liberal expectancy faces several difficulties, the most evident being the definition of the nature of ethnicity itself. This entails what we have in Chapter 1 referred to as the problem of 'constructed' as against 'grounded' ethnicity, and, in Chapter 3, the problem of intensity. As we argued there, the question of intensity is linked to the question of kinship since kinship ties are often seen as blood–emotion ties which account for the intensity of ethnicity. The reference to an 'explosive revival' of ethnicity suggests this notion of intensity, reflecting common-sense ideas of blood and kith and kin. The paradox of modernity is not that ethnic ties have remained important, belying the decline-of-kinship and decline-of-ethnicity thesis. It is that if ethnicity has survived it is not necessarily and not always tied to kinship in the way that Durkheim, for example, portrayed it – an extension of the natal milieu. In other words if ethnicity has survived it is not the same social form as projected in the social proposition of the liberal expectancy.

This also entails the conclusion that if ethnicity has an intensity, commonly portrayed as 'irrationality', it does not derive, or does not necessarily derive from its links to kinship. If ethnicity has survived in situations where it is called upon, as an instrumental form of indi-vidual and collective action, then what has survived is not 'illiberal' ethnicity as a denial of the liberal expectancy, but the ingenuity of people in situating their action and constructing collective forms.

The cultural proposition

In the quotation from Hutchinson which began this chapter 'world trade and mass communications' are seen as the solvents of local cultures and the harbingers of a certain cultural uniformity that sets aside ethnic diversity. These global influences are the suggested source of homogenisation. The Gellner (1983) argument, that the creation of states entails the creation of nation-states, is another. This is because, it is argued, the functioning of the state requires a measure of cultural uniformity – specifically a *lingua franca* becomes a necessity and local languages are deemed inefficient. The homogenisation of culture entails the creation of a nation. The argument that ethnicity has survived as a 'refutation' of the cultural proposition of the liberal expectancy entails the argument that what is surviving in 'ethnicity' is cultural difference – almost precisely the opposite, of course, of the Barthian argument. Indeed it is often apparently the case that ethnic boundaries are 'hardened' even while cultural uniformity increases and progresses (Barth 1969).

Ethnicity in Britain survives in the form of a series of fluid ethnic identities, in part the product of the vitality and vigour of the young people who have responded to their parents' expectations, to the social warmth, coolness, and hostility of others, and the subtleties of relationships generated by new patterns of friendship, marriage and collegiality. The stimulus of social change and the simultaneously angry despairing and hopeful responses of people generate cultural changes some of which are captured by the term ethnicity – and by notions of 'hybridity', and the shifting ground of gender expectations and aspirations (Werbner and Modood 1997, Yuval-Davis 1997). But to say here that there is a 'survival' of ethnicity does not say that there is a widening of the cultural differences between 'ethnic groups' which were culturally distinct and are becoming more so.

In the USA, it is not being argued that the apparent vitality of white ethnicities is a consequence of heightened cultural diversity and difference. Waters' (1990) inspection of ethnic identities via qualitative responses to census questions suggests that ethnic identities persist in the face of cultural assimilation or 'Americanisation' and Yinger (1994), in his review of acculturation and assimilation, finds himself asking why ethnic identities persist at the same time as cultural differences diminish. One of the most telling of Waters' observations is that when people were asked to describe the distinctiveness of the ethnicity with which they identified, people from many different origins described the same set of characteristics – a family closeness, caring for the elderly, a sense of loyalty and communal values. This suggests very strongly that people are describing the same experience – the experience of people who, over a generation or two or more, have moved from countries and circumstances where family solidarity was more important, to an increasingly individualistic style of life in urban American. The same sentiments would be reported by people who had not migrated at all.

In the former Soviet Union much of the evidence assembled by Valery Tishkov (1997) indicates that cultural differences had significantly diminished under the influence of the centralised state and 'official' communist values. This was in part a state-inspired cultural homogenisation – the Soviet state undoubtedly mistrusted religion and discouraged, suppressed, and persecuted the faithful, and Russification brought Russian as the *lingua franca* to a multilingual country. But it was also part of a process of secularisation and modernisation as people across the Soviet Union adopted Russian as the language of social mobility. In Muslim areas of the country, Tishkov argues, Islamic faith and observance was minimal and remains so after the collapse of the Soviet state. Both the Soviet and post-Soviet state assiduously recorded language and ethnic identity – the Soviet state in affirming a claim to respect all 'nationalities' within the Union and the post-Soviet states in mobilising cultural difference as the basis for state formations. In both cases they ran counter to the actual diminution of cultural difference, a salutary example of the civic order – the state – insisting on particularism even where it foundered. People named a nationality for themselves because they were asked to, and having named a nationality felt obliged to claim that they spoke the corresponding language – even when they did not (Tishkov 1997).

The evidence of declining religious observance and faith, and of diminishing use of 'minority' languages, is accompanied by new ethnonational claims made by political elites seeking to secure support and legitimacy within a region (Tishkov 1997). Thus the 'revival' of Islam in Central Asian states could be interpreted quite differently from the conventional view of long-suppressed religious instincts reemerging and ethnonational identities springing free from imperial control. New political elites in local states seek to restore religious observance and faith – at least outwardly – among a largely indifferent population and to preserve the titular language as a cultural confirmation of the new nation-state. Again cultural particularism is a construction of a state elite conscious of the value of cultural identities in securing support for the state. It is this, rather than an upsurge of suppressed cultural difference, that is the key factor here. In the former Soviet Union and in the USA (see

Schlesinger 1991) it is not a revolution of cultural difference but a change in the valuation of culture.

The review of the liberal expectancy does not, therefore, result in the resounding case for the demise of Universalism and the survival or revival of ethnic particularism. The evidence is mixed and complex, a contrast of principle and practice in the economic and political contexts and in, the social and cultural contexts, at least as much evidence for narrowing cultural difference as for diversity. This suggests that what is recognised as a revival of ethnic particularism in culture identity and politics is in fact precisely the opposite. What we may be seeing in all three is a new form of expression of universalistic values and a convergence in culture around the relentless march of individualism. In other words, the central core value is human dignity and opposition to all affronts to human dignity and this dignity is expressed as the sanctity of the human individual. In stressing respect for cultures, languages and identities, people are opposing indignity, indifference, and the impersonal treatment of individuals, in articulating political aspirations as ethnonationalism, people are demanding enhanced devolved political democracy. The argument that the core element of ethnically framed identities is demand for respect of the individual would explain why cultural advocates have to balance demanding respect for 'our culture' against a compelling and constraining construction of 'our culture' as uniform and fixed. In this sense it – the so-called revival of ethnicity – may be seen as the latest twist in Durkheim's (1898) contradiction – how to reconcile the growth of individualism with social solidarity.

The evidence is mixed and complex in another sense, that is, the picture is different in the different contexts we have discussed. In the economic and political spheres the evidence is not of the demise of universalistic values but of the continued tension between principle and practice – universalistic principle and particularistic practice. This is similar to Balibar and Wallerstein's (1991) conclusion with regard to the 'zigzag' of Universalism and particularism in capitalist societies. In the cultural and social contexts the evidence again is not the 'unexpected' survival of ethnic particularisms. Rather it is of the emergence of new forms of ethnic expression, despite the actual decline of ethnic solidarities in the sociological sense of kinship and community and despite the narrowing of cultural difference. Central to these new forms of ethnic expression are the elaboration of ethnicities (Hall 1992) and the revaluation of cultures. This revaluation of cultures and identities, is different in its implications from any suggestion that the processes of broad cultural convergence have come to a halt or even gone into reverse. The formula 'value-my-culture/value-me' may turn out to be more significant for its second half than its first.

In a similar way, ethnonationalism may be understood as a means of achieving a just and universalistic civic order rather than a deviation from it. If a wider civic order is unable to confer equal respect and access to resources to all its cultural and regional components then, wherever there is a coherent whole within the existing state system, we can expect ethnonationalisms to raise the possibility that respect, dignity and all due material benefits can be better guaranteed by some form of devolution of power, from small increments of local autonomy all the way to secession and the creation of a new state. This is precisely the kind of problematic with which Charles Taylor has grappled in essays on the possibilities of cultural diversity consistent with statehood, inspired by the 'problem' of Quebec in Canada. In other words, can there be a recognition of French-Canadian culture, of French Canada/Quebec as a distinct society, which is at the same time consistent with the survival of a Federal Canada as a civic order. We have referred at several points earlier to the politics of recognition and the politics of redistribution. Taylor (1992) here has elucidated the problem of Universalism as a form of individualism – the recognition of the worth of the human individual – and the recognition of culture not as a form of 'particularism' but as part of the politics of recognition. It is worth looking closely at Taylor's argument.

The politics of recognition

The starting point is a distinction between honour societies and dignity societies:

> Honor in the *ancien regime* sense is intrinsically linked to inequalities. For some to have honor in this sense, it is essential that not everyone have it... As against this notion of honor we have the modern notion of dignity, now used in a universalist and egalitarian sense, of the inherent 'dignity of human beings or of citizen dignity... this concept of dignity is the only one compatible with a democratic society. (Taylor 1992, p. 27)

Thus is initiated the 'discourse of recognition' which Taylor describes as being played out on two levels, that of identity and that of public rights:

> In the politics of universalism the equal dignity of all citizens [is emphasised] and what is to be avoided at all costs is the existence of first class and second class citizens... The development of the modern notion of identity has given rise to a politics of difference. There is of course a universalist basis to this as well, making for the overlap and confusion between the two... The underlying demand is a principle of universal equality. The politics of difference is full of denunciations of discrimination and refusals of second class citizenship. This gives the principle of universal equality a point of entry within the politics of dignity... it asks that we give acknowledgement and status to something that is not universally shared. (Taylor 1992, pp. 38–9)

The culture–communities 'trapped' within a wider system – such as in Taylor's examples, Canadian Indians and French Canadians – are not rejecting the Universalist principles of the wider (Federal Canadian) system but insisting that it has failed them: the supposedly neutral set of difference-blind principles of the politics of equal dignity is in fact a reflection of one hegemonic culture.

We can be sure that Taylor would say the same about gender as about ethnicity, with difference-blind principles turning out to favour males.

From here it becomes clear that Taylor believes in the possibility of a reconciliation of the principles of Universalism and difference, or the recognition of difference as a central element of the proper practice of Universalism. This must be achieved both without neglecting those truly shared civic values and without descending into utter relativism and subjectivism as some advocates of non-hegemonic cultures are prone to do:

> One has to distinguish the fundamental liberties that ought to be unassailably entrenched from privileges and immunities that are important but can be revoked or restricted. (Taylor 1992, p. 59)

The emphasis on culture as the site of change and of assertion of minority rights has the effect of projecting education, schools and universities as the centres within which these contests are crucially decided.

Taylor's essay in the reconciliation of Universalism and difference has provided this much more textured and elaborate account, more intelligible than any claim that what we are witnessing is the survival and revival of particularism or the demise of Universalism. The rights to 'life, liberty, due process, free speech, and free practice of religion' he speaks of as the fundamental ones which 'ought never to be infringed'. At the heart of these fundamentals is the pivotal value of human dignity. Once people have become attached to this idea – the idea of their own worth, of each person's in-principle equality with all others – affronts to it are hard to take. This is true of individuals in the particular sense, but also of individuals as participants in a collective identity. There is no earthly imaginable reason in contemporary society why any individual should be or can be asked to accept that they are less worthy than others. If any ideological current or social practice asserts or implies that a category of people are less worthy, then this is a daily affront to all individuals who acknowledge themselves to be one of this category.

This kind of argument would accord with Modood's observation that two decades of economic disadvantage and racial discrimination did not unify British South Asian Muslims and prompt them into political action in the way that was achieved by an insult to their Islamic faith (Modood 1992).

The politics of cultural difference pose very considerable difficulties – as the case of Quebec, much on Taylor's mind, illustrates – but we can expect, with Taylor, that they will not prove insurmountable. And when they cite the language of universal rights – as do, for example, the claims of indigenous peoples – they are evidence of a certain robust survival of 'Universalism' rather than its contradiction. To be sure the leaders of some modernising states are apt to describe the language of human rights as a western discourse, designed to perpetuate global inequalities. If demands to improve the 'human rights record' are reasonably seen to be mere opportunism of the rich countries, then this argument will be persuasive. But it is equally hard to imagine that some key elements of the Universalist discourse and its concomitant cultural individualism, once they take hold, will simply be dissolved in a welter of 'difference'.

What is less easy to imagine is that the indignities of inequality will be as in-principle solvable as the indignities of cultural recognition. To be told that the language one speaks is a lesser language, that one's darker or lighter skin is a mark of inferiority, that one's faith is only a step away from blind ignorance or superstition, or that as a woman one is inherently less able or apt for some task or responsibility – all these are increasingly insufferable indignities. But abject poverty is its own indignity, as is relative poverty in the midst of affluence, because of the desperation it imparts and because of the human message it conveys.

In one sense the homogenisation implied by Hutchinson's phrase 'the unification of the world through international trade and mass communications' (see beginning of this chapter) has, in fact, partially succeeded. By contrast with the purview of the 1960s and 70s, the American or Western capitalist project can be viewed as having massively succeeded. The socialist empire has evaporated with, Yugoslavia and Chechenya apart, hardly a puff of smoke. The possibility of socialism in South America and the Caribbean has for the time being at least, virtually disappeared. The USA has intervened decisively wherever it saw its interests threatened – in Chile, Guyana, Jamaica and Grenada and in a protracted struggle with Cuba. These have been triumphs not of democracy and human rights but of capitalism's impulse to crush socialism. Through most of the former Soviet Union, eastern Europe and almost all of South East Asia, India, and large parts of Africa including South Africa, open avowal of market economics has replaced any lingering socialist aspirations. It is impossible to tell how long this will hold. But it has been at enormous cost in terms of the perpetuation and exacerbation of poverty and of inequalities both within and between nation-states. At the time of writing we witness the crises of confidence in the economies of South East Asia, and evidence of gross inequalities within them. If these economic facts assert themselves in direct or indirect forms of the politics of the dispossessed it is not because in the end it is economic facts which are decisive but because these combine critically and in contradictory fashion with the message of human dignity.

Conclusion: social theory and ethnicity

My initial intention in this book was to set the analysis of ethnicity squarely within the context of economic and political structure and process. The chapters on 'ethnicity the class context' and 'ethnicity the political context' illustrate some of the characteristic settings within which ethnic mobilisations and racialised politics have emerged. These contexts include the ethnicisation of the division of labour and the class structure in such a way that ethnicity, class and economic position, inform each other; historically, this is a function or consequence of migrant labour voluntary and involuntary, and of the racialisation of class processes in post-slavery societies. At the same time, in many of the societies discussed we witness an economic marginalisation of dispossessed indigenous peoples almost invariably coupled with cultural demoralisation under the influence of an imposed hegemonic cultural system. The political context has partly been framed by the class dimensions of ethnicity, and by the racialisation of virtually the whole range of social relationships in societies dominated by a discourse of 'race'.

Part of our intention was also to draw back from a positivistic view of ethnic groups as ancestrally bounded entities in favour of a view which acknowledges common history and experience while also understanding the way in which ethnic and racialised identities are constructed in ways which can and do change; these identities may have no determinate relationship to the boundaries of common culture or kinship. It is evident that in all this a more telling place has to be granted to the concept of culture than was, until the last decade or so, characteristic of post-war sociology. For all the occasional excesses of post-modernists there are, as for example in the writings of Rattansi, leaps in the sociological imagination, especially in the field of ethnicity, which may not have been possible without the implicit and explicit critique of foregoing positivistic or Marxist sociology. While accepting much of the argument that ethnicities are socially constructed we did not accept the critique of primordialism advanced by several sources, since this is simply based on a misunderstanding of the Geertz (1973) argument. Indeed the distinction between primordial and civic is close in intellectual import to the 'universal' 'particular' theoretical constructions of later scholars of whom Balibar and Wallerstein (1991) is a key example.

In closing we may be permitted some broad strokes of the pen, careful and modest, if speculative. The strong strand of Marxist thinking in the analysis of ethnicity has contributed a great deal, not (and not alone) least in providing a critique of the forlorn hope of devising theories of racial or ethnic relations. Robert Miles (1993) has led the way in this respect and has fruitfully applied elements of Marxist thinking to the political economy of racism in capitalist social orders. At the same time a Marxist frame which aspired to capturing the *tout court* social realities of ethnicity and racism within a political economy framework has come to recognise its limitations. This is nowhere better exemplified than in Miles' (1994b) acceptance of the centrality of the politics of culture in the defining of (capitalist) nation-states – the discourse of race runs alongside and interpenetrates the discourse of nation. The weight attached in this book to the colonial and post-colonial frame in forming the racialisation and ethnicisation of social structures and processes is not inconsistent with Miles' argument; these frames are not the beginning and the end of the story. They are important in establishing the context of ethnicities and in informing a world view which, over several centuries, has come to dominate globally. But it is also evident that ethnicities and racisms must be viewed as being reproduced in contexts historically set by, but travelling beyond, the colonial and post-colonial frame. Indeed the historical context of nation-state formation in Europe constitutes a setting which has a centre of gravity at least partially independent of the colonial setting. As Miles has argued, the contemporary context of labour and capital in Europe forms a continuing setting for the working out of ethnic identities and racialised politics.

There must, however, be doubts about the claims of this kind of framework to comprising a comprehensive view of ethnicity and racism. In saying this I am much taken by three sets of evidence or argument. The first is that racisms, nationalisms, and ethnic and ethnonational formations persisted under communist regimes at least as forcibly as under capitalist regimes of the West. These were evident during communist regimes as much as in the aftermath of their collapse and sometimes for suspiciously parallel kinds of reasons – the search for people to blame, the arbitrary use of ethnically identified groups in specific labour contexts, the processes of definition of nations and of cultural 'levelling' under the impetus of industrialisation and 'modernisation'.

The emergence of nationalisms, ethnonationalisms and forms of racism in the wake of the collapse of communism cannot be satisfactorily explained by either the thesis of reawakening of suppressed identities or the argument that in the instant of becoming 'capitalist' these former socialist states immediately and instantly exhibited all the vices – racism included – of the capitalist form. Some of the principal sources of ethnonationalism in former socialist states must be related to political rather than economic processes, as peoples have sought to protect themselves within a state framework which promised to guarantee them securities which the former state no longer could or never did. Where the insecurity and destabilisation of political structures were greatest, the resort to ethnonational identities was most compelling and desperate, as in Yugoslavia.

The second is that the alliance of nation construction with racism on a broader definition can be found in contexts quite outside either the colonial/post-colonial frame as normally constituted, or the capitalist political economy frame. The case of China was explored in Chapter 2. It is evident that Dikötter's (1992) is not the only possible interpretation of the construction of Chinese nationhood and culture but it is also evident that it contains powerful themes which echo what has been regarded as racism in the West. As we suggested, the fixed gaze of Western scholars on Europe as the source of racism may be the last ironic twist of ethno- or Euro-centrism. It should also remind us that very little of this book concerns China and India which together constitute approaching half of the world's population. News reports (BBC World Service) of 27 July 1997 spoke of ethnic conflicts in western China when ethnic populations, the Uighurs, most of whom identify themselves as Muslims, showed signs of discontent with centralised Chinese rule. This was inspired, the report suggested, by the new freedoms of their Muslim neighbours in the former Soviet Union (Kazakhstan) with whom they might claim an ethnic solidarity. It may be some time before we begin to understand the forms which ethnicity and ethnic conflict will take in the world's largest nation-state.

The third is that the persistence of long historical antipathies and forms of oppression in Europe – towards Jews and Romanies above all – are not easily placed within either a colonial/post-colonial or capitalist political economy framework. To be sure the modern manifestations of anti-Semitism can be partially 'understood' as expressions of exclusivist German nationhood within an imperial project; and as products of class antagonisms in post-First World War Germany. And there is continuity between the valuation of order, science and classification and the bureaucratised programmes of genocide in the Third Reich. But such explanations are at best partial and I am conscious of all those manifestations of genocidal hatreds – surfacing in capitalist and socialist Europe, within and beyond fascist Germany – which fall only partially within the explanatory frameworks discussed in this volume.

Finally, we may reflect on the dynamic and hopeful dimensions of an emphasis on ethnicity rather than 'race'. Far from seeing the 'ethnicity perspective' as an escape from the harsh realities of racism, we may see it as an emphasis on the real potential of people and peoples to define themselves both in terms of what is particular to them and in terms of what they share with all others. This reflects the fact that the emphasis on culture in contemporary sociology is in part an emphasis on agency and indeterminacy. If we can construct ethnicities we can also both deconstruct and reconstruct them. This is the same message as feminists have propounded – if an important element of a gendered social order is the social construction of 'femininity' and the role of women, then the task is to deconstruct it. If the persistence of ethnicity is constituted by the particular affirmations of universal human dignity rather than the murderous definition of others unworthy of respect or even life, then ethnicity may offer hope rather than despair.

Bibliography

Ackerman SE (1986) Ethnicity and trade unionism in Malaysia: a case study of a shoe workers union, in Lee R (ed.), pp. 145–67.

Adam H (1971) *Modernizing Racial Domination: the Dynamics of South African Politics*, Berkeley, University of California Press.

Adam H and Giliome H (1979), *Ethnic Power Mobilised*, New Haven, CT, Yale University Press.

Adam H and Moodley K (1993) *The Opening of the Apartheid Mind: Options for the New South Africa*, Berkeley, University of California Press.

Adams R (1934) The unorthodox race doctrine of Hawaii, in Reuter EB (ed.) *Race and Culture Contracts*, New York, McGraw-Hill.

Adams R (1937) *Interracial Marriage in Hawai'i: a Study of the Mutually Conditioned Processes of Acculturation and Amalgamation*, New York, Macmillan.

Aluli NE and Davianna Pomaika'i McGregor (1994) The Healing of Kaho'olawe, in Hasager and Friedman (eds).

Anderson B (1983) *Imagined Communities: Reflections on the Origin and Spread of Nationalism*, London, Verso.

Anthias F (1992) Connecting 'race' and ethnic phenomena, *Sociology* **26**(3): 421–38.

Anthias F and Yuval-Davis N in association with Harriet Cain (1992) *Racialized Boundaries, Race, Nation, Gender, Colour and Class and the Anti-racist Struggle*, Routledge, London.

Apple R and Apple P (1979) *Land, Liliu'okolani and Annexation*, Honolulu, Top Gallant Publishing.

Aptheker H (1987) *American Negro Slave Revolts*, New York, International Publishers.

Asaratnam S (1970) *Indians in Malaysia and Singapore*, Kuala Lumpur, Oxford University Press.

BBC World Service (1997) Ethnic conflict in China, 27 July.

Back L (1993) Race identity and nation within an adolescent community in South London, *New Community*, **19**(2): 217–34.

Baldwin J (1965) *Nobody knows my Name*, London, Corgi.

Balibar E and Wallerstein I (1991) *Race Nation, Class Ambiguous Identities*, London, Verso.

Ball W and Solomos J (eds) (1990) *Race and Local Politics*, London, Macmillan.

Ballard R (1992) New clothes for the emperor? The conceptual nakedness of the British race relations industry, *New Community*, **18**: 481–92.

Ballard R (ed.) (1994) *Desh Pardesh: the South Asian Presence in Britain*, London, Hurst & Co.

Ballard R (1996) Negotiating race and ethnicity: exploring the implications of the 1991 census, *Patterns of Prejudice*, **30**(3): 3–34.

Banton M (1977) *The Idea of Race*, London, Tavistock.

240   *Ethnicity: Modernity, Racism, Class and Culture*

Banton M (1983) *Racial and Ethnic Competition*, Cambridge, Cambridge University Press.

Banton M (1987) *Racial Theories*, Cambridge, Cambridge University Press.

Banton M (1988) *Racial Consciousness*, London, Longman.

Banton M and Harwood J (1975) *The Race Concept*, Newton Abbott, David & Charles.

Banton M and Mansor MN (1992) The study of ethnic alignment: a new technique and an application in Malaysia, *Ethnic and Racial Studies*, **15**(4): 599–613.

Barany Z (1995) The Roma in Macedonia: ethnic politics and the marginal condition in a Balkan state, *Ethnic and Racial Studies*, **18**(3): 515–32.

Baron DE (1990) *The English Only Question: An Official Language for Americans*, New Haven, CT, Yale University Press.

Barot R (ed.) (1996) *The Racism Problematic: Contemporary Sociological Debate on Race and Ethnicity*, Lampeter, Edwin Mellen Press.

Barot R, Bradley H and Fenton S (eds) (1999) *Ethnicity, Gender and Social Change*, London, Macmillan.

Barringer H, Gardner RW and Levin MJ (eds) (1995) *Asians and Pacific Islanders in the United States*, New York, Russell Sage Foundation.

Barth F (ed.) (1969) *Ethnic Groups and Boundaries: The Social Organization of Culture Difference*, London, Allen & Unwin.

Bauman, Z (1989) *Modernity and the Holocaust*, Cambridge, Polity Press.

Beechert ED (1985) *Working in Hawaii: A Labor History*, Honolulu, University of Hawai'i Press.

Bennett C (1995) *Yugoslavia's Bloody Collapse, Causes, Course and Consequences*, London, Hurst.

Berger M (1952) *Equality by Statute*, New York, Columbia University Press.

Bhachu P (1991) Culture, ethnicity and class amongst Punjabi Sikhs in 1990s Britain, *New Community*, **17**(3): 401–12.

Biddiss MD (ed.) (1979) *Images of Race*, Leicester, Leicester University Press.

Billig M (1995) *Banal Nationalism*, London, Sage.

Blassingame JW (1979) *The Slave Community: Plantation Life in the Ante-bellum South*, New York, Oxford University Press.

Boas F (1982) *Race, Language and Culture*, Chicago, University of Chicago Press.

Bonacich E (1972) A theory of ethnic antagonism: the split labor market, *American Sociological Review*, **81**: 601–28.

Bonacich E (1976) Advanced capitalism and black/white relations in the United States: a split labor market interpretation, *American Sociological Review*, **41**: 34–51.

Boston TD (1988) *Race, Class and Conservatism*, London, Unwin Hyman.

Boulanger CL (1996) Ethnicity and practice in Malaysian unions, *Ethnic and Racial Studies*, **19**(3): 660–80.

Boyce DG (1991) *Nationalism in Ireland*, 2nd edn, London, Routledge.

Bradby H (1999) Negotiating marriage: young Punjabi women's assessment of their individual and family interests in Barot, Bradley and Fenton (eds).

Bradley H (1996) *Fractured Identities: Changing Patterns of Inequality*, Cambridge, Polity Press.

Brass PR (1985) Ethnic Groups and the State, in Brass PR (ed.) *Ethnic Groups and the State*, Beckenham, Croom Helm.

Brass PR (1991) *Ethnicity and Nationalism: Theory and Comparison*, New Delhi, Sage.

Brown C (1984) *Black and White Britain: The Third PSI Survey*, London, Heinemann.

Brown C and Gay P (1985) *Racial Discrimination: 17 Years After the Act*, London, Policy Studies Institute.

Buchanan AR (1977) *Black Americans in World War II*, Santa Barbara, CA, Clio.

Buck EB (1993) *Paradise Remade*, Philadelphia, PA, Temple University Press.

Buck EB (1984–5) The Hawaii Music Industry, *Social Process in Hawaii*, vol. 31.

Camejo P (1976) *Racism Revolution, Reaction 1861–1877*, New York, Monda Press.

Carter B, Green M and Halpern R (1996) Immigration policy and the racialization of migrant labour; the construction of national identities in the USA and Britain, *Ethnic and Racial Studies*, **19**(1): 135–57.

Carter B, Harris C and Joshi S (1987) The 1951–55 Conservative government and the racialisation of black immigration, in James W and Harris C (eds) *Inside Babylon: The Caribbean Diaspora in Britain*, London, Verso.

Carter J (1997) *Ethnicity, Equality and the Nursing Profession*, unpublished doctoral dissertation, University of Bristol.

Castles S and Kosack G (1985) *Immigrant Workers and Class Structures in Western Europe*, Oxford, Oxford University Press.

Castles S and Miller MJ (1993) *The Age of Migration: International Population Movements in the Modern World*, Basingstoke, Macmillan.

Castles S with Booth H and Wallace T (1984) *Here for Good: Western Europe's New Ethnic Minorities*, London, Pluto Press.

Cell JW (1982) *The Highest Stage of White Supremacy: The Origins of Segregation in South Africa and the American South*, Cambridge, Cambridge University Press.

Chinen JJ (1958) *The Great Mahele: Hawai'i's Land Division of 1848*, Honolulu, University of Hawai'i Press.

Cleaver E (1970) *Soul on Ice*, London, Panther.

Cohen A (ed.) (1974) *Urban Ethnicity*, London, Tavistock Publications.

Colley L (1992) *Britons: Forging the Nation 1707–1837*, New Haven, CT, and London, Yale University Press.

Connor W (1973) The politics of ethnonationalism, *Journal of International Affairs*, **27**(1): 1–21.

Connor W (1993) Beyond reason: the nature of the ethnonational bond, *Ethnic and Racial Studies*, **16**(3): 373–90.

Cornell S (1996) The variable ties that bind: content and circumstances in ethnic processes, *Ethnic and Racial Studies*, **19**(2): 265–89.

Crick B (1995) The sense of identity of the indigenous British, *New Community*, **21**(2): 167–82.

Curtin PD (1964) *The Image of Africa*, Madison, WI, University of Wisconsin Press.

Dabydeen D (1985) *Hogarth's Blacks: Images of Blacks in Eighteenth Century English Art*, Kingston upon Thames, Dangaroo Press.

Dabydeen D and Samaroo B (1987) *India in the Caribbean*, London, Hansib Publishing.

Daily Telegraph (1997) Hague slaps down Tebbit on race, 8 October.

Daws G (1968) *Shoal of Time: A History of the Hawaiian Islands*, Honolulu, The University of Hawai'i Press.

Degler CN (1971) *Neither Black Nor White: Slavery and Race Relations in Brazil and the United States*, New York, Macmillan.

Denitch B (1994) *Ethnic Nationalism: The Tragic Death of Yugoslavia*, London, University of Minnesota Press.

Diamond L and Plattner MF (eds) (1994) *Nationalism Ethnic Conflict and Democracy*, London and Baltimore, MD, John Hopkins University Press.

Dikötter F (1992) *The Discourse of Race in Modern China*, London, Hurst & Co.

Dikötter F (ed.) (1997) *The Construction of Racial Identities in China and Japan*, London, Hurst & Co.

Dollard J (1937) *Caste and Class in a Southern Town, White Caste Agression Against Negroes*, New York, Doubleday.

Donald J and Rattansi A (1992) *'Race', Culture and Difference*, London, Sage.

Douglass F (1962) *The Life and Times of Frederick Douglass, Written by Himself*, New York, Macmillan.

Drake St Clair and Cayton HR (1962) *Black Metropolis: A Study of Negro Life in a Northern City*, vols 1 and 2, New York, Harper & Row.

Draper T (1970) *The Rediscovery of Black Nationalism*, New York, Viking Press.

Dresser M (1986) *Black and White on the Buses: The 1963 Colour Bar Dispute in Bristol*, Bristol, Bristol Broadsides.

Dudley MK and Keoni KA (1990) *A Call for Hawaiian Sovereignty*, Honolulu, Na Kane O Ka Malo Press.

Durkheim E (1898) L'individualisme et les intellectuels, *Revue Bleue*, 4th Series, 10 pp. 7–13.

Durkheim E (1899) Notes sur l'antisemitisme in Dagan M *Enquête sur l'anti-semitisme*, Stock, Paris.

Dzidzienyo A and Casal L (eds) (1979) *The Position of Blacks in Brazilian and Cuban Society*, Minority Rights Group pamphlet number 7, London, Minority Rights Group.

Elkins SM (1976) *Slavery: A Problem in American Institutional and Intellectual Life*, Chicago, University of Chicago Press.

Eller JD and Coughlan R (1993) The poverty of primordialism: the demystification of ethnic attachments, *Ethnic and Racial Studies*, 16(2): 187–201.

Epstein AL (1978) *Ethos and Identity*, London, Tavistock.

Eriksen TH (1991) *Languages at the Margins of Modernity: Linguistic Minorities and the Nation-state*, Oslo, International Peace Research Institute.

Eriksen TH (1992) *Us and Them in Modern Societies: Ethnicity and Nationalism in Trinidad, Mauritius and Beyond*, Oslo, Scandinavian University Press.

Eriksen TH (1993a) Formal and informal nationalism, *Ethnic and Racial Studies*, 16(1): 1–26.

Eriksen TH (1993b) *Ethnicity and Nationalism: Anthropological Perspectives*, London, Pluto Press.

Essien-Udom EU (1962) *Black Nationalism: The Rise of the Black Muslims in the USA*, Harmondsworth, Penguin.

Evans G (1997) *Responding to Crises in The African Great Lakes*, London, Oxford University Press.

Expresso (Lisbon) (1997) Crimes em Nome da Cor, 7 June.

Fafe JF (1990) *Nação: fim ou metamorfose*, Lisbon, Imprensa Nacional Casa de Moeda.

Fardon R (1987) African ethnogenesis: limits to the comparability of ethnic phenomena, in Ladislav H (ed.) *Comparative Anthropology*, Oxford, Blackwell, pp. 168–88.

Featherstone M (ed.) (1990) *Global Culture: Nationalism, Globalization and Modernity*, London, Sage.

Fenton AF (1997) *E mau na hana no'eau o Hawai'i: craftspeople, public institutions and the perpetuation of tradition in Hawai'i*, unpublished masters dissertation, University of Edinburgh.

Fenton S (1979) Haoles and Hawaiians: ethnicity in the mid-Pacific, *New Community*, **VIII**(2): 262–71.

Fenton S (1980) Race, class and politics in the work of Emile Durkheim, in *Sociological Theories, Race and Colonialism*, Paris, Unesco.

Fenton S (1984) *Durkheim and Modern Sociology*, Cambridge, Cambridge University Press.

Fenton S (1987) Ethnicity beyond compare, review of Horowitz D (1985) *Ethnic Groups in Conflict*, *British Journal of Sociology*, **28**(2): 272–82.

Fenton S (1988) Health work and growing old: the Afro Caribbean experience, *New Community*, **14**: 426–43.

Fenton S (1996) Counting ethnicity: social groups and official categories, in Levitas R and Guy W (eds) *Interpreting Official Statistics*, London and New York, Longman.

Fielding S (1993) *Class and Ethnicity: Irish Catholics in England, 1880–1939*, Buckingham, Open University Press.

Financial Times (1996) Czech company report, 8 November, p. 3.

Financial Times (1998) Country cousins take rap for rising crime in Shanghai, 8/9 August.

Fleras A and Elliot JL (1992) *The Nations Within: Aboriginal State Relations in Canada, the United States, and New Zealand*, Toronto, Oxford University Press.

Fontaine P-M (ed.) (1985) *Race, Class and Power in Brazil*, Los Angeles, UCLA Center for Afro American Studies.

Foot P (1965) *Immigration and Race in British Politics*, Harmondworth, Penguin.

Foot P (1969) *The Rise of Enoch Powell*, Harmondsworth, Penguin.

Franklin JH (1943) *The Free Negro in North Carolina 1790–1860*, New York, WW Norton & Co.

Fraser N (1995) From redistribution to recognition? Dilemmas of justice in a post-socialist age, *New Left Review*, **212**: 68–93.

Frazier EF (1957) *Black Bourgeoisie: The Rise of a New Middle Class*, New York, Free Press.

Fredrickson GM (1972) *The Black Image in the White Mind: The Debate on Afro-American Character and Destiny, 1817–1914*, New York, Torchbook, Harper & Row.

Fredrickson GM (1981) *White Supremacy: A Comparative Study of American and South African History*, New York, Oxford University Press.

Fredrickson GM (1988) *The Arrogance of Race: Historical Perspectives on Slavery, Racism and Social Inequality*, Hanover, New England, Wesleyan University Press.

Fryer P (1984) *Staying Power: The History of Black People in Britain*, London Pluto Press.

Furnivall JS (1948) *Colonial Policy and Practice*, Cambridge: Cambridge University Press.

244   *Ethnicity: Modernity, Racism, Class and Culture*

Gans H (1979) Symbolic ethnicity: the future of ethnic groups and culture in America, *Ethnic and Racial Studies*, **2**(1): 1–20.

Gans H (1994) Symbolic ethnicity and symbolic religiosity: towards a comparison of ethnic and religious acculturation, *Ethnic and Racial Studies*, **17**(4): 577–92.

Geertz C (1973) *The Interpretation of Cultures*, New York, Basic Books.

Gellner E (1983) *Nations and Nationalism*, Oxford, Blackwell.

Gellner E (1992) *Postmodernism Reason and Religion*, London, Routledge.

Gellner E (1994) *Encounters with Nationalism*, Oxford, Blackwell.

Genovese ED (1971) *The World the Slaveholders Made*, New York, Vintage Books.

Genovese ED (1976) *Roll, Jordan, Roll: The World the Slaves Made*, New York, Vintage Books.

Gerth HH and Wright Mills C (1961) *From Max Weber: Essays in Sociology*, London, Routledge & Kegan Paul.

Geschwender J (1980–81) Lessons from Waiahole-Waikane, *Journal of Social Process in Hawaii*, **28**: 121–35.

Glazer N and Moynihan DP (1963) *Beyond the Melting-pot*, Cambridge MA, Harvard University Press (reprinted 1970, MIT Press).

Glazer N and Moynihan DP (eds) (1975) *Ethnicity: Theory and Experience* Cambridge, MA, Harvard University Press.

Glenny M (1990) *The Rebirth of History, Eastern Europe in the Age of Democracy*, Harmondsworth, Penguin.

Glenny M (1992) *The Fall of Yugoslavia: The Third Balkan War*, London, Penguin.

Goddard VA, Llobera JR and Shore C (eds) (1994) *The Anthropology of Europe: Identities and Boundaries in Conflict*, Oxford, Berg.

Goffman E (1969) *The Presentation of Self in Everyday Life*, Harmondsworth, Penguin.

Goldberg DT (1993) *Racist Culture: Philosophy and the Politics of Meaning*, Oxford, Blackwell.

Goldberg DT (ed.) (1994) *Multiculturalism: A Critical Reader*, Oxford, Blackwell.

Gordon P (1989) *Fortress Europe? The Meaning of 1992*, London, The Runnymede Trust.

Gossett TF (1965) *Race the History of an Idea in America*, New York, Schocken Books.

Grillo RD (1974) Ethnic identity and social stratification on a Kampala housing estate, in Cohen (ed.).

Grosby S (1994) The verdict of history: the inexpungeable tie of primordiality: a response to Eller and Coughlan, *Ethnic and Racial Studies*, **17**(1): 164–71.

Grosfoguel R (1997) Colonial Caribbean migrations to France, the Netherlands, Great Britain and the United States, *Ethnic and Racial Studies*, **20**(3): 594–612.

Guardian (1852) Anti-Catholic Riot in Stockport, 4 July.

Guardian (1995) It is true I killed your parents. It is true. I had orders, 1 May.

Guardian (1997a) Muslim riots shake China, 11 February.

Guardian (1997b) Symbols of the Old South under seige, 11 February.

Guardian (1997c) Census re-think, 27 June.

Guardian (1997d) China joins scramble for black gold, 29 September.

Guardian (1998) On Australia's sorry day it's goodbye to Botany Bay, 26 May.

Guillaumin C (1972) *L'idéologie raciste: genèse et langage actual*, Paris and The Hague, Mouton.

Guillaumin C (1995) *Racism, Sexism, Power and Ideology*, London, Routledge.

Gutman H (1977) *The Black Family in Slavery and Freedom 1750–1925*, New York, Vintage.

Hall S, Critcher C, Jefferson T, Clarke J and Roberts B (1978) *Policing the Crisis; Mugging, the State and Law and Order*, London, Macmillan.

Hall S (1992) New Ethnicities in Donald and Rattansi (eds).

Handler R (1988) *Nationalism and the Politics of Culture in Quebec*, Wisconsin, University of Wisconsin Press.

Handlin O (1973) *The Uprooted*, Boston, MA, Little, Brown.

Handy ESC, Emory KP, Bryan EH, Buck PH and Wise JH (1965) *Ancient Hawaiian Civilization*, Tokyo, Charles E. Tuttle.

Handy ESC, Emory KP, Bryan EH, Buck PH, Wise JH *et al.* (1981) *Ancient Hawaiian Civilization*, Rutland, VT, Charles E. Tuttle.

Hasager U and Friedman J (eds) (1994) *Hawai'i: Return to Nationhood*, Copenhagen, International Work Group for Indigenous Affairs.

Hawai'i Advisory Committee to the United States Commission on Civil Rights, (1991) *A Broken Trust, The Hawaiian Homelands Program: Seventy Years of Failure of the Federal and State Governments to Protect the Civil Rights of Native Hawaiians*, Western Regional Office, US Commission on Civil Rights.

Hawai'i State Department of Health (1993) Health Surveillance Program. Special Tabulation, Honolulu.

Hazlehurst K and Hazlehurst C (1989) Race and the Australian conscience: investigating aboriginal deaths in custody, *New Community*, **16**(1): 35–48.

Hechter M (1975) *Internal Colonialism*, London, Routledge.

Hermann JS (1981) *The Pursuit of a Dream*, New York, Oxford University Press.

Hirschmann C (1986) The making of race in colonial Malaya: political economy and racial ideology, *Sociological Forum*, **1**(2): 330–61.

Hirschmann C (1987) The meaning and measurement of ethnicity in Malaysia, *Journal of Asian Studies*, **46**(3): 552–82.

Hobsbawm E (1990) *Nations and Nationalism Since 1780: Programme, Myth Reality*, Cambridge, Cambridge University Press.

Hobsbawm E and Ranger T (eds) (1983) *The Invention of Tradition*, Cambridge, Cambridge University Press.

Hoel B (1982) Contemporary clothing sweatshops, Asian female labour and collective organisation, in West IJ (ed.) *Work, Women and the Labour Market*, London, Routledge & Kegan Paul.

Holmes C (ed.) (1978) *Immigrants and Minorities in British Society*, London Allen & Unwin.

Holmes C (1988) *John Bull's Island: Immigration and British Society 1871–1971*, Basingstoke, Macmillan.

Honolulu Advertiser (1996) Cayetano says OHA claim could reach $1.2 billion, 18 September.

Hormann BL and Lind AW (eds) (1996) Ethnic sources in Hawai'i, *Social Process in Hawai'i*, **29**.

Horowitz DL (1985) *Ethnic Groups in Conflict*, Berkeley, CA, University of California Press.

Horowitz DL (1989) Incentives and behavior in the ethnic politics of Sri Lanka and Malaysia, *Third World Quarterly*, **14**(4): 18–35.

Hosking G (1985) *A History of the Soviet Union*, London, Fontana.

Huggins N, Kilson M and Fox D (eds) (1971) *Key Issues in the Afro-American Experience*, New York, Harcourt Brace.

Hughes R (1987) *The Fatal Shore*, London, Pan Press.

Husbands CT (1991a) The mainstream right and the politics of immigration in France: major developments in the 1980s, *Ethnic and Racial Studies*, **14**(2): 170–98.

Husbands CT (1991b) The support for the Front National, analyses and findings, *Ethnic and Racial Studies*, **14**(3): 383–417.

Husbands CT (1994) Crises of national identity as the 'new moral panics': political agenda setting about definitions of nationhood, *New Community*, **20**(2): 191–206.

Husin Ali S (1991) Development, social stratifications, and ethnic relations: the Malaysian case, in Samarasinghe and Coughlan (eds), pp. 96–118.

Hutchinson J (1987) *The Dynamics of Cultural Nationalism*, London, Allen & Unwin.

Hutchinson J and Smith AD (eds) (1996) *Ethnicity*, Oxford, Oxford University Press.

Iganski P and Payne G (1996) Declining racial disadvantage in the British labour market, *Ethnic and Racial Studies*, **19**(1): 113–34.

Independent (1998) Queensland casts a vote for racism, 15 June.

James CLR (1938) *The Black Jacobins: Toussaint L'Ouverture and the San Domingo Revolution*, London, Allison & Busby.

Jenkins R (1986) Northern Ireland: in what sense 'religions' in conflict?, in Jenkins R, Donnan H and McFarlane G, *The Sectarian Divide in Northern Ireland Today* (Occasional paper No. 41), London, Royal Anthropological Institute.

Jenkins R (1997) *Rethinking Ethnicity: Arguments and Explorations*, London, Sage.

Jeshurun C (1993) Malaysia: the Mahathir Supremacy and Vision 2020, *South East Asian Affairs*, pp. 203–23.

Jesudason JV (1990) *Ethnicity and the Economy, the State, Chinese Business and Multinationals in Malaysia*, Oxford, Oxford University Press.

Jomo KS (1988) *A Question of Class: Capital, the State and Uneven Development in Malaya*, New York, Monthly Review Press.

Jones A (1994) Gender and ethnic conflict in ex-Yugoslavia, *Ethnic and Racial Studies*, **17**(1): 115–35.

Jordan W (1968) *White Over Black*, Baltimore, MD, Penguin.

Kame'eleihiwa L (1992) *Native Land and Foreign Desires: Pehea La E Pono Ai?*, Honolulu, Bishop Museum Press.

Kanahele GS (1996) The New Hawaiians, *Social Process in Hawai'i*, **29**: 13–21.

Kearney H (1989) *The British Isles: A History of Four Nations*, Cambridge, Cambridge University Press.

Keesing RM (1989) Creating the Past: Custom and Identity, in the *Contemporary Pacific*, **1**(1–2): 19–42.

Kennedy S (1959) *Jim Crow Guide to the USA*, London, Lawrence & Wishart.

Kent NJ (1993) *Hawaii: Islands Under the Influence*, Honolulu, University of Hawai'i Press.

Khan JS (ed.) (1998) *Southeast Asia Identities*, Singapore, South East Asia Studies.

Khan JS and Loh Kok Wah F (1992) *Fragmented Vision: Culture and Politics in Contemporary Malaysia*, Sydney, Allen & Unwin.

Kiberd D (1996) *Inventing Ireland: The Literature of the Modern Nation*, London, Vintage.

Kiernan VG (1969) *Lords of Human Kind: European Attitudes to the Outside World in the Imperial Age*, Harmondsworth, Penguin.

Klein HS (1967) *Slavery in the Americas: A Comparative Study of Cuba and Virginia*, London, Oxford University Press.

Kolsto P (1996) The new Russian diaspora, an identity of its own? Possible identity trajectories for Russians in the former Soviet Republics, *Ethnic and Racial Studies*, **19**(3): 609–40.

Kupchan CA (ed.) (1995) *Nationalism and Nationalities in the New Europe*, Ithaca, NY, Cornell University Press.

Kuper I (ed.) (1975) *Race, Science and Society*, Paris, Unesco Press.

Kymlicka W (1989) *Liberalism, Community and Culture*, Oxford, Clarendon.

Kymlicka W (1995) *Multicultural Citizenship: A Liberal Theory of Minority Rights*, Oxford, Clarendon.

Lacy D (1972) *The White Use of Blacks in America*, New York, McGraw-Hill.

Laczko LC (1994) Canada's pluralism in comparative perspective, *Ethnic and Racial Studies*, **17**(1): 20–42.

Lal V (1990) *Fiji: Coups in Paradise*, London, Zed Books.

Lawrence D (1974) *Black Migrants White Natives*, London, Cambridge University Press.

Lawson S (1992) Constitutional change in Fiji: the apparatus of justification, *Ethnic and Racial Studies*, **15**(1): 61–84.

Layton-Henry Z (1984) *The Politics of Race in Britain*, London, George Allen & Unwin.

Lee R. (ed.) (1986) *Ethnicity and Ethnic Relations in Malaysia*, Center for South East Asian Studies, Northern Illinois University.

Lee R (1990) The state religious nationalism and ethnic rationalization in Malaysia, *Ethnic and Racial Studies*, **13**(4): 483–501.

Lee SM (1993) Racial classifications in the US census 1890–1990, *Ethnic and Racial Studies*, **16**(1): 75–94.

Lévi-Strauss C (1975) Race and History in Kuper (ed.)

Levitas R (ed.) (1986) *The Ideology of the New Right*, Cambridge, Polity Press.

Lewis P (1994) *Islamic Britain, Religion Politics and Identity among British Muslims*, London, I.B. Tauris.

Liliu'okalani (1964) *Hawai'i's Story by Hawai'i's Queen*, Tokyo, Charles E. Tuttle.

Lim MH (1985) Affirmative action, ethnicity and integration: the case of Malaysia, *Ethnic and Racial Studies*, **8**(2): 250–76.

Lind AW (1938) *An Island Community: Ecological Succession in Hawaii*, Chicago, University of Chicago Press.

Lind AW (1955) *Hawai'i's People*, Honolulu, University of Hawai'i Press.

Lind AW (1996) Race and ethnic relations: an overview, ethnic sources in Hawai'i, *Social Process in Hawai'i*, **29**: 110–27.

Linnekin J (1983) Defining tradition: variations on the Hawaiian identity, *American Ethnologist*, **10**: 241–52.

Linnekin J and Poyer L (eds) (1990) *Cultural Identity and Ethnicity in the Pacific*, Honolulu, University of Hawai'i Press.

Lipton M (1985) *Capitalism and Apartheid: South Africa, 1910–1986*, Aldershot, Wildwood House.

Little S (1994) *Sri Lanka: The Invention of Enmity*, Washington, DC, The United States Institute of Peace Press.

Litwack LF (1961) *North of Slavery, The Free Negro in the Free States 1790–1860*, Chicago, University of Chicago Press.

Litwack LF (1980) *Been In the Storm So Long, the Aftermath of Slavery*, London, Athlone Press.

Lloyd C (1994) Universalism and difference: the crisis of anti-racism in the UK and France, in Rattansi and Westwood (eds).

Lloyd C and Waters H (1991) France: one culture, one people? *Race and Class*, **32**(3): 49–65.

Lloyd PC (1974) Ethnicity and the structure of inequality in a Nigerian town in the mid-1950s, in Cohen (ed.).

Loomis A (1976) *For Whom Are the Stars? Revolution and Counter-revolution 1893–1895*, Honolulu, University of Hawai'i Press.

Lorimer DA (1978) *Colour, Class and the Victorians: English Attitudes to the Negro in the Mid Nineteenth Century*, Leicester, Leicester University Press.

MacDonald S (ed.) (1993) *Inside European Identities*, Oxford, Berg.

McGarry J and O'Leary B (eds) (1993) *The Politics of Ethnic Conflict Regulation*, London and New York, Routledge.

McKay J (1982) An exploratory synthesis of primordial and mobilisationist approaches to ethnic phenomena, *Ethnic and Racial Studies*, **5**(4): 395–420.

MacKenzie M Kapilialoha (ed.) (1991) *Native Hawaiian Rights Handbook*, Honolulu, Native Hawaiian Legal Corporation.

Magas B (1993) *The Destruction of Yugoslavia, Tracing the Break-up 1980–92*, London, Verso.

Malaysia: Seventh Malaysia Plan 1996–2000, Kuala Lumpur, Per Cetakan Nasional Malaysia Berhad.

Malcolm X (1968) *The Autobiography of Malcolm X*, Harmondsworth, Penguin.

Malik K (1996) *The Meaning of Race: Race History and Culture in Western Society*, London, Macmillan.

Marable M (1983) *How Capitalism Underdeveloped Black America*, London, Pluto Press.

Marable M (1984) *Race, Reform and Rebellion*, London, Macmillan.

Mare G (1993) *Ethnicity and Politics in Southern Africa*, London, Zed Books.

Mariappan K (1996) Micro and Macro Ethnicity: Ethnic Preferences and Structures in Malaysia, unpublished dissertation, University of Bristol.

Marks S and Trapido S (eds) (1987) *The Politics of Race, Class and Nationalism in Twentieth Century South Africa*, London, Longman.

Marquand D (1995) After Whig imperialism. Can there be a new British identity?, *New Community*, **21**(2): 183–94.

Marx AW (1998) *Making Race and Nation: A Comparison of the United States, South Africa and Brazil*, Cambridge, Cambridge University Press.

Mason D and Jewson N (1992) Race equal opportunity policies and employment practice: reflections on the 1980s, prospects for the 1990s, *New Community*, **19**(1): 99–112.

Massey DS and Denton NA (1993) *American Apartheid: Segregation and the Making of the Underclass*, Cambridge, MA, Harvard University Press.

Maude HE (1981) *Slavers in Paradise: The Peruvian Slave Trade in Polynesia, 1862–1864*, Stanford, CA, Stanford University Press.

May S (1998) Language and education rights for indigenous peoples, Maori in Aotearoa/New Zealand, *Language,Culture and Curriculum*, **11**(3).

May S (1999) *Language Education and Minority Rights*, London, Longman.

Meier A and Rudwick W (1976) *From Plantation to Ghetto*, New York, Hill & Wang.

Miles R (1982) *Racism and Migrant Labour*, London, Routledge & Kegan Paul.

Miles R (1989) *Racism*, London, Routledge.

Miles R (1993) *Racism After 'Race Relations'*, London, Routledge.

Miles R (1994a) A rise of racism and fascism in contemporary Europe? Some skeptical reflections on its nature and extent, *New Community*, **20**(4): 547–62.

Miles R (1994b) Explaining racism in contemporary Europe, in Rattansi and Westwood (eds), pp. 189–221.

Miles R and Phizacklea A (eds) (1979) *Racism and Political Action in Britain*, London, Routledge & Kegan Paul.

Miles R and Phizacklea A (1984) *White Man's Country: Racism in British Politics*, London, Pluto Press.

Miller D (1995) Reflections on British national identity, *New Community*, 21(2): 153–66.

Milne R (1981) *Politics in Ethnically Bi-polar States*, Vancouver, University of British Columbia Press.

Modood T (1992) *'Not Easy Being British': Colour, Culture and Citizenship*, London, Trentham Books and Runnymede Trust.

Modood T and Werbner P (1997) *The Politics of Multiculturalism in the New Europe: Racism Identity and Community*, London, Zed Books.

Modood T, Beishon S and Virdee S (1994) *Changing Ethnic Identities*, London, Policy Studies Institute.

Modood T, Berthoud R, Lakey J, Nazroo J, Smith P *et al.* (1997) *Ethnic Minorities in Britain, Diversity and Disadvantage*, London, Policy Studies Institute.

Montagu A (ed.) (1964) *The Concept of Race*, New York, Free Press.

Moody A (1968) *Coming of Age in Mississippi: An Autobiography*, London, Peter Owen.

Mulgan R (1989) *Maori, Pakeha and Democracy*, Auckland, Oxford University Press.

Nagata JA (1974) What is a Malay? Situational selection of ethnic identity in a plural society, American Ethnologist, **1**(2): 331–50.

Nagata JA (1976) The status of ethnicity and the ethnicity of status: ethnic and class identity in Malaysia and Latin America, *International Journal of Comparative Sociology*, **17**(3–4): 242–60.

Nagel J (1994) Constructing ethnicity: creating and recreating ethnic identity and culture, *Social Problems*, **14**(1): 152–76.

Nagel J and Snipp CM (1993) American Indian social, economic, political and cultural strategies for survival, *Ethnic and Racial Studies*, **16**(2): 203–35.

Nash M (1989) *The Cauldron of Ethnicity in the Modern World*, Chicago, University of Chicago Press.

Native Hawaiian Data Book (1996) State of Hawai'i, Office of Hawaiian Affairs.

Nawawi MN (1990) *Plural Societies*, pp. 56–67.

Nisbet RA (1967) *The Sociological Tradition*, London, Heinemann Educational.

Norton R (1977) *Race and Politics in Fiji*, Queensland, University of Queensland Press.

Obeyesekere G (1992) *The Apotheosis of Captain Cook. European Mythmaking in the Pacific*, Chichester, Princeton University Press.

Observer (1995) The battered slaves of the Gulf, 1 October.

Observer (1995) Four million Filipina maids work abroad, 1 October.

O'Hare WP, Pollard KM, Monn TL and Kent MM (1991) African Americans in the 1990s, *Population Bulletin*, **46**(1): 1–39.

Okamura JY (1981) Situational ethnicity, *Ethnic and Racial Studies*, **4**(4): 452–63.

Oliver DL (1975) *The Pacific Islands*, Honolulu, University Press of Hawai'i.

Ollman B and Birnbaum J (eds) (1990) *The United States Constitution*, New York, New York University Press.

Omi M and Winant H (1986) *Racial Formation in the United States*, London, Routledge & Kegan Paul.

Paine R (1992) The claim to aboriginality: Saami in Norway, in Grønhaug R, Haaland G and Henriksen G (eds) *The Ecology of Choice and Symbols: Essays in Honour of Frederick Barth*, Bergen, Alma Mater.

Parekh B (1995) The concept of national identity, *New Community*, **21**(2): 255–68.

Parkin F (1971) *Class Inequality and Political Order*, London, McGibbon and Kee.

Patterson O (1975) Context and choice in ethnic allegiance: a theoretical framework and Caribbean case study, in Glazer and Moynihan (eds).

Pearson D (1990) *A Dream Deferred: The Origins of Ethnic Conflict in New Zealand*, Wellington, Allen & Unwin.

Phizacklea A (1999) Gender and transnational labour migration, in Barot, Bradley and Fenton (eds).

Phizacklea A and Miles R (1980) *Labour and Racism*, London, Routledge & Kegan Paul.

Phizacklea A and Wolkowitz C (1995) *Home Working Women: Gender, Racism and Class at Work*, London, Sage.

Pinkney A (1976) *Black Nationalism in the United States*, Cambridge, Cambridge University Press.

Poliakov L (1974) *The Aryan Myth: A History of Racist and Nationalist Ideas in Europe*, Brighton, Sussex University Press.

Prejean Nakoa (1994) Kanaka Maoli and the United Nations, in Hasager and Friedman (eds).

Puette WJ (1988) *The Hilo Massacre: Hawai'i's Bloody Monday August 1st 1938*, Honolulu, University of Hawai'i Press.

Ramet SP (1996) *Balkan Babel, the Disintegration of Yugoslavia from the Death of Tito to Ethnic War*, Oxford, Westview Press.

Ramet SP (1996) Nationalism and the 'idiocy' of the countryside: the case of Serbia, *Ethnic and Racial Studies*, **19**(1): 70–87.

Ratnam KJ (1965) *Communalism and the Political Process in Malaya*, Kuala Lumpur, University of Malaya Press.

Rattansi A (1994) 'Western' racisms, ethnicities and identities in a 'postmodern' frame, in Rattansi A and Westwood S (eds) *Racism, Modernity and Identity on the Western Front*, Cambridge, Polity Press.

Rattansi A and Westwood S (1994) *Racism, Modernity and Identity, on the Western Front*, Cambridge, Polity Press.

Rawick GP (1972) *Sundown to Sunup, The Making of the Black Community*, Westport, CT, Greenwood.

Reitz JG and Breton R (1994) *The Illusion of Difference: Realities of Ethnicity in Canada and the United States*, Toronto, C.D. Howe Institute.

Rex J (1973) *Race Colonialism and the City*, London, Routledge & Kegan Paul.

Rex J (1983) *Race Relations in Sociological Theory*, 2nd edn, London, Routledge & Kegan Paul.

Rex J (1986) *Race and Ethnicity*, Milton Keynes, Open University Press.

Rex J (1997a) The problematic of multinational and multicultural societies, *Ethnic and Racial Studies*, **20**(3): 455–73.

Rex J (1997b) The concept of a multicultural society, in Guiberneau M and Rex J (eds) *The Ethnicity Reader: Nationalism, Multiculturalism and Migration*, Cambridge, Polity Press.

Rex J and Guiberneau M (eds) (1997) *The Ethnicity Reader: Nationalism, Multiculturalism and Migration*, Cambridge, Polity Press.

Rex J and Mason D (eds) (1986) *Theories of Race and Ethnic Relations*, Cambridge, Cambridge University Press.

Rich PB (1986) *Race and Empire in British Politics*, Cambridge, Cambridge University Press.

Robertson R (1992) *Globalization Social Theory and Global Culture*, London, Sage.

Rodrigucz C and Cordero-Guzman H (1992) Placing race in context, *Ethnic and Racial Studies*, **15**(4): 523–42.

Roff WR (1994) *The Origins of Malay Nationalism*, Oxford, Oxford University Press.

Roosens EG (1989) *Creating Ethnicity: The Process of Ethnogenesis*, London, Sage.

Rosas F and Rollo MF (1998) *Língua Portuguesa: A Herança Comum*, Lisboa, Assirio & Alvim.

Rose EJB in association with Deakin N, Abrams M *et al.* (1969) *Colour and Citizenship, A Report on British Race Relations*, London, Oxford University Press.

Said EW (1985) *Orientalism: Western Conceptions of the Orient*, London, Peregrine.

Said EW (1991) *Orientalism: Western Conceptions of the Orient*, Harmondsworth, Penguin.

Samad Y (1992) Book-burning and race relations: political mobilisation of Bradford Muslims, *New Community*, **18**(4): 507–19.

Samarasinghe SWR and Coughlan R (eds) (1991) *Economic Dimensions of Ethnic Conflict*, London, Pinter.

Sarawak Tribune (1997) Over one million illegal immigrants in Malaysia, 2 April.

Sayyid B (1997) *Fundamental Fear*, London, Zed Books.

Scarr D (1984) *Fiji: A Short History*, Sydney, Allen & Unwin.

Schermerhorn R (1970) *Comparative Ethnic Relations: A Framework for Theory and Research*, New York, Random House.

Schlesinger AM (1991) *The Disuniting of America: Reflections on a Multicultural Society*, New York, WW Norton & Company.

Schmidt JD, Hersh J and Fold N (eds) (1998) *Social Change in South East Asia*, Harlow, Longman.

Shaw A (1988) *A Pakistani Community in Britain*, Oxford, Blackwell.

Shils E (1957) Primordial personal sacred and civil ties, *British Journal of Sociology*, **8**(2): 130–45.

Shyllon F (1977) *Black People in Britain, 1555–1833*, London, Oxford University Press.

Siddique S and Shotam NP (1982) *Singapore's Little India: Past, Present and Future*, Singapore, Institute of South East Asian Studies.

Silber L and Little A (1995) *The Death of Yugoslavia*, Harmondsworth, Penguin.

Silberman C E (1964) *Crisis in Black and White*, Vintage Books, New York.

Sivanandan A (1982) *A Different Hunger: Writings on Black Resistance*, London, Pluto Press.

Skultans V (1999) Gender and ethnicity in Latvian narrative experience, in Barot R, Bradley H and Fenton S (eds) *Ethnicity, Gender and Social Change*, London, Macmillan.

Small S (1994) *Racialised Barriers: The Black Experience in the United States and Englands in the 1980s*, London, Routledge.

Smith AD (1981) *The Ethnic Revival in the Modern World*, Cambridge, Cambridge University Press.

Smith AD (1986) *The Ethnic Origin of Nations*, Oxford, Blackwell.

Smith AD (1991) *National Identity*, Harmondsworth, Penguin.

Smith AD (1992) National identity and the idea of European unity, *International Affairs*, **68**(1): 55–76.

Smith AD (1995) *Nations and Nationalism in a Global Era*, Cambridge, Polity Press.

Smith B (1985) *European Vision and the South Pacific*, 2nd edn, New Haven, CT, Yale University Press.

Smith MG (1965) *The Plural Society in the British West Indies*, Berkeley, University of California Press.

Solomos J (1988) *Black Youth, Racism and the State*, Cambridge, Cambridge University Press.

Solomos J and Back L (1996) *Racism and Society*, London, Macmillan.

Spoonley P, McPherson C and Pearson D (1996) *Nga Patai: Racism and Ethnic Relations in Aotearoa/New Zealand*, Palmerston North, Dunmore Press.

Spoonley P, McPherson C, Pearson D and Sedgwick C (eds) (1984) *Tauiwi: Racism and Ethnicity in New Zealand*, Palmerston North, Dunmore Press.

Srinivasan S (1992) The class position of the Asian petty bourgeoisie, *New Community*, **19**(1): 61–74.

Stannard D (1989) *Before the Horror: The Population of Hawai'i on the Eve of Western Contact*, Honolulu, Social Science Research Institute, University of Hawai'i.

Stannard DE (1992) *American Holocaust, The Conquest of the New World*, Oxford, Oxford University Press.

Stanton W (1960) *The Leopard's Spots: Scientific Attitudes Towards Race in America, 1815–1859*, Chicago, University of Chicago Press.

Steinberg S (1981) *The Ethnic Myth: Race Ethnicity and Class in America*, Boston, Beacon Press.

Stone M (1981) *The Education of the Black Child in Britain: The Myth of Multiracial Education*, London, Fontana.

Takaki R (1984) *Pau Hana*, Honolulu, University of Hawai'i Press.

Tamura EH (1994) *Americanization, Acculturation, and Ethnic Identity: The Nisei Generation in Hawaii*, Urbana and Chicago, University of Illinois Press.

Taylor C (1992) *Multi-culturalism and The Politics of Recognition*, Princeton, Princeton University Press.

Taylor CM (1994) *Multiculturalism: Examining the Politics of Recognition*, Princeton, Princeton University Press.

Thoburn JM (Bishop) (1892) *India and Malaysia*, New York, Hunt & Eaton.

Thomas WI (1966) *On Social Organisation and Social Personality,* Chicago, University of Chicago Press.

Bibliography 253

The Times (1965) The Dark Million, 18–27 January.

Tiryakian EA (1971) The principles of 1789 and sociology, in Tiryakian EA (ed.) *The Phenomenon of Sociology*, New York, Appleton Century Crofts.

Tishkov V (1997) *Ethnicity, Nationalism and Conflict In and After the Soviet Union: The Mind Aflame*, London, Sage.

Tonkin E, McDonald M and Chapman M (eds) (1989) *History and Ethnicity*, Association of Social Anthropologists, monograph no. 27, Routledge.

Tönnies F (1963) *Community and Society*, New York, Harper & Row.

Trask Haunani K (1991) Natives and anthropologists: the colonial struggle, *Contemporary Pacific*, **3**(1): 111–17.

Trask Haunani K (1993) *From a Native Daughter: Colonialism and Sovereignty in Hawai'i*, Maine, Common Courage Press.

Trollope A (1991) *The Bertrams*, Oxford, Oxford University Press.

Turnbull C (1948) *Black War: The Extermination of the Tasmanian Aborigines*, Melbourne, Lansdowne Press.

Turner BS (1994) *Orientalism Postmodernism and Globalism*, London, Routledge.

US Bureau of the Census (1993) Census of Population. Social and Economic Characteristics, Hawaii CP-2–13, Washington.

Uyehara M (1977) *The Hawaii Ceded Lands Trusts; Their Use and Misuse*, Honolulu, Hawaiiana Almanac Publishing.

Vallieres P (1971) *White Niggers of America*, Toronto, McClelland & Stewart.

Vann Woodward C (1951) *Origins of the New South 1877–1913*, Baton Rouge, Louisiana State University Press.

Vann Woodward C (1963) *Tom Watson: Agrarian Rebel*, New York, Oxford University Press.

Vann Woodward C (1964) *American Counterpoint*, Boston, Little, Brown.

Varigny C de (1981) *Fourteen Years in the Sandwich Islands: 1855–1868*, Honolulu: University of Hawai'i Press.

Vertovec S (1992) *Hindu Trinidad: Religion, Ethnicity and Socio-Economic Change*, London, Macmillan.

Virdee S (1995) *Racial Violence and Harassment*, London, Policy Studies Institute.

Wade P (1985) Race and class: the case of South American blacks, *Ethnic and Racial Studies*, **8**(2): 233–49.

Walker R (1990) *Ka Whawai Tonu Matou: Struggle Without End*, Auckland, Penguin.

Wallman S (ed.) (1979) *Ethnicity at Work*, London, Macmillan.

Walvin J (1973) *Black and White: The Negro and British Society*, London, Allen & Unwin.

Walvin J (1983) *Slavery and the Slave Trade: A Short Illustrated History*, Jackson, MS, University Press of Mississippi.

Washington BT (1945) *Up from Slavery, an Autobiography*, London, Oxford University Press.

Waters MC (1990) *Ethnic Options: Choosing Identities in America*, Berkeley, CA, University of California Press.

Watson G (1970) *Passing for White*, London, Tavistock.

Wayland SV (1997) Religious expression in public schools: kirpans in Canada, hijab in France, *Ethnic and Racial Studies*, **20**(3): 545–61.

Weber E (1976) *Peasants into Frenchmen, the Modernization of Rural France 1870–1914*, Stanford, CA, Stanford University Press.

Werbner P and Modood T (1997) *Debating Cultural Hybridity: Multicultural Identities and the Politics of Anti-racism*, London, Zed Books.

Werbner R and Ranger T (eds) (1996) *Post Colonial Identities in Africa*, London, Zed Books.

Wieviorka M (1994) Racism in Europe: Unity and Diversity, in Rattansi and Westwood (eds).

Wilkie M (1994) Anti-discrimination law in Australia, *New Community*, **20**(3): 437–54.

Williams C (1994) *Called Unto Liberty*, Clevedon, Multi-lingual Matters.

Williams R (1958) *Culture and Society 1780–1950*, New York, Harper & Row.

Wilson WJ (1980) *The Declining Significance of Race*, Chicago, University of Chicago Press.

Wilson WJ (1987) *The Truly Disadvantaged; The Inner City, the Underclass and Public Policy*, Chicago, University of Chicago Press.

Wolf E (1982) *Europe and the People without History*, Berkeley, University of California Press.

Wolpe H (1988) *Race, Class and the Apartheid State*, Paris, Unesco.

Woo D (1990) The 'overrepresentation' of Asian Americans: red herrings and yellow perils, *Sage Race Relations Abstracts*, **15**(2): 3–36.

Yelvington KA (ed.) (1993) *Trinidad Ethnicity*, London, Macmillan.

Yin Hua Wu (1983) *Class and Communalism in Malaysia: Politics in a Dependent Capitalist State*, London, Zed Books.

Yinger MJ (1994) *Ethnicity*, New York, State University of New York Press.

Young C (ed.) (1993) *The Rising Tide of Cultural Pluralism. The Nation State at Bay?*, Madison, WI, University of Wisconsin Press.

Yuval-Davis N (1993) Gender and Nation, *Ethnic and Racial Studies*, **16**(4): 621–633.

Yuval-Davis N (1997) *Gender and Nation*, London, Sage.

Zeitlin IM (1968) *Ideology and the Development of Sociological Theory*, Englewood Cliffs, NJ, Prentice-Hall.

Author Index

A

Anthias 3, 49, 51, 54–7, 165, 166, 210

B

Balibar 13, 15, 58, 70, 77, 98, 100, 184, 219, 230, 235
Bonacich 36
Boston 131, 133, 134
Boulanger 149, 190, 191
Bradley 53–5, 175

C

Camejo 15, 127, 138
Connor 90, 91

D

Dikötter 52, 53, 83–5, 86, 237
Durkheim 47, 96, 97, 100, 102, 103, 227, 230

E

Eriksen 6, 11, 14, 18, 28, 30–2, 46, 59, 65, 68, 90, 94, 107, 190, 200

F

Fenton 2, 29, 48, 55, 96, 100, 164, 175, 195, 198, 201
Fredrickson 15, 62, 67, 77, 78

G

Gans 95, 215
Geertz 26, 101–6, 110, 112, 176, 222, 235
Gellner 36, 38, 39, 46, 68, 171–3, 202, 203, 222, 228
Glenny 7, 11, 52, 84

H

Hall 166, 230
Hirschmann 1–3
Husbands 37, 170, 207, 208, 219

J

Jenkins 39, 95
Jomo 144, 146

K

Khan 1, 14, 19, 20, 149, 191, 223
Kymlicka 67, 217

L

Lee, S 2, 3
Lind 152, 154–7, 169, 197
Litwak 122, 123, 180
Loh Kok Wah 1, 14, 19, 20, 149, 191, 223

M

Marx 42, 96, 160
May 9, 14, 15, 46, 176
Miles 5, 37, 48, 50, 62, 67, 89, 159, 163, 164, 166, 205–7, 220, 235, 236
Modood 54, 165, 166, 168, 210, 211, 228, 233

P

Patterson 30, 32, 34
Phizacklea 37, 55, 56, 163, 166, 205, 207

R

Rattansi 48, 212, 214, 215, 220, 221, 223, 235
Rex 22, 25, 31, 39, 48, 50

Subject Index

A

ancestry 2–4, 6–8, 10, 16, 19, 22, 24, 26, 27, 29, 37, 41, 42, 58, 62, 64, 67, 84, 90, 91, 95, 122, 124, 151–3, 156, 157, 163, 168, 171, 173, 179, 183, 194, 195, 201, 204, 222
anthropology 70, 74, 80
anti-semitism 100, 220, 237
Australia 32, 40, 41, 43, 74, 117, 157, 161, 172, 173, 175, 198, 204, 210

B

Bosnia 18, 109, 202, 217, 218
Brazil 25, 31, 41, 42, 53, 71, 74, 158, 162
Britain 2, 4, 9, 25–7, 30, 31, 33–5, 38, 47–9, 53–7, 68, 71, 91, 95, 96, 112, 117, 135, 139, 141, 158–66, 168, 169, 172, 178, 191, 192, 201, 203–5, 207–10, 213, 219, 225, 228

C

Canada 32, 37, 41, 64, 65, 158, 161, 173, 201, 204
capitalism 28, 29, 33, 44–6, 48–53, 59, 60, 71, 72, 77, 83, 96–9, 101, 117, 130, 148, 167, 177, 189, 205, 208, 209, 220, 234
Catalans 9, 57, 218
categories 1–3, 11, 13, 17–19, 21, 23, 24, 31, 42, 44, 47, 52, 61, 63, 67, 72, 74, 78–9, 85, 92, 106, 116, 124, 136, 138, 143, 155, 163, 168, 170, 171, 190, 191, 208
census terms 2–4, 19, 21, 61, 68, 91, 157, 228
China 52, 53, 82, 84–5, 91, 117–19, 141, 142, 154, 155, 169, 185, 199, 237

choice 19, 22, 57, 89, 94, 106, 189, 190, 222, 226
citizenship 14, 23, 39, 43, 54, 89, 101–3, 105, 113, 115, 140, 166, 172, 173, 177–9, 185–7, 203, 206, 209, 226, 232
class 8, 14, 23, 25, 26, 30, 42, 44, 45, 47–9, 51, 52, 55, 70, 75, 77–8, 82–3, 95, 97, 98, 100, 101, 105, 114–22, 124–34, 136, 137, 139–41, 143–9, 152–7, 159–69, 171, 176, 178, 180, 186–9, 191, 193, 195, 208–10, 215, 221, 223–5, 232, 234, 235, 237
classification 5, 6, 10–12, 15–20, 22, 23, 27, 31, 42, 43, 48, 59, 61, 62, 65, 73, 219, 237
colonialism, colonial, post-colonial 3, 13, 20, 22, 25, 26, 28–30, 32, 38–40, 43–6, 48, 50–3, 59, 61, 71, 74, 80, 82, 101, 102, 112, 119–21, 141–4, 151, 156–8, 169, 177, 178, 184, 185, 191–4, 197, 208, 209, 211, 213, 216, 219, 220, 236, 237
constraint 17, 18–19, 20, 53, 54, 88, 89, 91, 92, 95, 96, 189, 190, 192, 193, 201
contextualisation 21, 22, 24, 29, 51, 58, 112
Croatia 7, 11, 18, 202
cultural devaluation 41, 43, 46, 47, 50, 53, 89, 157, 210, 218
culture 5, 6, 8–10, 12–14, 19, 20, 22–7, 29, 37–9, 41–3, 45–53, 57, 58, 62, 64–5, 67, 68, 70, 75, 83, 84, 85, 88, 94, 97, 99, 103–5, 116, 136, 137, 139, 149, 152, 153, 157, 167, 170, 171, 173, 174, 176, 177, 182–6, 195, 196, 198–207, 210,